BIBLICAL
RESISTANCE
HERMENEUTICS
IN THE
CARIBBEAN
CONTEXT

ORAL THOMAS

author·HOUSE·

AuthorHouse™
1663 Liberty Drive
Bloomington, IN 47403
www.authorhouse.com
Phone: 833-262-8899

Published by AuthorHouse 04/14/2025

ISBN: 979-8-8230-4408-0 (sc)
ISBN: 979-8-8230-4407-3 (e)

Library of Congress Control Number: 2025904413

Print information available on the last page.

CONTENTS

FOREWORD

In his 1980 Synod Charge, Anglican Bishop of Jamaica, Neville deSouza, called on the Church and its leaders to "stand by the people as the Lord stood by Israel". deSouza spoke in a Jamaica embroiled in a socio-political struggle against social disenfranchisement and historical damnation.

This call, at the time it was made, does not come as a surprise at all. Theologians and Church leaders, for the most part, seemed to have been wedded to an understanding that Christian doctrine ought not to mix with one's social existence. That there ought to be a separation between religious life and social life.

It would seem, then, that local theologians and Church leaders, having denied the proclamation carried in the gospel of Matthew, had shied away from an interpretation of biblical narrative which would allow them to join in the people's struggles for social change and social justice. While embracing personal salvation as an aspect of Christian witness, the Church and its leaders failed to realize that Christian doctrine was a critical element in human liberation. That the Church must participate in the fight against the degradation of human life.

St. Matthew Chapter 25 confirms this mission: "For, I was enhungered and ye gave me meat: I was thirsty and you gave me drink: I was a stranger and you took me in: naked and you clothed me: I was sick and you visited me: I was in prison and ye came unto me".

This failing has been explicitly addressed in this academic offering,

Biblical Resistance Hermeneutics within a Caribbean Context, authored by Antiguan theologian, teacher and practitioner of the faith Rev. Dr. Oral Thomas, who is also former President, United Theological College of the West Indies (UTCWI). Given his academic acumen and his practical and social experiences, Rev. Thomas is well placed to produce such a refreshing and timely text.

Thomas, a Minister of Religion in the Methodist Church in the Caribbean and the Americas (MCCA), makes a case for understanding the bible as a tool of resistance in the interest of the people and their sociopolitical ambitions. For too long the bible has not given agency to a people seeking a just place in their societies. Hence, he advises that the bible should be read through the lens of resistance. If this is carried through, the bible becomes a weapon of resistance and a tool of change.

This advice, which is carried in the offer of a hermeneutic interpretation of the bible coupled with a reflective analysis of Caribbean society, bears great significance in the "sociality" of our people's existence. The text emphasises that one needs to understand the critical nature of biblical texts as products of social processes, social contradictions and societal change.

By applying the principles and methods of biblical interpretation to an understanding of the complex nature of society's forward movement, Thomas has brought a welcome and significant voice to how the bible is to be read, understood and applied. This makes Thomas' work exciting and yet sobering.

Writing in the context of national liberation movements which emerged in the region in the 1970s and to which some of us subscribed or were a part, Thomas offers an eye-opener which calls us to appreciate how the bible texts can and have laid the basis for social transformation. At the time, the understanding was that religion, the bible, had no place in such movements which focused only on the material aspects of life. You may be taken aback to learn that a particular hermeneutic interpretation of biblical texts has the potential to become a 'weapon of struggle'. Those who believe in the power of the Spirit on its own to effect social change will appreciate how the Spirit and the Being can work together to address social change issues.

Biblical Resistance is guaranteed to satisfy the queries and reservations of scholars, theologians, historians, the ecclesial population, those involved in politics, and 'revolutionaries. It makes interesting reading for all, regardless of their religious views, theological disposition, Christian preferences, ideological views, political proclivities and social leanings. It makes a good read for all.

His significant offer seeks, in my view, to lay to rest the dichotomy between religious life and social existence embraced by some religious leaders and 'revolutionary' thinkers.

Having read Thomas' work, you will conclude, as Thomas does, that a hermeneutic and contextualised interpretation of the bible narrative is critical to understanding Christian doctrine as an effective tool of analysis in the liberation movements, the people's movement, for social change.

This work has undoubtedly undermined the disjuncture between the Christian doctrine and social issues of poverty and related social problems.

Judith Soares

INTRODUCTION

The Case for a Resistant Biblical Hermeneutic within the Caribbean Context

Biblical hermeneutics can be a weapon in the struggle within the complex interplay of theology, ideology, politics, and economics. However, it can also dilute the revolutionary potential or dull the revolutionary edge of social forces advocating for social justice. Therefore, a contextualized reinterpretation of biblical texts is crucial to the effectiveness of these texts as analytical tools within people's movements for social change.

The work *"Biblical Resistance Hermeneutics within a Caribbean Context,"* published in 2010, served several purposes:

(i) **Made a case** for a biblical resistant hermeneutic within the Caribbean context by arguing that biblical interpretation in the Caribbean involves **less** agency in understanding biblical texts as products of social forces and struggles and more in how the biblical text articulates its messages and contextual relevance for the church and society.

Critically **examine** the historical and contemporary shortcomings of Caribbean hermeneutical practice.

(ii) **In** the context of national liberation movements for social justice, it primarily focused on the role of biblical text interpreters in the process of liberation.

(iii) **Identified** a significant gap in theologians' and practitioners' understanding of biblical texts as products of social processes, contradictions, and foundational elements of societal change.

(iv) **Emphasized** the practical importance of interpreting biblical texts within any socio-cultural context and period of Caribbean history. This is essential for driving societal change, as these texts were not produced in isolation but rather from a specific viewpoint grounded in particular social conditions.

The work focuses on the state of biblical interpretation in the Caribbean rather than the historical context of its 2010 publication. It continues to generate fresh urgency and relevance for this generation of Caribbean hermeneuts. It is also significant for countries in the Global South with similar characteristics and experiences of colonialism and Empire. Moreover, the work consistently provokes, instructs, and inspires independent thought and action. It is a pedagogical tool, a call to conscience, and an activist agenda.

In its 2010 edition, the work examines biblical interpretation within the context of weekly Sunday worship experiences. These weekly Sunday worship services in the Caribbean reflect a widespread tradition of attendance that prioritizes seeking spiritual uplift over connecting with who God is and what God does concerning their lived realities. Regardless of the weather or the preacher and liturgist, we gather in village and city chapels for Sunday worship despite disagreements about clean, unfashionable, or trendy clothing. Since the lyrics of the hymns sung do not emerge from the crucible of Caribbean social realities, and the prayers offered are not always spontaneous, and the biblical proclamations focus on those who sinned rather than those who were sinned against, the worship experience feels unreal as it is disconnected from the particularities of lived realities.

More specifically, while concern is expressed and prayers are offered for victims of violence, injustice, the hungry, the naked, and the ill, regardless of the nature of the social ills or injustices, such concern and prayers do not lead to social action or well-planned strategies for resistance that expose the systems and practices in society that foster violence, injustice, and social deprivation. We attend worship, offer our prayers or have them provided for us, sing hymns, listen to proclamations from the Bible, and then return home, only to wake up on Monday morning and go to work, school, play, and shop for the rest of the week, waiting for the weekly Sunday worship experience once again. Therefore, worship appears to be an escape from reality, a space more for, if not solely for, personal reflection rather than for agency and radical social change.

However, the proclamation from the Bible is central to the worship experience. For many, preaching is the most essential activity within this setting. It's common for individuals to attend worship services based on who is preaching. The pulpit holds critical importance in the Caribbean. Aside from open-air political meetings during election season, no other event or institution in the Caribbean commands such a captive audience and recognized authority, where people willingly gather en masse to hear the "truth" proclaimed and open themselves to change and challenge[1]. Nevertheless, the proclamation from the pulpit in the Caribbean is one of those activities that fails to grant social forces and struggles the agency needed to regard the Bible as an effective agent of social change.

Two factors contribute to this lack of agency in the proclamation from the Bible. One is the disconnection between religious life and the

---

[1] C.H.L. Gayle & W.W. Watty, eds., **The Caribbean Pulpit, An Anthology** (St. Michael, Barbados: Cedar Press, 1983), p. v

specifics of social existence. William Watty identifies several misguided antitheses in the dialectics of perspectives in traditional Caribbean biblical theological formulations that elucidate this disconnection[2]. Watty argues that, in the Bible, the essential contrast is not between belief in God and atheism but between belief in God, atheism, and belief in false gods; not between the spiritual and the material but between the spiritual and the material concerning the sensual; not between the sacred and the secular but between the sacred and the secular concerning the profane; not between creation and salvation but between creation, salvation, and what it means to be human in a world where the environment is continually destroyed and exploited, and in which the gap between rich and poor widens[3]. Here, it is less about duality and more about a complex array of unacceptable alternatives to spirituality. This disconnection between faith and the specifics of social realities is based on an understanding that cannot claim the Bible as its source or authority.

This text highlights two aspects of a proclamation from the Bible in the Caribbean pulpit. First, preachers are not inclined to either lead by example in their commitment to social justice or call for a type of social involvement that would not lead to a resigned acceptance of the status quo, the depreciation of material concerns, the co-option and complicity of religion in oppression, or an otherworldly faith focused on compensation in the hereafter. In reality, a proclamation from the pulpit stops short of "offending" the ruling class and embodying the Gospel for fear of criticism regarding involvement in "politics." Consequently, it has not been convinced that engagement with the material and profane is a salvific act.

The other factor, which is a fundamental failure in Caribbean hermeneutical practice and the primary concern of this study, is that

---

[2] William W. Watty, **From Shore To Shore, Soundings in Caribbean Theology** (Barbados: Cedar Press, 1981), p. 35
[3] Ibid. pp. 35-39

less emphasis is placed on understanding biblical texts as products of social forces and struggles, understood as socio-ideological productions. Instead, **more focus is given** to how the biblical text communicates its message, interpreting it as it stands and considering its contextual relevance for the church and society. This fundamental failure represents an unforced error in biblical hermeneutical practice within a Caribbean context.

Background

What has happened and is happening thus far is that much of the literary work on Caribbean biblical theology and hermeneutics tends to focus on reading strategies centered on the literary-rhetorical characteristics of biblical texts or how the text conveys its meaning. This approach derives meaning from biblical texts mainly for spiritual truth and formation while also providing answers for existential realities[4]. Most studies have concentrated on the meaning of biblical texts concerning lived experiences, focusing on the world in front of the text (Hamid 1971, 1973, 1977; Gayle C Watty, 1986; Kirton, 1982; *Caribbean Journal of Religious Studies* 1987, 1991, 1992, 1993, 1995; Deane 1980; *Caribbean Lenten Booklet Series; Caribbean Christian Living Series; Fashion Me A People Series 1S81*). Even when the exegetical starting point for biblical interpretation is existential realities, the emphasis remains on the text's literary features (Mulrain, 1995, 1999; Persaud, 2000; James, 2000; Nicholas, 1993; Jagessar, 2002).

---

[4] Idris Hamid ed., **In Search of New Perspectives,** San Fernando, Trinidad, 1971; *Troubling Of The Waters,* San Fernando, Trinidad, 1973; ed. Idris Hamid, *Out Of The Depths,* San Fernando, Trinidad, 1977; ed. Kortright Davis, *Moving Into Freedom,* Bridgetown, Barbados, 1977; William Watty, *From Shore To Shore,* CEDAR Press, Barbados, 1981; Noel Leo Erskine, *Decolonising Theology,* Orbis Books, Maryknoll, New York, 1981; Hemchand Gossai & Nathaniel Samuel Murrell, *Religion, Culture and Tradition in the Caribbean*, Macmillan, 2000.

Therefore, a Caribbean biblical hermeneutical practice must focus on the interests and practices that shaped the biblical writers' interpretations of the realities they convey. In this context, the following question merits investigation: To what extent have biblical texts, as socio-ideological productions and products of social practice, been empowered to condition or influence the interpretation of the Bible in the Caribbean, or are they doing so currently?

Focusing on the meaning of biblical texts for lived realities in Caribbean biblical hermeneutics is a critical response to one of the legacies of colonialism upon the church: the failure to understand the significance of faith and the challenges to faith within its local context[5]. This inability to grasp the historical realities in which God is revealed stems from the fact that Christianity was introduced to the Caribbean through conquest. A gospel of submission to authority (God and "Massa"), a spiritualized understanding of salvation that neglects the material dimension, and a teaching of futuristic eschatology were proclaimed. Such proclamations and teachings legitimized and sustained an unjust economic and political system that benefited the colonizing empire. Religion served the interests of the empire.

The intention, however, is not to suggest that the reading strategy aimed at contextualization is incorrect or even irrelevant. Caribbean hermeneutes do strive to contextualize faith. Nevertheless, for Caribbean biblical hermeneutics to challenge oppressive structures of spirituality and theology, it must emphasize the socio-ideological interests and social practices that have shaped the theological understanding of the biblical text and contextual realities. The underlying assumption is that it seeks to be relevant, meaningful, effective, and resistant and to claim the Bible as its authority. In this regard, Caribbean biblical hermeneutics must balance focusing on biblical texts as products of socio-historical

---

[5] Allan Kirton, *"Current Trends in Caribbean Theology and the Role of the Church"*, **Caribbean Quarterly**, Vol. 37, No. 1, p. 102

practices and addressing the specificities and nuances of Caribbean contextual realities.

On the contrary, I contend that biblical texts are historically and contextually conditioned. They reflect the socio-historical and ideological interests and practices of the contexts from which they emerged. In other words, biblical texts originated from specific contexts and were written from particular perspectives. Three phases are involved in the composition of biblical texts. First, there was the original experience, which was not recorded as it unfolded; second, the collective memory of that experience; and third, the ideological and theological interpretation of the experience.[6] An ideological and theological agenda is present in biblical texts. Accordingly, biblical texts are "readings" of social realities—events, structures, systems of society, values, roles, institutions, social class, conflicts, and behaviors—in which their authors lived. Biblical texts do not create themselves; writers produce them. Biblical texts are written documents that are passive yet not neutral or disinterested. Therefore, understanding who wrote what and why is crucial.

For instance, biblical scholars have suggested that there are four versions of Jewish history or the history of Israel in the Hebrew Scriptures, known as JEPD: J, the Jahwist account, justified David's rule (950-922 b.c.e.); E, the Elohist account, justified Jeroboam I's revolt against Judah (South) (800-750 b.c.e.); D, the Deuteronomist history, justified the revival of state religion under Josiah (722 b.c.e.); and P, the Priestly account, posited the right of priests to rule Judah (South) and show loyalty to Persia (586)[7]. Therefore, Israel's history was written from various perspectives, reflecting contradictory and conflicting

---

Bible Today (London: SCM Press, 1994)

[6] Notes from class lecture by R.S. Sugirtharajah

[7] See Robert B. Coote & Mary P. Coote, **Power, Politics and the Making of the Bible** (Minneapolis: Fortress Press, 1990), pp. 4-9; and David Robert Ord & Robert B. Coote, **Is the Bible True? Understanding the**

social and political interests and practices among different groups with contrasting positions[8]. A case in point is the conquest tradition—the settlement of the Israelite tribes in Canaan after "their" Exodus from Pharaoh's oppressive Egypt. However, after they arrived in Canaan, they showed no regard for the human rights of those they encountered in the land. The once oppressed now oppress.

Moreover, in discussing the purpose of the two Gospel accounts of Jesus's life, R.S. Sugirtharajah contends that the Gospel of Mark uses the Kingdom of God as an alternative to all imperial kingdoms. The Gospel of Luke is about accommodating Roman power, in which Jesus is a religious reformer who poses no threat to Roman control[9]. Therefore, writers of the one life of the same Jesus produce two accounts to suit their particular audiences, interests, concerns, and issues.

Stuart Hall explains that when newscast events are not shown live, they are represented through the aural-visual language of television.[10] In this context, as it follows the 'rules' of language, the event transforms into a story. In other words, an "event becomes a 'story' before it can become a communicative event."[11] Therefore, this explanation positions the Bible as a 'story': the events do not merely reflect reality; they are signified practices.[12] Consequently, they are specific productions of historical and social events and relations that require a decoding strategy to empower the material and ideological conditions that shaped the text.

The point I am making here is that the Bible is a "produced"

[8] Ibid.
Bible Today (London: SCM Press, 1994)
[9] R.S. Sugirtharajah, **The Postcolonial Biblical Reader** (Massachusetts: Oxford, Victoria: Blackwell Publishing, 2006), p. 68
[10] Stuart Hall, *"Encoding and Decoding in the Television Discourse"*, Paper presented to the Council of European Colloquy on "Training in the Critical Reading of Television Language", University of Leicester, September 1973, p. 2
[11] Ibid.
[12] Itumeleng J. Mosala, **Biblical Hermeneutics and Black Theology in South Africa** (Grand Rapids, Michigan: William B. Eerdmans Publishing Company, 1989), p. 124

text[13]. It reflects Israel's socio-historical practices—an account of how successive generations lived and contemplated the promise of salvation. Thus, both the text creators and the text itself convey information and actively shape a version of the reality depicted. Biblical texts take sides. Therefore, this study focuses on the socio-ideological interests and practices that influenced or shaped the text's production and its resulting theological perspective.

In other words, to further emphasize, my primary concerns are what is produced (the text itself, who wrote what and why) and the agency it embodies; who is reading what, how they are reading it, and the agency this reading holds; and how the produced text and its interpretation allow for the subversion or resistance against oppressive systems and structures, ultimately facilitating social transformation.

Furthermore, the concern regarding biblical texts as products and the agency they receive highlights that the factors preceding exegesis— one's presuppositions, praxis, social location, and hermeneutical suspicion—are both valid and critical. What occurs before exegesis is also determinant of how exegesis is conducted. Therefore, I acknowledge that all three aspects—what happens before, during, and following interpretations—are essential to the hermeneutical process. Nonetheless, I focus on the agency attributed to biblical texts as products. Still, I keep a critical perspective on what transpires before and after exegesis, as well as the agency assigned to the social forces and struggles that shape the culture of exegetes.

Therefore, I am locating and interpreting the Bible within the context of faith experiences and the struggle for authenticity and relatedness to the specifics of social realities. Additionally, I am creating a *space* and an imagined counter-reality to unreality and disconnection through which to interpret the Bible. In the worship experience,

---

[13] J. Severino Croatto, **Biblical Hermeneutics: Towards a Theory of Reading as Production of Meaning** (Maryknoll, NY: Orbis Books, 1987), pp. 66-67

particularly in the Caribbean, interpreting the Bible holds the most significant potential for social good. Placing the interpretation of the Bible within the context of worship does not diminish its value in personal and family devotional exercises or in weekday Bible study sessions, where, admittedly, it is not purposefully and critically engaged for social change. Instead, in terms of sheer numbers and opportunities, it is during the weekly Sunday worship experiences that possibilities abound. Those fifty-two opportunities each calendar year represent the most significant untapped potential for social change in the Caribbean.

However, if the interpretation of biblical texts is to have agency in effecting social change, one must deepen one's understanding of these texts as products of social forces and struggles. Essentially, suppose worship experiences are to remain honest and the pulpit or the proclamation from the Bible within those experiences is to be meaningful, significant, effective, and a cultural tool of resistance. In that case, the social forces and struggles of worshippers' experiences and culture, alongside the social forces and struggles that shaped biblical texts, cannot be viewed as unrelated to the specific social realities.

Furthermore, if the disconnection and irrelevance of spiritual and theological structures, the gap between faith and social realities in Caribbean faith experiences, and biblical hermeneutical practices are to be authentic, integrated, and united. The existing oppressive structures and their causes must be identified, opposed, and transformed.

As such, I will need to understand how and why resistance develops. By resistance, I refer to the construction of a consciousness that challenges, exposes, and overcomes those social systems and practices that oppress. Chris Mullard identifies four movements in the conceptual framework of resistance[14]: first, the protection of interests and power by the ruling class, which necessarily requires oppression and repression;

---

[14] Chris Mullard, **Race, Power and Resistance** (London, Boston, Melbourne: Routledge & Kegan Paul, 1985), pp. 38, 47-48, 172-173

second, this protection leads to the relative "powerlessness" of the ruled, which in turn generates a consciousness of an alternative social order; third, the ruling class responds with even more oppressive and repressive measures to legitimize its supremacy; and fourth, factions of interest are consequently established, with the ruling class working to safeguard its power and interests while the ruled strive to build power to transform the unjust social system.

While I will use Mullard's four movements to determine where resistance occurs and what drives agency in Caribbean biblical hermeneutical practices, I will also examine whether the particularity and uniqueness of the Caribbean context assist in answering how and why resistance develops differently from Mullard's four movements. Additionally, I will remain keenly aware of whether the three elements of the resistance ethic exert any influence. These three elements are: *separating* oneself from any socio-economic and political system that is not organized with the community's well-being as its ultimate goal; *denouncing* the hidden intentions or overt pretensions of any social system that is structured for hegemony; and proclaim*ing* God's judgment on any socio-economic system that oppresses[15].

Resistance, however, is less problematic than I suggested here. I have a limited understanding of resistance to actions outside the system. However, what happens externally is not exclusive from what happens internally (opposition).[16] Resistance and opposition are not antagonistic relatives. Sometimes, the opposition employs tools from outside the system for reform. For example, the psychosocial resistance of slave women in the Caribbean during slavery—manifested through uncooperative acts

---

[15] See Dagoberto Ramirez Fernandez *"The judgment of God in the Multinationals: Revelation 18"* in Leif E. Vaage ed. **Subversive Scriptures – Revolutionary Readings of the Christian Bible in Latin America** (Pennsylvania: Trinity Press International, 1997), pp. 96-100
[16] M. Certeau, *"On The Oppositional Practices of Everyday Life"* **Social Text**, 1980 3:3-43

like strikes, malingering, insubordination, control of fertility, and (h) ideology[17]—occurred within the system but did not undermine the goal of resisting racial and socio-economic domination. Thus, there is no single form of resistance but rather a syncretism of resistance and opposition. Nevertheless, the type of resistance this study focuses on is running away to contest domination or as an anti-hegemonic stance (Philemon).

In summary, my conclusion from this background check of Caribbean biblical hermeneutical practice is that **less** agency is given to the materiality of the contexts surrounding biblical texts during interpretation and **more** to their literary-rhetorical features and contextual relevance, resulting in minimal resistance against oppressive systems. This imbalance in agency is illustrated in the work of George Mulrain, a former tutor at the United Theological College of the West Indies in Jamaica. Mulrain acknowledges, "When a passage of Scripture is properly expounded, one ought to be in a position to know more about the historical facts behind that passage and its context, *but perhaps more importantly, its meaning for today.*"[18] (Emphasis mine). However, Mulrain also recognizes that in studying biblical texts, "we need to know something about those who wrote them, *and in whose interests they were written...bearing in mind that the Bible itself was written from a biased perspective.*"[19] (Emphasis mine). In other words, there is no dispute about emphasizing biblical texts' contemporary meaning and contextual relevance. The disagreement is that the socio-ideological interests and social practices that create biblical texts are not given agency.

---

[17] Robert Beckford, **Dread and Pentecostalism, A Political Theology for Black Church in Britain** (London: SPCK, 2000), p. 103

[18] George Mulrain, *"Is There a Calypso Exegesis?"* in R.S. Sugirtharajah ed., **Voices From the Margins – Interpreting The Bible in The Third World** (Maryknoll: Orbis/SPCK, 1995), p. 37

[19] Ibid., p. 38

Aim

Therefore, this study develops a biblical resistant reading strategy within a Caribbean context that seeks to come to grips with and gives agency to both the material conditions from which biblical writers produced texts and the particularities and peculiarities of Caribbean socio-historical realities. Fulfilling this aim addresses the need to give agency to the material conditions from which biblical texts emerged, which is absent in the Caribbean biblical hermeneutical practice. Here, the purpose is not to recover biblical texts' original audience, message, and intention. Neither is it to recount the actual history or artifactual evidence as against focusing on the epigraphical evidence, the confession of faith in God that portrayed the world (interpretation of reality) in which the writers lived and discovered themselves in the light of faith in God. Instead, it is to understand or to see that biblical communities lived as part of a real, inhabited world, with real people and places[20] while uncovering and emphasizing the ideologies, social forces, and relationships that shaped the biblical writers' interpretations of their social realities.

Therefore, I am endeavoring to establish a connection between the "readings" of the socio-historical realities of biblical writers and the Caribbean readers of biblical texts. A biblical resistant reading strategy requires giving self-conscious attention to the world, interests, or practices that influenced the production of the text (*behind the text*), the writer's interpretation of reality (*on the text*), and the influences and experiences that shape the reader's understanding (*in front of the text*) or the specific nuances of the interpreter's context. The production and reading of biblical texts are forms of social action. Through these modes of social action, all three hermeneutical moves—behind the text, on or within the text, and in front of the text—intersect to form a

---

[20] Norman Gottwald, **The Hebrew Bible – A Socio-literary Introduction** (Philadelphia: Fortress Press), pp. 35-78

biblically resistant hermeneutic within a Caribbean context. Essentially, the resistant reading strategy identifies the biblical ideologies, struggles, and social practices one is hermeneutically engaging with.[21]

A brief overview of the influences and experiences that shape the Caribbean reader of biblical texts is essential to demonstrate that the mode of existence is resistance. In the interpretive process, biblical texts are not isolated from a given historical context or conjuncture; they are influenced by the social forces at play. Likewise, interpreters exist within their own historical and social contexts.

The Caribbean is a "created" community. The indigenous inhabitants of the Caribbean – Tainos, Caribs, and Arrawaks – were mercilessly exterminated by the marauding colonialists of the fifteenth and sixteenth centuries. Africans, against their will, and later Asians as indentured laborers, were brought to the Caribbean not to settle the islands but specifically for plantation labor. Thus, from its inception, the Caribbean was intended to serve purposes that were extrinsic to, or not in the interest of, its own economic and political advancement and development.

Furthermore, the Caribbean has never fully controlled its decision-making processes or the forces and systems of production. When individuals are stripped of the right to self- definition or to declare who or what they are and are denied the chance to pursue self- determination or shape their future, they become powerless. This powerlessness is a cause, not just a symptom, of removing the opportunity for self-definition and self-determination. The roots of this powerlessness continue to shape the interpretation of scripture in the context of the Caribbean.

This brief historical overview of the Caribbean reveals that the frameworks of our spirituality and socio-political economy are deeply

---

[21] Mosala, **Biblical Hermeneutics**, p. 122

intertwined with, dominated by, and controlled by foreign forces and influences, making resistance our mode of existence.

Given that our mode of existence is resistance, it will be crucial to distinguish and resist the causes of powerlessness by isolating and examining the issues of decision-making and production. This includes understanding how others perceive us and how we view ourselves and addressing our social relations to production and power within Caribbean societies. Consequently, this study will advocate for recognizing the agency of the socio- historical and existential realities of the Caribbean reader of biblical texts and the ideological or dominant influences on those realities while also acknowledging that biblical texts are ideological productions and products of social practices: history conditions theology, and the reader's culture shapes or conditions exegesis[22].

I am claiming that interpreting biblical texts is also influenced by the interpreter's social, economic, cultural, and religious context. A disinterested interpreter does not exist. I am undertaking this study as a powerless Afro-Caribbean male Methodist. My main concern is that biblical texts are socio-ideological products. I am interested in exploring the agency of Caribbean peoples' social forces and struggles in the interpretive process. In this study, my voice represents that of a Caribbean subaltern who lives in a context shaped by geopolitical and economic hegemony.

Despite my interest in the socio-historical realities of the Caribbean, this study will advance a resistant reading strategy that starts with the biblical text as evidence of the social environment in which it was produced. This study differs significantly from the typical approach in Caribbean biblical hermeneutical practice by interpreting the ideology,

---

[22] George Mulrain *"Is There A Calypso Exegesis?"* in R.S. Sugirtharajah ed. **Voices From the Margin – Interpreting The Bible in the Third World** (ORBIS/SPCK, 1995), p. 42

social forces, and relationships that shape biblical texts. As mentioned earlier, in Caribbean biblical hermeneutical practice, there is a tendency to begin either with an analysis of the literary features of the biblical text or with how the biblical text communicates its messages, before moving on to biblical-theological reflections on the social realities of readers or the meaning of the biblical text for their lived experiences[23].

Regardless of the starting point, focusing on biblical texts as products remains essential. The question is what occurs "there." Contextual realities do not always have to be the starting point for interpretation to be liberating. Reexamining the biblical text within its socio-historical context is valid and relevant, offering liberating possibilities. A socio- structural analysis of biblical texts is more likely to reveal and challenge oppressive and exploitative systems and structures in society, highlighting the need for social transformation. This potential arises from a resistant reading strategy that emphasizes socio-structural realities. It effectively exposes, challenges, and questions the nature of social relationships, systems, and structures embedded within biblical texts and societies.

Methodology

No one mode of reading the Bible will suffice for interpretation. To develop a Caribbean biblically resistant hermeneutic, an interdisciplinary approach is necessary. As such, postcolonialism, associated with R.S. Sugirtharajah's reading strategy, and the historical-materialist approach,

---

[23] Stephen Jennings *"The Word in Context: The Essential Criterion For Doing and Reflecting Authentic Caribbean Theology"* in **Caribbean Journal of Religious Studies**, Vol. 8 No. 2 April 1988, pp. 1-10

in the manner of Itumeleng J. Mosala[24] and as critiqued by Gerald O. West[25], are the analytical concepts that will serve as the tools of analysis.

Postcolonialism

For Sugirtharajah, postcolonialism primarily concerns detecting, questioning, challenging, and exposing how the dominated are represented by the dominant, the link between power and knowledge, and the tracking down of ideologies in plots and characterizations in texts and their interpretations; as such, postcolonialism is interested in biblical writers' versions of reality and how that reality is re-inscribed in interpretation.[26] Since this study is interested in the socio-ideological agenda and social practices that produced biblical texts, postcolonialism is a critical analysis tool.

Historical-materialist approach

For Mosala, the historical-materialist approach focuses on uncovering the social, gender, class, vested interests, social practices, and struggles in biblical texts. Within the oppressive context of apartheid South Africa, where Mosala developed his biblical interpretive approach, identifying the socio-structural issues in biblical texts was a crucial first step to fostering critical discourse in the liberation struggle. There are three key aspects of the historical-materialist approach that I will address: the nature of the mode of production—whether communal, tributary, or capitalistic; the formation of socio-economic classes based on their relationship to the mode of production; and the ideological

---

[24] Itumeleng J. Mosala, **Biblical Hermeneutics and Biblical Theology in Southern Africa** (Grand Rapids, MI: Eerdmans, 1989)

[25] Gerald West, **Biblical Hermeneutics of Liberation: Modes of Reading the Bible in the South African Context** (Pietermaritzburg: Cluster Publications, and Maryknoll NY: Orbis Books, 1991).

[26] R.S. Sugirtharajah, **The Postcolonial Biblical Reader** (Massachusetts, Oxford, Victoria: Blackwell Publishing, 2006), p. 88

manifestations that emerge from the mode of production[27] and its associated social class structure.

I am emphasizing that ideological manifestations are not solely a product of class struggle. Richard Horsley argued that Roman imperial power relations relied not only on armies, taxes, and administrative systems, but also on the imperial cult—temples, shrines, images, sacrifices, and festivals.[28] Nevertheless, my focus is on the fundamental material relationships within the Roman Empire and the socio-ideological agenda and social practices that shaped those material relationships, particularly in relation to the socio- historical context of Philemon. This emphasis on the ideology and social practices produced by the material relationships in Philemon, rather than the imperial cult, aligns with the Caribbean context of this study.

Modes of Reading the Bible

West advocates for multiple Bible "reading" approaches without prioritizing a[29] single method. He argues for the integration of all three hermeneutical moves in biblical interpretation—namely, the context behind the text, the content within the text, and the implications in front of the text—to engage with biblical texts as they relate to specific human conditions within a framework of faith, emphasizing both personal and social transformation. This reading strategy aligns with my interest as it empowers the materiality of the biblical text and the context of the interpreter.

All three reading strategies—postcolonialism, historical-materialism,

---

[27] Mosala, **Biblical Hermeneutics**, p. 103

[28] Richard Horsley ed., **Paul and Empire, Religion and Power in Roman Imperial Society** (Pennsylvania: Trinity Press International, 1997) p. 23-4 ; see also, Richard Horsley, *"Submerged Biblical Histories and Imperial Biblical Studies"* in R.S. Sugirtharajah, **The Postcolonial Bible** (Sheffield: Sheffield Academic Press, 1998), pp. 162-67

[29] West, **Biblical Hermeneutics of Liberation**, p. 157

and contextual Bible study—are essential for analyzing a resistant hermeneutic, such as what is envisioned here within the Caribbean context. Paying attention to the socio-ideological interests and social practices that shaped the theological interpretation of biblical texts will influence the development of this biblical resistant hermeneutic. As a result of employing postcolonialism, historical-materialism, and contextual Bible study as analytical tools, the following questions will serve as the foundation for analysis, not just to frame and shape the discussion but as a reading strategy to identify, track, and reveal the imperial intentions and assumptions that inform and influence the production of biblical texts and the social dynamics at play in the context of readers:

1. *From what or whose point of view is the text written?*
2. *What socio-ideological and theological interests are shaping the text or are shaped by it?*
3. *In what type of situation, and as part of what social struggle, did people write this text in this manner?*[30]
4. *Whose voice is silenced or heard in the text? How are the marginalized represented or understood? Are they being spoken to? Do they have a voice?*
5. *What are the sources of conflict and tension stemming from vested interests and social practices in the text?*

Moreover, other proponents of the historical-materialist approach are drawn into the discussion. For example, the work of Norman K.

---

[30] Christopher Rowland & Mark Corner, **Liberating Exegesis: The Challenge of Liberation Theology to Biblical Studies** (London: SPCK, 1991 2nd. edition), p. 143

Gottwald[31], Richard A. Horsley[32] C.L.R. James[33] and Fernando F. Segovia[34] is referenced, as they all make critical contributions to the perspective that ideology, social forces, and relationships shape and influence the "reading" of social realities.

Additionally, Paul's letter to Philemon in the New Testament serves as the chosen biblical text due to its parallels with the Caribbean experience of slavery and the potential it holds for developing a resilient biblical-theological hermeneutic. Clearly, slavery in the first century differs in nature and character from the slavery practiced during the golden age of colonialism in the Caribbean. Nonetheless, Philemon remains relevant, as the principles of justice, dignity, self-determination, and self-definition do not change with shifting circumstances. An oppressed individual or community, whether in the first century or the twenty-first century, remains oppressed, just as the Caribbean continues to be oppressed.

Philemon is a significant case for biblical interpretation in Caribbean social history. Like Caribbean societies with their history of colonialism and cultural imperialism, the faith community in the household of Philemon—and by extension, the broader community of faith—was challenged to find a liberating practice within the oppressive structure of the Roman Empire. Moreover, mirroring the Caribbean experience of slavery, Onesimus lacks a voice or say in his future; he has no right to self-definition or self-determination.

---

[31] Norman K. Gottwald, ed. *The Bible and Liberation: Political and Social Hermeneutics* (Maryknoll: Orbis Books, 1993, revised ed.)
The Tribes of Yahweh: A Sociology of the Religion of Liberated Israel 1250–1050 B.C.E., (Maryknoll: Orbis Books, 1979)
[32] Richard A. Horsley ed., *The Bible and Liberation: Political and Social Hermeneutics* (Maryknoll: Orbis Books, 1993, revised ed.)
[33] C.L.R.James, *Beyond A Boundary* (London: Stanley Paul & Co., 1963)
[34] Fernando F. Segovia ed., *Reading From This Place vol.1 Social Location and Biblical Interpretation in the United States* (Minneapolis: Fortress Press, 1995)

Illustrative Material

The work, however, does not focus entirely on theoretical analysis. Illustrative materials are gathered from primary sources through focus groups of about one hundred seventy-five (175) individuals across six Caribbean countries to support the main theoretical concepts. The perspectives of as wide a spectrum as possible were gathered from trained or ordained and non-ordained Christian educators from various confessional groups— Baptists, Pentecostals, Methodists, Moravians, Bible Believers Fellowship, and Catholics— across diverse age ranges regarding what might constitute the elements of a Bible study, sermon, or lesson using the letter of Philemon. Although the sample of one hundred seventy- five individuals in six Caribbean countries may seem small, the findings can be quantified and support the conclusions drawn.

Gathering material from the focus groups was conducted for two purposes. First, to discover the prevailing or contemporary biblical reading strategy or strategies within the Caribbean context, especially regarding Philemon; and second, to ascertain which aspect(s) or combination(s) of the hermeneutical process – *behind the text* (the ideological interests and social practices that influenced the biblical writer's perspective), on or *within the text* (how the text conveys its message), and *in front of the text* (the experiences and influences that shape the reader's interpretation of biblical text) –shape the "reading" strategies.

A two-stage process approach was adopted for the exercises. First, groups were divided into smaller units of four or five people, addressing the same questions or issues and reporting back to the group. Each group was asked to read Philemon and then respond to the following questions: How would you interpret this letter? What reading strategy would you use to understand it? What would you say this letter is about? What was the purpose of writing this letter? Next, after the groups made their responses, they received feedback on their findings.

In addition to being a practitioner of biblical hermeneutics as a pastor for the past seventeen years, conducting the seminars allowed me to engage with and observe biblical hermeneutics in a Caribbean context. There was no detachment from the process. Principal theoretical ideas are integrated with practical data applications, systematically collected and analyzed to develop a grounded theory.[35] Consequently, the potential for change 'on the ground' in biblical hermeneutical practices within a Caribbean context was noted.

Structure

The work features six chapters in its revised version, which include an introduction, foreword, conclusion, and afterword.

Chapter 1 explores **the Bible's role in Caribbean biblical hermeneutics** and its impact on the social histories of nations primarily affected by British conquest and colonialism. How the Bible is interpreted and understood is essential for its function as a tool for advocating liberation and social change in Caribbean societies.

In examining the Bible's role in Caribbean biblical hermeneutics, the chapter alsocritically assesses **the history and development of biblical hermeneutics within the Caribbean context**. It divides Caribbean social history into three specific historical periods, which will serve as the foundation for analyzing each period:

- Colonial   1492 -1838
- Post-"Emancipation":   1838-1960s
- "Independence":   1960s onwards

The division into specific historical periods serves three purposes:

---

[35] See B. Glaser & A. Strauss, **The Discovery of Grounded Theory** (Chicago: Aldine De Gruyter, 1967), pp. 2-6; Glaser and Strauss define grounded theory as theory brought into relation to data, so there is no mismatch between theory and empirical data (p. 6).

first, to highlight and identify the significant shifts in social relations and socio-historical contexts; second, to explore the biblical "reading" strategies used by the interpreters mentioned in each period, along with the consequences of those strategies; and third, to understand the biblical texts that Caribbean hermeneutes engage with. In other words, these specific periods are not merely about the overall sequencing of events in Caribbean social history.

Additionally, in chapter one, I examine what provides or hinders agency to resistance within the biblical interpretive strategies of the interpreters mentioned, whether in the socio- historic context from which the biblical texts emerged or in the socio-historical circumstances of the interpreters.

Tracking the contours of Caribbean biblical hermeneutical practice in this manner allows for evaluating whether agency is granted to the ideological agenda and social practices that create biblical texts, as well as the socio-historical realities of the Caribbean. Furthermore, it enables an examination of what occurs in the stages prior to exegesis— such as praxis, presuppositions, social location, and hermeneutical suspicion—and what follows, or in other words, the social consequences of interpreting biblical texts.

The Bible's role in Caribbean biblical hermeneutics is reflected in the chapter "A History and Development of Biblical Hermeneutics within a Caribbean Context" from the 2010 edition.

In **Chapter 2, biblical hermeneutical practices within the Caribbean context** are analyzed based on the findings of the empirical study conducted in six Caribbean countries and the reading strategies identified in biblical hermeneutical practices in Caribbean social history.

To support the claim that biblical texts are products of dominant socio-ideological interests, theological perspectives, and social systems and practices, **Chapter 3** places **Philemon within its context** by focusing on the socio-ideological and theological agenda, alongside the socio-economic and political practices that contributed to its creation. The crucial issue here is verse 16, particularly the meanings of "in the Lord" and "in the flesh." When the faith community gathers *(House church)*, Philemon and Onesimus are brothers. However, when they disperse to live their lives in the community *(Household)*, they assume the roles of enslaver and enslaved person. Can Philemon be both Onesimus's master and brother, while Onesimus is simultaneously Philemon's slave and brother? In this context, is Paul advocating for manumission? If that is the case, understanding Paul's intention through the lens of manumission risks reducing a personal, yet profoundly important, issue to a mere Master-slave relationship, thereby overlooking the communal significance and implications of this text for the institution of slavery itself. The challenge here is that Paul becomes ensnared in his dichotomies and the grip of the Empire: there are no male or female distinctions, yet women are expected to remain silent in the church; there are no distinctions between Jew or Gentile, yet Paul himself is a Pharisee among Pharisees; and there are no enslaved persons or free individuals, yet Onesimus must return to an enslaver.

Before addressing these issues, however, we must consider verses 1 and 12. Verse 1 indicates that the matter of Onesimus's return to Philemon is not just between them; it also demands public attention and a collective solution. Do we not have a model of an egalitarian system and social relations that exists independently of distinctions, serving as an alternative to Roman rule?[36] Furthermore, if we interpret "sending back" in verse 12 as a technical term for "runaway," what exactly does "runaway" imply? Did Onesimus truly "run away"? Was achieving reconciliation prioritized over social justice? Or does the issue lie in "the stark distinction between the treatment of individual slaves by their respective masters and the broader inhumanity of slavery as an

---

[36] Horsley, **Submerged Biblical Histories**, p. 165

institution"?[37] Alternatively, was "runaway" a form of resistance from Onesimus? Moreover, if the priority was neither social justice nor the inhumanity of slavery, what then explains Paul's complicit, pacifist, or less-than- revolutionary stance?

Placing Philemon in its 'context' allows for an evaluation of the interpretations *of Philemon chapter 4* by examining its appropriation by both pro- and anti-slavery advocates, as well as enslaved individuals from liberal, liberationist, and postcolonial viewpoints. One significant silence in Philemon is the lack of Onesimus's voice. Is Paul's voice the sole one present, or could it represent the voice of the emerging church? If it does, is the emerging church cautious about being perceived as an alternative model of egalitarianism or as a challenge to the power dynamics of the Roman Empire?

Consequently, the interpretations of Philemon are assessed to determine whether Philemon has been separated from its socio-historical context during its appropriation and with what interpretive outcomes, or how biblical scholarship has interpreted Philemon. Specifically, I am interested in the socio-ideological perspectives through which the cited interpreters approached Philemon to ascertain whether it was perceived and understood as a site of struggle. Essentially, I aim to uncover, first, how the socio-ideological and theological agendas present in Philemon influence these interpretations; second, to evaluate whether it is the rhetorical features of the letter or the experiences and influences surrounding their contextual realities that shape the cited interpreters' reading strategies and agency; and third, to investigate where resistance is or is not occurring.

Chapter 5 develops **a resistant biblical hermeneutics reading strategy tailored for a Caribbean context** by merging insights from both practice and theory. In other words, the biblical resistant

---

[37] Moses I. Finley, **Ancient Slavery and Modern Ideology** (London: Chatto & Windus, 1980) p. 122

hermeneutic is not merely an intellectual exercise or abstract analysis. Rather, it places strong emphasis on commitment to and engagement in social struggle as a means of social transformation.

Chapter 6 proposes and evaluates *the implications of developing a biblically resistant hermeneutic within a Caribbean context,* focusing on oppressive structures of spirituality and theologies, biblical hermeneutical practice, and the challenge against oppressive systems and structures in Caribbean societies. Seven implications of the work are discussed.

(i) *Defining the Bible*: This work differentiates between the Bible and the word of God. In this context, the Bible is considered an "action," representing the practiced signified or the 'story' of a particular group's socio-historical experience during a specific time in their pursuit of becoming the people of God. In this sense, while the Bible remains a revelation, it is not merely dictation. Who God is and what God does are encapsulated in that 'story,' but not at the expense of other 'stories' reflecting God's involvement in human history.

(ii) *"Reading" the Bible*: Furthermore, one consequence of this work is the necessity to select appropriate reading strategies for interpreting biblical texts in preaching, teaching, and study. This choice is not only demanded of trained theologians but also of countless Christian educators and disciples who bear the responsibility of conveying the Bible's message without the advantage of formal training. Essentially, the issue here relates to how meaning is derived from biblical texts and whether such meaning can exist independently of social engagement, that is, without becoming existentially involved in the lived realities of the people to whom one preaches and among whom one lives.

(iii) Examin*ing theology from non-traditional perspectives*: Another consequence of this work is the essential concern it raises about questioning and revealing the structure of social relations involved in decision-making and the production within Caribbean economies and societies. The existing structures appear to have led to widespread economic poverty and unemployment among the population.

Investigating the causes and systemic issues related to economic poverty and mass unemployment will provide biblical-theological insights. Here, questions are raised, and issues are highlighted through examples that allow for an analysis of the *budgets* for Antigua and Barbuda for the years 2001 and 2006, as well as the 2001 census, to address systemic problems and assess the quality of life for Caribbean people.

(iv) *Understanding the foundation and framework of Caribbean religions*: A deep exploration of Caribbean social realities may reveal that there may not be a singular Caribbean theology, but rather multiple perspectives in Caribbean theologies. Nevertheless, it remains essential to express theological viewpoints grounded in the social forces, struggles, and the urgent call for human dignity and social justice among Caribbean peoples.

(v) *Structuring spirituality against resistance*: This work takes seriously the fact that the Caribbean is a community "created" by Europeans, despite the brave efforts of the Caribs, Arawaks, Maroons, and all those who revolted and continue to revolt against foreign domination and oppression. Central to the European colonial enterprise was a worldview that deemed it the right, even the duty, of Europeans to impose themselves on unsuspecting peoples. The inspiration for this enterprise was rooted in theology. Key to this theology was the assertion that God is apathetic—God neither "knows" nor "experiences" the suffering endured by human beings or the colonized. This view presents Christianity as non-incarnational and as an otherworldly hope that dismisses the significance of the material conditions of this world. Two consequences of such imposed views for Caribbean peoples included alienation from their lived realities and the domestication of religious faith.

(vi) *Engaging folk culture worship:* The aim here is to create worship experiences centered on the community's interests, serving as counter-cultural or radical spaces of resistance.

(vii) *Cultural Expressions as Hermeneutical Practices*: One implication of this work is that culture shapes theological reflections. The Caribbean is culturally diverse, featuring many nationalities, ethnicities, and cultures. Two cultural expressions that bridge the divide are cricket and carnival. This work employs cricket and carnival as epistemological lenses and means of understanding to examine the contextuality and historical process of developing perspectives in Caribbean theologies. In other words, this work uses culture to interpret oppressive structures in spirituality and theology.

In summary, the work maintains tension, granting agency and providing conjuncture[38]. On one hand, the **agency** relates to the experiences of marginality and injustice faced by people, fostering a critical consciousness that leads to praxis and interpreting biblical texts as products of social forces and struggles. Where such agency is present, ideological agendas and ruling class ideas are identified and exposed. On the other hand, **conjuncture** encompasses an awareness of the significance and impact of socio- economic and political circumstances, both local and international, on one's community. The tension between agency and conjuncture fosters resistance and inspires the envisioning of an alternative social world, providing strategies for bringing that alternative social world into existence. Wherever such envisioning occurs—whether in worship experiences, Bible study sessions, or

---

[38] Brian Meeks, **Narratives of Resistance – Jamaica, Trinidad, the Caribbean** (Jamaica: The University Press of the West Indies, 2000), p. 58

communities of interest—that space is not an escape from reality but a space of reality where strategies for social change and resistance are nurtured to re-engage with lived experiences[39].

Finally, the work *concludes by* emphasizing the necessity of analytical concepts as advocated by Caribbean social scientists like C.L.R. James, George Lamming, and Walter Rodney, in comprehending how social forces and struggles both shape and are shaped by social realities, which serve as contexts for engaging in theology and developing biblical "reading" strategies.

The conclusion will be followed by an **afterword** from Dr. Steed Davidson, the Executive Director of the Society for Biblical Literature (SBL) and a Caribbean biblical scholar, who will evaluate the work and its significance for ongoing biblical interpretation in the Caribbean. Additionally, there will be a **foreword** by Dr. Judith Soares, a retired Senior Lecturer and Tutor/Coordinator of the Women and Development Unit at The University of the West Indies, School of Continuing Studies, Barbados.

---

[39] Ibid. p. 93

PART ONE

A CRITICAL ASSESSMENT OF THE HISTORY AND DEVELOPMENT OF BIBLICAL HERMENEUTICS WITHIN THE CARIBBEAN

CHAPTER 1

THE BIBLE'S ROLE IN CARIBBEAN BIBLICAL HERMENEUTICS

Introduction

In Caribbean Christianization and civilization, the cross arrived before the Bible. When Columbus landed by chance on the Caribbean island of Guanahani in the Bahamas in October 1492, his first act was to plant a cross. He renamed the island San Salvador (Saint Savior or liberator). Columbus renamed islands wherever chance took him in the Caribbean during his four voyages (1492, 1493, 1498, 1502). By doing so, he usurped the right of Caribbean inhabitants to self-definition and self- determination in the name of the Spanish crown. For five centuries thereafter, Britain, France, and Holland followed in Spain's footsteps to conquer, rule, and dominate through massacre, cultural genocide, slavery, and indentureship. Imperial and commercial interests drove their involvement in the Caribbean. Consequently, the order – cross first, 'civilization' second – meant that Christianization was subordinated to 'civilization,' with the Bible faithfully serving domination.

When Columbus sailed to the Caribbean in 1493, accompanied by the Benedictine friar Boyl and other missionaries to the indigenous Arawaks and Carib Indians, he landed on Hispaniola. On January 6, 1494, a worship service was held in Hispaniola to mark their safe arrival, including Scripture and song. The arrival of the Bible was celebrated. However, by the end of the year, Boyl and others returned to Spain, disturbed and troubled by the unjust and cruel treatment inflicted on the indigenous people in the name of Christianity. Their unexpected return was an early omen of the sanction the Bible was expected to provide for such cruelties.

Throughout the centuries, Caribbean history has been the narrative and song of a specific people's fight to free themselves from imposed foreign values, customs, and control. These battles against domination and oppression, as well as the quest for emancipation, shaped the context and interpretive approaches of Caribbean Biblical hermeneutical practice.

In the following, I will explore the role of the Bible in the social history of countries significantly impacted by British conquest and colonialism. This social history can be divided into three overlapping periods.

The periods are as follows:

- Colonial: 1492-1838
- Post-"emancipation":   1838-1959
- "Independence":   1960s- onwards

Dividing Caribbean social history into these distinct periods serves three purposes. First, these periods provide a picture of the context for interpreting each period's socio-historical realities (material conditions). Second, they indicate the agency attributed to these realities in the adaptations of the biblical story. Third, they help identify the various interpretive approaches used. Each new historical period introduced a different theological stance and, consequently, a different interpretive method or practice.

This approach to the task does not aim to explore the entire history of the Caribbean, as that exceeds the scope of this study. Instead, the main areas of British conquest and colonialism will serve as the focus of biblical hermeneutics, specifically Jamaica, Barbados, Guyana, and the Leeward Islands. My interest in these periods centers around emphasizing the material conditions of the Caribbean context and their influence on biblical hermeneutical practices as they relate to the readers of the biblical texts, their social location, reading strategies, choice of texts, meaning- making, understanding of the Bible, instances of resistance, and the social consequences or effects of the hermeneutics (see Tables on pp.56, 76, and 93).

Additionally, dividing Caribbean social history into the periods of Colonial, Post-"emancipation," and Post-"independence" situates both Caribbean readers of biblical texts and foreign missionaries who engaged with these texts in a Caribbean context within their socio-historical framework. Furthermore, the reading strategies are situated within the prevailing biblical criticism of each period, highlighting how the cited reading strategies either reflected or challenged the dominant biblical thought of their time.

During the colonial period, readers engaged in a hermeneutical practice focused on the original audience, message, and intention. What mattered was what the text meant and what it meant historically. In biblical criticism, this hermeneutical practice is referred to as *historical criticism*. In historical criticism, the *readers' social location, presuppositions, culture, and experiences* were considered irrelevant, as only the text itself mattered.[40] The readers' task was to extract meaning *from* the text, rather than imposing meaning onto it. A notable exception to this reading strategy, despite the era's suppression of indigenous voices,[41] was that of Sam

---

[40] ¹Fernando F. Segovia & Mary Ann Tolbert, **Reading From This Place – Social Location and Biblical Interpretation in the United States Volume 1** (Minneapolis: Fortress Press, 1995), p. 13

[41] Fernando F. Segovia, **Decolonizing Biblical Studies - A View From the Margins** (Maryknoll, New York: Orbis Books, 2000), pp. 147-150

Sharpe, who interpreted the oppressive socio-economic circumstances through the biblical texts with revolutionary outcomes.

The post-"emancipation" period marked an era where biblical criticism underwent a paradigm shift from text-dominant approaches to reader-oriented reading strategies, or *literary criticism*. In literary criticism, the focus is on the artistic or rhetorical features of the text, including who wrote what, how, and the meaning that arises from the interaction between the reader and the text. *This indicates* that the reader's social location, presuppositions, culture, and experiences are of little consequence, and there is less emphasis on the text's socio-economic, political, and ideological dimensions. Nevertheless, the reading strategies employed by readers during this period reflected the influences of their socio-economic, political, and cultural contexts, thereby illustrating that "every reader is historically and socially conditioned."[42] Moreover, these reading strategies signify the emergence and dominance of liberation hermeneutics within Caribbean biblical hermeneutical practice, highlighting the theological readings and implications of socio-economic, political, and cultural realities in light of faith based on the Bible.

Against this background of interest in the social realities of readers, in the post-"post-independence" period, "readers 'read' biblical texts from within specific locations and with specific interests in mind".[43] My interest, therefore, in this post-"post-independence" period is not limited to the different reading strategies that different readers employed but extends to why different readers "read" in different ways. The tables on pages 56,76, and 93 show that the various ways of reading resulted from the positionality of readers – race, gender, religion, class, ethnicity, ideology – or the mixed status and marginalized subject or dominant

---

[42] Fernando F. Segovia & Mary Ann Tolbert, **Teaching the Bible – The Discourses and Politics of Biblical Pedagogy** (Maryknoll, New York: Orbis Books, 1998), p. 123

[43] Segovia, **Decolonizing Biblical Studies**, p. 43

positions[44] the readers embodied and to which they belonged.[45] In biblical criticism, this reading strategy where attention is given to the socio-economic, political, and cultural circumstances of both the context of the biblical text and readers and the ideological commitment and stance of readers[46] is known as *cultural criticism*.

Postcolonial criticism of biblical studies is absent from the tracking of Caribbean biblical hermeneutical practice and, therefore, from tables 56, 76, and 93 below, but it significantly influences this study. The pioneer of postcolonial criticism in biblical studies is R.S. Sugirtharajah, who first introduced this approach in 1996[47]. While historical, literary, and cultural criticism typically focuses on either the biblical texts or the readers—or both—postcolonialism "perceives its task as critiquing, problematizing, and exposing contradictions and inadequacies in both the text and its interpretation."[48] For Sugirtharajah, this task is both historical and hermeneutical. It is historical because it genuinely engages with colonial domination and the suppression of the voice of the "other," thereby exposing "the imperial assumptions and intentions of biblical interpretation, as those who opposed them[49];" and it is hermeneutical in that it re-reads biblical texts from the perspective of postcolonial concerns such as creolization, 'home' as a different reality in the Diaspora, and multiculturalism.[50] In Caribbean biblical hermeneutical practice, the reading strategies of Sam Sharpe, Paul Bogle, Marcus Garvey, and Rastafarianism align with this postcolonial criticism of

---

[44] Mary Ann Tolbert, *"Reading For Liberation"* in Segovia & Tolbert, **Reading From This Place**, p. 266

[45] Segovia & Tolbert, **Reading From This Place**, pp. 28-31

[46] Ibid. p. 28

[47] R.S. Sugirtharajah, *"From Orientalist to Post-Colonial: Notes on Reading Practices"* **Asia Journal of Theology**, Vol. 10 No. 1, 1996, pp. 20-27

[48] R.S. Sugirtharajah, **Voices From the Margins, Interpreting the Bible in the Third World**, revised and expanded third edition (Maryknoll, New York: Orbis Books, 2006), p. 5

[49] Ibid. p. 72

[50] Ibid.

biblical studies, challenging hegemony and discriminatory colonial representations.

Colonial era: 1492–1838

Socio-historical and political realities and forces

Natal alienation[51]

The period from 1492 to 1838 marks the beginning and "legal end" of slave trading in the Caribbean. This era was characterized by genocide, slavery, and indentureship. Against their will, Africans were brought to the Caribbean to labor on sugar plantations as slaves. In Africa, they had professions, families, and a sense of dignity and worth. Thus, in their homeland, they were socialized and civilized.

However, when forcibly taken by slave traders in Africa and purchased by European planters in the West Indies, they instantly became merchandise or property of the plantation owners. All rights and any sense of human worth and dignity were forcibly stripped away. For instance, the baptismal records from the Anglican churches of St. Dorothy's, Old Harbour, and the cathedral in Spanish Town, both in Jamaica, indicated that only the name of the plantation and the racial designation mattered to the white European curate, rather than the complete identity of the slave.

---

[51] The term comes from Orlando Patterson who holds "slaves were not allowed to integrate the experience of their ancestors into their lives; to inform their understanding of social reality with inherited meanings of their natural forbears; or to anchor the living present in any conscious community of memory" see in *Slavery and Social Death* (Cambridge, Massachusetts: Harvard University Press, 1982), p. 5

Table 1: 1 Identification of slaves
Example: St. Dorothy's Anglican
Church, Old Harbour, Jamaica

Condition	Estate (1811-1879)
Sambo	Old Yarmouth
Mustee	Sutton's Estate
Negro	Colbeck's Estate
Mullet	Bushy Park
Mulatto	Windsor Estate
Black Boy	Mckenzie Estate[52]

Commodification and exploitation of Black humanity

The insults of dehumanization and demoralization were compounded by the further injury of commodification, or thingification, as slaves were listed in estate inventories alongside cattle, horses, shovels, hoes, forks, and picks. Richard Peres, a British historian, noted that 'in all the inventories found among the West Indian archives, it was quite uncommon for the mill, cauldron, still, and buildings to account for more than one-sixth of the total capital; in most plantations, one-tenth would be the mark. By far the greatest capital items were the value of the slaves and the acres planted in cane by their previous labor[53]. During this era, black humanity held value only within the framework of slavery. Yet, black humanity existed outside of and before slavery and achieved significant accomplishments and civilization.

Furthermore, besides denying the enslaved Africans their humanity and suppressing their capacity for realising their full human potential,

---

[52] Cited in *Caribbean Journal of Religious Studies*, April 1996, vol. 17 No.1, p.28
[53] Richard Peres, **Planters and Merchants** (Cambridge [England], published for the economic history review at the university press, 1960), p. 24; See also Douglas Hall, *'Incalculability as a Feature of Sugar Production During the Eighteenth Century'*, in **Journal of Caribbean History**, Vol.35: 1, 2001, pp.82-83.

the system was further consolidated by the fact that this inhuman condition was written into the laws of the lands. The Barbados *Act for the better ordering and governing of Negro slaves of April 1668* regarded Africans as belonging to the animal kingdom and thereby not worthy to occupy the same socio-geographic space as the Whites.[54] The Act states in its preamble:

> Whereas a very considerable part of the wealth of this Island consist of Negro slaves...It is hereby ordained and enacted ...that...all Negro slaves in all courts of judicature, and other places within this Island shall be held, taken and adjudged to to be Estate Real, and not chattel, and shall descend unto the heir and widow of any person dying intestate according to the manner and custom of lands of inheritance held in fee-simple.[55]

Women and children were not spared these indignities. The principle of partus sequitur ventrem (the child follows the mother's status regardless of the father's race) was applied without mercy. Essentially, this principle facilitated stockbreeding and sexual exploitation. A woman's worth and dignity were reduced to and measured by her reproductive capacity to produce a 'herd of subhuman labor units.'[56]

Both in fact and in law, Africans were treated as property, with slave masters exerting absolute control and power over the slaves. Indignity

---

[54] Hillary Beckles, **Black Rebellion in Barbados, The Struggle Against Slavery, 1627-1838** (Bridgetown: Caribbean Research and Publication Inc., 1987), p.24

[55] Ibid. p. 24

[56] Angela Davis, **Women, Race and Class** (Reading, Berks: Cox & Wyman Ltd., 1981), p. 15; but see also pp. 3-29, 'The Legacy of Slavery: Standards for a New Womanhood', where Davis shows that oppression of women is not only a consequence of economic determinism but has multiple causes such as class, race, and gender.

was further compounded as slave owners viewed slaves as extensions of their will, seeing themselves as gods who recognized no power beyond their own over these individuals.[57] Not only were the slaves stripped of their humanity, but they also lost their self-determination and freedom, including the right to govern and direct their own lives.

Furthermore, in the economic system of plantation slavery, the enslaved Africans were organised into gangs along lines of ethnic divisions. The policy was not to keep too large a number of any single ethnic group together on a single plantation who spoke the same language and were from the same family, kinship, folklore, religious, economic, and political systems[58]. The logic was that if ethnic groups had been left to form economic and social power bases, they would have been a direct challenge to the plantocracy's strength, effectiveness, and viability and a security danger. This was a policy of divide to rule. Through this schema, however, the slaves lost touch with aspects of their identity through language and cultural practices.

Complicity and duplicity of the church

For the enslaved people, the situation became worse. The Plantocracy also influenced the church, the salt of the earth. There was no one in the world to call on but Thee. During a visit to Barbados, Richard Ligon, a British colonial historian of the 1900s, recounted how a slave named Sambo expressed his wish to become a Christian[59]. Ligon relayed this request to Sambo's owner, who replied as follows:

---

[57] Noel Leo Erskine, **Decolonizing Theology, A Caribbean Perspective**, (Maryknoll, New York: Orbis Books, 1981), p. 39

[58] Don Robotham, *"The Development of a Black Ethnicity in Jamaica"*, in Rupert Lewis & Patrick Bryan, eds., **Garvey: His Work and Impact** (Trenton, New Jersey: 1994), p. 26

[59] Alfred Caldecott, **The Church in the West Indies, West Indian Studies No. 14**, (London: Frank Cass & Co. Ltd., 1st Published 1898, Reprinted 1970), p. 65

that the people of the Iland were governed by the laues of England, and by those laues we could not make a Christian a slave.[60]

Ligon responded that Sambo's request was different in that he was not asking for a Christian to become a slave but for a slave to become a Christian. The slave owner replied:

> that it was true that there was a great difference in that: But being once a Christian, he could no more account him a slave, and so lose the hold they had on them as slaves by making them Christian; and by that means should open such a gap, as all Planters in the Iland would curse him."[61]

It is to be noted here that Ligon took Sambo to the slave owner, not to the church or the pastor for an inherently religious matter. This was an unpretentious indication of the totality of the control of slave owners as well as the self-consciously complicit role of the church within the status quo. The church's knowingly complicit role stemmed largely from the fact that "the missionaries regarded slavery as a political rather than a moral institution, and based their work in the West Indies on accepting its legality." As someone well-versed in British history, Ligon should have recognized that the missionaries were on a predetermined mission.

Relations to production: role of slaves, plantocracy, and missionaries

Despite the observation that slaves were considered property, which explains the associated inhumane treatment, that perspective was unbalanced and biased.

---

[60] Caldecott, **The Church in the West Indies**, p. 65
[61] Caldecott, **The Church in the West Indies**, p. 65

Richard Pares, a British historian and scholar of the seventeenth century, argued that slaves were no fools. In his work, *Planters and Merchants*, he asserted that slaves possessed such technological abilities that they operated the plantations' productive systems. Pares provided the following assessment of the economic value of slaves:

> Yet, when we look closely, we find that the industrial capital was much greater than a sixth of the total value. With the mill, the boiling houses and they still went an army of specialists – almost all of them slaves, but nonetheless specialists for that.[62]

In other words, the slaves operated the plantations. It's not a stretch to argue that the "specialists," the slaves in the colonies, generated the wealth of British society during the industrial revolution of the seventeenth and eighteenth centuries. Despite all the justifications for disregarding slaves as human beings, they were far from ignorant.

Nevertheless, the socio-historical context of the era from 1492 to 1838 was, on one hand, characterized by alienation, oppression, and exploitation for the slaves, resulting in a profound loss of humanity, roots, identity, and freedom. On the other hand, for the plantocracy, it represented a period of dictatorial control over the society's economic, political, and religious decision-making structures. This context inherently shaped the Biblical interpretive approach adopted by some planters and missionaries. Before the missionaries arrived on Caribbean soil, they were already instructed on what to say and do. For example, the guidelines provided to missionaries by the Baptist Missionary Society can be seen as a model for all missionaries:

> You are quite aware that the state of society in Jamaica is very different from that under which it is our privilege

---

[62] Richard Pares, **Merchants and Planters,** p. 24

to live in this country, and that the great majority of its inhabitants are dependent upon their superiors in a degree altogether unknown here. The evidence of the fact will probably especially at first, be painful and trying to your feelings; but you must ever bear in mind that, as a resident in Jamaica, you have nothing whatever to do with its civil and political affairs; and with these you must never interfere...the Gospel of Christ you well know, so far from producing or countenancing a spirit of rebellion or insubordination, has a directly opposite tendency...let your instructions, both to young and old, be conceived in the spirit and corresponds with the directions an example of our Divine Teacher, as laid down in the New Testament at large; and then, whatever disposition may be felt to obstruct or misrepresent you, none will justly be able to lay anything to your charge.[63]

The missionaries arrived in the Caribbean not primarily on a mission but clearly with a purpose: to ensure that moral education and their religious efforts neither challenged nor undermined the institution of slavery[64]. They acted as willing accomplices, bowing to economic power as they chose to overlook any conflict between Christianity and slavery[65]. The missionaries saw no evil, heard no evil, and, more

[63] E. A. Payne, **The Baptists in Jamaica**, pp. 20-1, quoted in Francis Osborne, S.J. Coastlands and Islands, First Thoughts on Caribbean Church History, United Theological College of the West Indies, 1972
[64] Dale Bisnauth, **History of religions in the Caribbean**, (Kingston: 1989), p. 129
[65] See S. Jakobsoson, **Am I Not a Man and a Brother? British Missions and the Abolition of the Slave Trade and Slavery in West Africa and the West Indies 1786-1838** (Uppsala, 1972), pp. 287, 301-302, 561-562; **Baptist Missionary Society (BMS) Periodical Account V (1813)**, pp. 292- 293; J.H. Hinton, **Memoir of William Knibb, Missionary in Jamaica** (London:

importantly, did not speak out against the injustice of slavery. Never has it been truer that there is none so blind as one who refuses to see.

Biblical interpretive approaches

Below, I cite five hermeneutes from the colonial era. Their social status is particularly noted, as interpreters of biblical texts are always socially positioned and invested[66]: Count Zinzendorf, a Moravian missionary to the Caribbean from Germany; William Hart Coleridge, the Anglican bishop of Barbados sent from England, a member of the Parish Council and thus part of the establishment; George Liele, a former slave who became a Baptist missionary from Virginia, United States; Sam Sharpe, a domestic slave and Baptist preacher; and William Knibb, a Baptist missionary from England, who was a trained schoolteacher and an untrained academic theologian, arriving in Jamaica in 1825. Although these examples are few, they reflect the general biblical interpretive approach of the era and will support the conclusions drawn.

Uncritical retelling of the biblical story

With Genesis 1-2:4a and 9:18-27, Ephesians 5 & 6 and the moral and social responsibility of the church in the interpretive frame, **Count Zinzendorf** counseled slave converts in 1739 this way: Be true to your husbands and wives, and obedient to your masters and bombas. The Lord has made all ranks – kings, masters, servants and slaves. God has punished the first Negroes by making them slaves, and your conversion will make you free, not from the control of your masters,

---

1897), pp. 149-150; M. Turner, **Slaves and Missionaries, The Disintegration of the Jamaican Slave Society 1787-1834** (Urbana: 1982), pp. 8-10, 25, 76-77
[66] Fernando F. Segovia & Mary Ann Tolbert, **Teaching the Bible – The Discourses and Politics of Biblical Pedagogy** (Maryknoll, New York: 1998), p. 123

but simply from your wicked habits and thoughts, and all that makes you dissatisfied with your lot.[67]

In one stroke, the Count overlooked Ephesians 2:14, which states that the death of Jesus abolished the superstructure of superiority and inferiority, thereby providing the interpretive key and basis for the various relationships described in the Epistle, including those between parents and children, husbands and wives, and masters and slaves. He conveniently misrepresented God's purposes as Creator and within Creation, invoked his racist hermeneutic with an undisguised reference to the "curse"[68] of Ham in Genesis, and promoted an understanding of salvation that was highly individualistic and focused on the afterlife. Here, there was no analysis of the biblical text's context but rather a hasty attempt to highlight the significance of the text for contemporary situations. The failure to Analyze the context of the biblical text underscores the reality that practical application of scripture to context cannot occur without first examining the socio-historical environment that biblical writers navigated while shaping their interpretations of reality. When the intention is to uphold the status quo, critical analysis becomes unnecessary and even perilous, as the ends justify the means.

William Hart Coleridge, in a sermon to newly confirmed slaves, urged them to be obedient and submissive by referencing Ephesians 5:15-33, 1 Peter 2:11-25, 3:1, Titus 2:1-15, 3:1-2, and Romans 12:6-21. Coleridge proclaimed:

> In all things and every station, strive to approve
> yourself the chosen of God…being diligent as rulers,
> loyal as subjects; just and equal as masters, obedient as

---

[67] J.E. Hutton, **A History of Moravian Missions** (London: Moravian Publications Office, 1922), p.44;

[68] Cain Hope Felder, *"Racial Motifs in the Biblical Narratives"*, in R.S. Sugirtharajah, **Voices From The Margins, Interpreting the Bible in the Third World** (Maryknoll, New York: 1995), pp. 195-8; Here Felder posits that the curse was pronounced on Canaan, Ham's son, and not Ham.

servants; as parents kind, as children dutiful, faithful in marriage...liberal in wealth, contented in poverty, if bond, with goodwill doing service, if free, not using your liberty as a cloak of maliciousness, but as servants of the Lord.[69]

One is left to consider the bishop's intention as damning, if not ambiguous, in his reference to slaves as "rulers," "masters," "wealthy," and "free," as nothing was further from the reality. Bishop Coleridge's choice of biblical text is significant here. The texts from Ephesians, Peter, and Titus all come from a time when the church was accommodating to the patriarchal and hierarchical imperial Graeco-Roman society surrounding it. The liberating tendencies of egalitarianism and the inclusivity of the earlier Jesus Movement were practiced less and less. Additionally, the Roman text relates to submissiveness. Coleridge's biblical interpretive approach consistently reinforced the colonial strategy of instilling submission to authority. One can assert here that biblical hermeneutics, shaped by the social realities of the day, is not merely a hermeneutic of "convenience" but of "necessity." However, while Bishop Coleridge's hermeneutic of "necessity" was questionable under the circumstances, it was sincere.

In a document published on Christmas Day in 1795[70], George Liele's reading strategy, established in 1783, became evident. The articles in this document ended with the phrases "according to the word of God" or "agreeable to the word of God," followed by a proof-text. *Article 1* cited Matthew 3:1-3 and 2 Corinthians 6:14-18 to support the idea that

---

[69] William Coleridge, **Charges Delivered to the Clergy of the Diocese of Barbados and the Leeward Islands**, (London: J. G. & F. Rivington, 1835), pp. 263-264

[70] *"An Account of the Jamaican Baptists, with memoirs of George Liele"*, **General Baptist Repository vol. 1 Supplement 1802** (London: printed for the editor by J. Skirven, Ratcliff Highway), pp. 229-240

the Baptists' theological position aligned with that of the Anabaptists.[71] However, was the use of these texts a subtle way to address the ideology of racism within the slave society of his time? *Article 11* addressed public worship and the debate over whether Sunday was a 'legal' day of rest or worship, using[72] Mark 16:2-6 and Colossians 3:16 as proof-texts. This interpretation contradicted the official mandate that designated Sunday as a market day for slaves. *Article XV* evaluated the conditions for church membership, referencing 1 Peter 2:13- 16 and 1 Thessalonians 3:13 as proof-texts.[73] Here, these scriptures promoted showing deference to rulers. But were these verses employed to help regulate the behavior of congregants and alleviate the tension between plantation owners and slaves? *Article XVII* examined the punishment for the misconduct of slaves, citing 1 Timothy 1:6, Ephesians 6:5, and 1 Peter 2:13-21 as proof-texts.[74] While Liele's reading strategy does not separate biblical texts from their contexts, it opposes them.

A resistant reading[75] of the biblical text

Sam Sharpe was born in Montego Bay, Jamaica, in 1801 and, therefore, was not an uprooted African slave.[76] Although he was given the name of his owner, Samuel Sharp, Esq., Sharpe was known by the aliases "Schoolmaster Sharpe," "Daddy," and "Ruler" due to his reading and writing skills and the respect he earned in plantation society

[71] Ibid. p. 234
[72] Ibid.
[73] Ibid. p. 235
[74] Ibid. p. 236
[75] See R.S. Sugirtharajah, **Postcolonial Criticism and Biblical Interpretation** (Oxford: Oxford University Press, 2002) pp. 52-55, who has pointed out that resistant interpreters do not advocate the revolutionary overthrow of oppressive systems and structures. Rather, through and based upon a re-interpretation of the Bible, they seek to establish selfhood and dignity.
[76] Edward Kamau Brathwaite, **Wars of Respect, Nanny and Sam Sharpe**, Agency for Public Information, Kingston, Jamaica, 1977, p. 28

from his peers. Despite being treated well and kindly as a domestic slave, Sharpe's position within the social hierarchy of slavery and his awareness of the oppression and indignity experienced by slaves placed him in a different social and ideological position compared to his owner.

Sharpe's relatively humane domestic obligations and treatment did not dull his sense of justice and passion for his oppressed and exploited class. For Sharpe, it wasn't about how he or any individual was treated, but rather how the entire socio- economic and political system was designed to dominate and exploit Black people while granting social privilege and status to white individuals. Edward Kamau Brathwaite, a Caribbean poet and historian, vividly captures the dilemma of the house slave and field slave in which Sharpe was forced to imaginatively navigate in the contemporary era like this:

> Kind individuals treat their dogs, cats, and horses with compassion, yet treating slaves kindly is like adorning lepers with expensive and beautiful clothes. Those beautiful garments do not alter the condition of the leper. Similarly, kind treatment does not change the reality of a slave. Slavery is the most profound violation of the human spirit; kindness cannot rectify this violation. Only freedom can.[77]

Sharpe was a deacon in the Baptist church, specifically a black Baptist. Here, black does not refer to the color of Sharpe's skin but rather to the socio-political status marked by marginalization, domination, exploitation, and alienation within plantation society and economy, in contrast to the privilege and rank of whites. In the Baptist church, Sharpe encountered the biblical teachings of the missionaries and their efforts toward secular freedom through literacy campaigns and

---

[77] Transcript from a Jamaica Broadcasting Corporation TV play entitled Sam Sharpe in 1973 written by Edward Kamau Brathwaite.

the establishment of schools. The missionaries faced a philosophical dilemma in their evangelistic work: slaves could be spiritually free yet temporarily enslaved, meaning they could have free souls while being bound in body.[78] Sharpe resolved this dilemma between soul and body, presenting the missionaries with a 'new' hermeneutical key: spiritual freedom equals physical freedom, as no one can serve two masters.

What Sharpe did was organize a two-pronged attack on the plantation system of slavery. First, Sharpe centered his interpretive approach on his praxis, his daily struggle for freedom and equality in an oppressive and unjust society. He rooted the fight for freedom within the Biblical tradition of emancipation. The Exodus story, Luke 4:16-18, the Matthean teaching of Jesus that no man can serve two masters (Matthew 6:24), and Colossians 3:11 *(which states that in renewal there is no longer Greek and Jew, circumcised and uncircumcised, barbarian, Scythian, slave and free; but Christ is all and in all, NRSV)* formed the ideological basis for what was called the Baptist War of 1831[79]. Thus, he recognized and had reasons to demonstrate discontent with the oppressive political circumstances. Sharpe transformed the concept of religious freedom into civil freedom. Unlike the Maroons, Sharpe and his followers sought freedom not as rebels but as lawful human beings, a right upheld by law.[80]

Integral to Sharpe's praxis was the practice of 'religion.' Within plantation society and economy, 'religion' for Sharpe and his followers was not limited to the accepted doctrinal practices and beliefs, which were merely "a dispassionate system of God-talk and a code of behavior."[81] On

---

[78] Ibid. p. 30
[79] See Philip Sherlock, **Shout For Freedom: A Tribute to Sam Sharpe** (London: McMillan Education Limited, 1976), p. x
[80] Mary Turner, **Slaves and Missionaries – The Disintegration of Jamaican Society**, 1787- 1834 (Barbados, Jamaica, Trinidad & Tobago: University of the West Indies Press, 1998), p. 163
[81] [42] Gayraud S. Gilmore, **Black Religion and Black Radicalism** 3rd. ed. (Maryknoll, New York: Orbis Books, 1998), p. 29

the contrary, 'religion' related to a faith expression in God and the gods, emerging from the experiences of suffering and struggle, celebrating and advocating dignity, freedom, and self-identity. The use of the body in religious rituals, dreams and visions, and spirit was (re)-introduced in black Baptists' church practices. This understanding, which divided the Baptists into 'white' Baptists and 'black' Baptists, extended beyond a simple color divide; it represented the distinction between lived realities and worldviews. Blackness served as both a condition of oppression and the lens through which emancipation was viewed.

Second, Sharpe politicized and radicalized the attempt at disinterested reading of the Bible and 'religion' by the missionaries. He contrasted what he heard from the missionaries with what he and they read from the Bible – *if the Son therefore shall make you free, you shall be free indeed (John 8:36); you are bought with a price, be not ye the servants of men (1 Corinthians 7:23); there is neither Greek nor Jew, there is neither bond nor free (Galatians 3:28), no man can serve two masters (Matthew 6:24)* – against the backdrop of the material ease and privilege of the plantocracy, and the lives of degradation, alienation, and inauthenticity that he and his fellow slaves were forced to endure. Amid such lived realities, the political implications of exclusion and discrimination were clear to him, as were the political imperatives and consequences of rebellion. For Sharpe and his followers, politicizing biblical interpretation and 'religion' was a prerequisite for revolt and a means of social change.

Additionally, for Sharpe and his followers, the promised rewards in heaven for adhering to the ideals of the Christian faith were inadequate compensation for enduring the chattel and wage slavery of their era. Slaves sought freedom and tangible rewards in this present life. Sharpe approached the Bible from the perspective of the slaves' struggle between the powerful and the poor, leading to his distinct interpretation and course of action. It is possible for both the oppressed and the oppressor to read the same Scriptures yet arrive at different conclusions, as each starts from a different 'place' or epistemology.

Therefore, based on the understanding that before God and in Christ, all people were created equal in freedom and that no social distinctions existed, natural equality implied that a White man had no authority to enslave a Black man. This led to the emergence of a rebellion characterized by 'passive resistance.' After the Christmas holidays of 1831, slaves planned to cease work and refuse to labor until their freedom was recognized or granted, and a decision was made to compensate them for their work following appropriate negotiations. His aim was not a revolution or the violent overthrow of the institution of slavery. Sharpe envisioned a transformation of the socio-economic system that exploited labor, in which slaves had no say in determining the value of their labor, into a wage labor system where they would have bargaining power over their labor costs. This plan of 'passive resistance' demonstrated that Sharpe understood the impact of industrial strike actions on an industrial system at a time when the essential role of labor for productivity and profitability in a plantation economy was overlooked, treating labor as mere chattel instead.[82] The rebellion led by Sharpe contested the notion that slaves were merely mindless property, a perception that served as the tinder to which Sharpe and his followers literally struck a match.

This vision of wage laborers, however, put Sharpe at odds with his trusted comrades – Dover and Gardner – who sought not only bargaining power over the labor of slaves but also to become landowners or to control the productive forces of the plantation economy.[83] With no plan for a post-emancipation society in place, the strategy of 'passive

---

[82] Edward Kamau Brathwaite, **Wars of Respect**, p. 25
[83] Don Robotham *"The Development of a Black Ethnicity in Jamaica"* in **Garvey: His Work and Impact**, eds. Rupert Lewis and Patrick Bryan (New Jersey: Africa World Press, Inc., 1991), p. 37

resistance' escalated into a full-blown armed rebellion involving around twenty thousand slaves.

The rebellion was also ignited by the rumor that had reached the colonies, indicating that the authorities in Britain had already abolished slavery and that colonialists were denying the slaves their freedom, which they believed was their Divine right. Slaves felt that the plantation owners' dictates no longer held them bound. It was estimated that the rebellion caused around £1.5 million in property damage. This uprising was ruthlessly suppressed, with both innocent and guilty individuals paying the ultimate price for their resistances—death by hanging in the public square.[84] Although the colonists violently quelled the rebellion, the belief that the Bible opposed slavery remained strong. Hope for a better life in the afterlife transformed into hope for a better life after abolition[85]. The ideas of human equality and the view of bondage as unlawful and unbiblical (freedom and self-respect) formed the biblical foundation of the rebellion.

Scriptural allusions and quotations

William Knibb arrived in Jamaica at a time when revolts against slavery by the enslaved individuals in the colonies were becoming bolder and more frequent, and abolitionist sentiments against slavery were strengthening in Britain. His awareness of these events shaped his interpretive approach, evident in his use of scriptural allusions and quotations in letters to his mother and sister, as well as in his contributions to the anti-slavery debates in England[86]. For instance, framed by Isaiah 61:1-4 and Luke 4:16-18, he expressed in a letter to his mother that it "cheers the heart of your son which would otherwise

[84] The square in Montego Bay where the rebelling slaves were publicly hanged is named Sam Sharpe Square in their honour.
[85] Mary Reckford, "The Slave Rebellion of 1831", in **Jamaica Journal** 3 June 1969, p.27
[86] Hinton, **Memoir of William Knibb**, pp. 49, 66, 288-9

sink to proclaim liberty to the captives and the opening of prisons to them that are bound. This is a delightful employment, and I will dwell on it so that I may be thus employed." Knibb's interpretive approach focused primarily on using scriptural allusions and quotations. However, the source of interpretation and meaning was not the biblical text's original context but rather the prevailing material realities. Thus, the consequence challenged the status quo and fostered solidarity with the victims of injustice and inhumanity.

Outcome: social control & stability versus social reconstruction

The consequences of these interpretive strategies are summed up rather aptly by Benjamin La Trobe, a leader of the Moravian Church in Britain in 1768 and a promoter of foreign missions, in a letter to a friend in 1770: "these Negroes are also a proof that a genuine reformation in principle and practice is always inseparable from true conversion.... the magistrates themselves have more than once declared, the baptized Negroes are a greater security to them than their forts." The colonies were safer with Christian slaves than with battalion stations and fortresses. Indeed, one of the chief roles of missionaries was to complete the act of enslavement by enslaving people mentally so they believed slavery was their fate. Fundamentally, social security was of higher value than social justice, as taming the enemy within was considered more necessary and profitable than defeating the enemy without. In other words, the ideology of security and stability shapes hermeneutics.

Stability, however, depended on who was doing the interpreting and whose interests were being served by that interpretation. While the missionaries focused on law and order, emphasizing conformity and obedience, acceptance of the status quo, submission to authority, passivity, and docility, the enslaved people, led by Sharpe, sought equity within the system and structures of society. Their movement was not millenarian, lacking a prophetic figure announcing the will of God and an anticipated new world to be realized over time through divine intervention. Sharpe and other enslaved individuals did not aspire to create a new world but rather to gain freedom from chattel slavery and the unconditional right to sell their labor for wages. Thus, their goals were tangible and aimed at specific economic and social reconstruction.

Eisegetics and Exegetics

In the reading strategies of the foreign missionaries and slaves mentioned above, crucial factors included who interpreted and selected biblical texts. In this context, the Bible served both oppressive and liberating purposes[87]. There is often a significant difference between the "readings" of social reality provided by biblical writers and the interpretations of those realities by biblical interpreters[88]. When those in positions of power interpret scripture, their interpretations are frequently regarded as factual and normative, becoming ingrained societal norms. During slavery, the planters and missionaries who held power infused their biases, prejudices, and interests into their interpretations, overlooking the fact that biblical texts are products of socio-ideological interests and social practices. Consequently, they established and upheld social structures that sanctioned and legitimized the inferiority and subjugation of the slaves.

Consequently, in examining the reading strategies of foreign missionaries— such as the uncritical retelling of biblical stories, including scriptural allusions and quotations—it becomes clear that socio-historical realities are not granted agency in the interpretive process. As a result, the interpretation focuses on the literal meaning of

---

[87] R.S. Sugitharajah, **Postcolonial Criticism and Biblical Interpretation**, New York: Oxford University Press, pp. 117-22; see also Gerald O. West, **Contextual Bible Study**, Pietermaritzburg: Cluster Publications, 1993, p.53.
[88] Miguel A. De La Torre, **Reading the Bible From the Margins** (Maryknoll, New York: 2003), p. 4

biblical texts, lacking a serious intention to apply their significance or message to contemporary contexts. Interpretation is vulnerable to what Itumeleng Mosala refers to as 'the escapist option of textual selectivity,' a deliberate choice of texts that align with one's class and ideological interests.

However, when the oppressed—those without power, in this case, the slaves—were the ones interpreting, the materiality of biblical texts and contexts was given agency, shaping and informing the interpretive process. This resistant reading strategy employed by the system's victims challenged the status quo, fostered solidarity among them, and aimed at achieving tangible goals.

Another aspect of reading strategies is the difference between literalism— interpreting texts to mean exactly what they say—and literary criticism, which views biblical texts as conveying a message. In literalism, the reader's task is to extract meaning from the text rather than imposing their own interpretations. Here, the text's meaning is fixed; it applies universally, regardless of time or place. What it means in Britain is the same as in the Caribbean. In contrast, literary criticism emphasizes how the text communicates its meaning (its rhetorical features), placing the reader in a role that actively contributes to meaning-making. This distinction highlights the hermeneutical approaches in the reading strategies of the missionaries and Sharpe. The missionaries moved from the text to social reality without considering the ideological interests and social practices of the world in which the biblical writers lived. Conversely, Sharpe approached interpretation from a praxis or social struggle perspective, relating the text to lived experiences. While the missionaries' reading strategy reinforced the status quo, Sharpe's contributed to economic and social reconstruction, seeking to challenge the oppressive system— albeit as an unintended consequence for Sharpe and his fellow rebels.

In summary, resistance arose from Sharpe's or the slaves' interpretive reading strategy, not from the foreign missionaries' literal readings. The foreign missionaries' interpretive approach did not focus on the material concerns of alienation and the brutal exercise of power, which it legitimized, leading to complicit support for the status quo. In contrast, Sharpe and the slaves approached the biblical texts through the interpretive lens of alienation and brutal domination. Their push for an alternative social order stemmed from the Bible – particularly the Exodus story, Luke 14:16-18, and the creation story where all are equal before God. Thus, the resistant hermeneutic of Sharpe and the slaves consisted of four movements. First, the plantocracy protected its socio-economic and political interests and power through oppressive and repressive means, with tacit support from the church; second, the oppressed (Sharpe and the slaves) agitated for a just social order based on biblical principles of justice and equality; third, the plantocracy implemented additional oppressive measures to deny self-determination and self-identity, thereby legitimizing its power and creating camps of interest; and fourth, these camps of interest were in conflict. Therefore, for Sharpe and the slaves, both the materiality of the biblical texts and their context were significant; the result was neither justification nor legitimization of the status quo.

Thus, both the interpreter and the choice of biblical text are significant; neither the biblical text nor the interpreter is without Bias. Ultimately, every interpretation arises from who we are (identity), where we are (social location), and what we know (experience). Our identity, social location, and expertise influence what we articulate about God and how we understand God and the world.

Biblical reading strategies during the colonial period 1492 - 1838

Reader/ Interpreter	Social location	Biblical Texts	Socio-historical realities	Reading strategy	Location of meaning	Under standing of Bible	Consequences
Count Zinzendorf	Male, Missionary	Genesis 1-2:4a Ephesians 5&6					Acceptance of the status quo, pietism, escapism
Bishop William Hart Coleridge	Male, Missionary	Ephesians 5&6, 1Peter 2:11-25, Titus 2:1-13, 3:1-2, Romans 12:6-21	(cultural) genocide, slavery, indentureship	Uncritical retelling of the Biblical story	In the text	Authoritative	Submission to authority
George Liele	Male, former Slave	Mathew 3:1-3, 2 Corinthians 6:14-18, Mark 16:2-6, Colossians 3:16, 1Peter 2:11-25, 1 Thessalonians 3:13, 1Timothy 1:6, Ephesians 5&6,					Passivity and docility

Sam Sharpe	Male, Slave	Matthew 6:24, Luke 4:16-18, Colossia ns 3:11		A resista nt readin g of the Biblical text	Interac tion betwe en text and reader	Formative	Economic and social reconstruction
William Knibb	Male, Missionary	Luke 4:16-18		Scriptural allusions and quotations	Biblical texts		Solidarity with victims

Post-"emancipation" era: 1840-1959
Socio-historical and political realities and forces

The economics of dispossession

The abolition of slavery was fundamentally a shift in the foundation of labor exploitation[89]. The race-based ideology of the slavery era served to ensure an ample supply of a domesticated and unskilled labor force. Furthermore, freedom was superficial, as those who were "freed" lacked economic (land ownership) and political (involvement in decision-making) power. There existed a triangular hierarchy of domination[90] and a pyramid-like wealth system based on social stratification, which was directly linked to a system of property relations: the 'Backra' group (the White minority at the top) held economic and political power; this group included Governors, Planters, Attorneys, Government officials, Bookkeepers, Artisans, and Poor Whites, who constituted less than 5% of society; the 'Malatta' group (Brown, in the middle, which included

---

[89] Girvan, **Garvey: His Work and Impact**, pp. 15-16
[90] B.W. Higman, **Writing West Indian Histories** (London: Macmillan, 1999), pp. 194-195

free Blacks) enjoyed caste privileges, owned property, and refrained from forming any social organizations to challenge the status quo due to their privileged social position, as well as their material and status interests. They made up less than 10% of Caribbean societies; the 'Nayga' (the Black majority at the bottom) had no rights and lacked power; this group consisted of overseers, skilled and unskilled laborers, peasants, and African and Indian agro-proletarians, accounting for over 80% of the population. Emancipation represented no more than an intensification of exploitation characterized by the economics of dispossession.

Racially stratified society

Slavery, therefore, created a racially stratified society where wealth was concentrated in the hands of the white minority at the top of the pyramid. In this stratified society, being a person of consequence or worth meant being white or of fair complexion. Additionally, throughout the British colonies, except for the Baptists in Jamaica, ecclesiastical affairs and leadership were restricted to white expatriates.

Inculcation of British values

By being in control, the British could propagate their values and interpretation of the Bible and Christianity. Given this position of influence, it was inevitably English values that were instilled in Africans: education in English, adherence to the Christian religion, which is not inherently English, correct speech in English, being known by the company you keep, church membership in an established community, having a fair complexion, and a disdain for manual or agricultural labor[91]. In other words, in this racially stratified society, to be a person of consequence and worth meant being white or of fair complexion

---

[91] Bisnauth, **History of religions,** p. 202

and professedly Christian. Conversely, being black meant being socially inferior.

Furthermore, the British, who now formed a minority ruling class, solidified their grip on power by embracing the middle class. Members of the middle class occupied numerous positions within the Civil Service and related organizations. A grateful and pacified middle class allowed themselves to be anglicized in exchange for limited opportunities for upward social mobility through acquiring status symbols such as a secondary education, church affiliation, and gainful employment. They underwent a comprehensive enculturation program into an unfamiliar culture, which involved adopting British language, customs, and worldview. However, while the middle class lacked direct and substantial contact with the masses' struggles, they could not attain the freedoms and the economic and political power enjoyed by the ruling or leisured class[92]. Essentially, the minority British ruling class took on the role of the 'father who produced children and had to guard against being supplanted by them.'

The context, therefore, featured, on one side, privilege and power for the 'Backra' minority group and, on the other side, powerlessness and inferiority for the 'Nayga' majority group. In between, the 'Malatta' group, which looked down upon any association with the 'Nayga' majority, fearing it might jeopardize their opportunities for upward social mobility, was itself denied control over the decision- making processes and the production forces of society by the 'Backra' ruling minority. The guardians served as the gatekeepers, as the Backra minority group was both the guardian and gatekeeper for the Malatta and Nayga groups.

---

[92] C.L.R. James, **Beyond A Boundary** (London: Stanley Paul & Co., 1963), p. 52

The quest for political and economic self-determination

The post-emancipation era was also one in which the Caribbean peoples and their various governments sought to address their right to name themselves and to determine their own future and way of life. This was an undertaking that was easier said than done. The attempt to galvanise the region into one economic and political bloc, with the formation of the West Indian federation in the 1950s, failed with the withdrawal of Jamaica., Prime Minister of Trinidad and Tobago, Eric Williams, now famous mathematical dictum of, one from ten leaves nought, captured that failure. Never was a more serious blow dealt to regional unity. The Puerto Rican model of industrialization by invitation did not eliminate poverty and unemployment and so came to nothing. With the United States of America (USA) invasion of the Dominican Republic in 1965, the region was given another lesson in who controlled its right to self-determination.

But it wasn't all gloom and doom. The Cuban revolution in 1959 challenged the neo-colonial order, prompting other Caribbean nations to seek a development model beyond the revolution. If the Haitian revolution represented the awareness that Caribbean peoples could achieve self-determination, the Cuban revolution initiated the quest for self-definition[93]. The emergence of the Black Power movement in the Caribbean highlighted the reality that poverty could not be addressed without tackling issues of race and class in society. Additionally, the formation of CADEC in 1969 (Christian Action for Development in the Eastern Caribbean) aimed to confront the root causes of underdevelopment and poverty instead of merely providing relief.

Thus, the post-emancipation era was a time when Caribbean peoples struggled to recover from the trauma of slavery, discover their identities, and forge their path forward.

---

[93] Anna Grimshaw ed. **The C.LR. James Reader** (Oxford UK & Cambridge USA: Blackwell, 1992), p. 296

Biblical Interpretive approaches

In this section, I will refer to the work of Paul Bogle, Marcus Garvey, Rastafarianism, and Philip Potter. The social contexts of these interpreters are particularly interesting, as they interpret texts from specific social positions that shape their understanding[94]. The reading approach shared by all four interpreters primarily involves a critical reinterpretation of the biblical text, where the reader significantly contributes to the meaning through social engagement. A crucial factor here is the reader's ideological perspective and commitment.

Resistant reading strategies
Paul Bogle

Paul Bogle, a Baptist deacon and National Hero of Jamaica, and his followers centered their biblical interpretive strategy on the oppressive material conditions in which souls lived, rather than solely focusing on the need for soul salvation. The base for his ministry operations was the village chapel in Stony Gut, located in St. Thomas-in-the-East. For Bogle, the chapel represented the seat of a just God, and it was responsible for judging the Courthouse, which was the dispenser of justice for the people of God. Consequently, the failure of the Courthouse to ensure justice was viewed as a symbol of injustice and oppression. Thus, the Courthouse became the focal point for protests in 1865. In Bogle's perspective, the Courthouse had fallen out of alignment with the chapel.

Bogle's religious beliefs were shaped by his admiration for the Psalms and Isaac Watts' hymns, especially those influenced by the Psalms[95]. He was known to carry the Psalms of David along with additional hymns by Isaac Watts.

---

[94] Fernando F. Segovia, **Decolonising Biblical Studies: A View From the Margins** (Maryknoll: Orbis Books, 2000), pp. 5, 9–32

[95] Devon Dick. Masters Thesis unpublished written to advocate that Paul Bogle was a Christian Hero; see also Clinton Hutton, PhD Thesis *Colour for Colour:*

Bogle's hermeneutical key was the Last Judgment, based on Psalms 11, 50, and 143[96]. However, judgment was not deferred to some distant future time. In the protest and advocacy of the people, God was delivering judgment against the current ruling class. Bogle and the people's struggles were against flesh, blood, and the rulers of this age. Bogle stood in the tradition of the Psalms, which assert that God wills justice and righteousness (Psalms 96-99). Earthly authorities are responsible for administering justice and righteousness (Psalm 72:1-7), which precisely entails the crushing of oppression. When the lives of the poor and needy are especially threatened and vulnerable, God highlights them for special attention (Psalm 72:12-14; 82). Bogle's praxis, his daily fight for justice for the poor, and his belief that God is on the side of the poor fueled his advocacy and protests for social justice, shaping his exegetical strategy. In other words, Bogle approaches the biblical text through engagement in and out of a real-life context.

Marcus Garvey

Marcus Garvey was born in August 1887 in St. Ann's Bay, Jamaica, about sixty years after the "emancipation" of slaves in the Caribbean, and died in 1940. As one of Jamaica's national heroes, Garvey was better known for his political activism than his theology. However, his politics were never separated from his religious praxis.

In Garvey's interpretive approach, the focus and the starting point of biblical interpretation was his involvement in the socio-cultural and political realities of the community. The reason for this approach was experiential. The experience of racism that came first in his pre-teen years and later in professional life was of profound effect. His white girlfriend was instructed not to communicate with him on her arrival in Scotland from Jamaica to attend school because he was black. Likewise,

---

Skin for Skin (1992)
[96] Ibid. p. 36

in his sojourns in Latin America as a migrant worker, he became sickened by the subjugation and abuse of Black Workers in the fields, mines, and cities based on skin colour. In the United States of America, he saw that the same race-based theory held as Blacks had to bear the burden of economic and political discrimination, racial violence, and the violation of constitutional rights following World War 11.

Principally, Garvey's Biblical reading strategy emerged from his experiences of seeing

Blacks regarded and treated as inferior and chattel.

Out of these experiences of racial discrimination and political and economic exploitation, the biblical creation narrative found in Genesis and Psalm 68:31 shaped Garvey's understanding of human origin, purpose, and emancipation. Over time, the Creation narrative, along with Africa and the people of African descent, became the organizing principle of his biblical interpretative approach. The fundamental issue for Garvey was that the denigration, racial discrimination, and political and economic exploitation of Black people undermined God's intentions as Creator within the created order.

Garvey argued that human identities originate from God. As a result, this eliminated any exclusive claims on God by any race. In the *Universal Negro Catechism* of the African Orthodox Church, it was stated that any race could connect with God. The catechism provided the following answers to the questions raised about the nature and understanding of God:

Q. What is the color of God?

A. A spirit has neither colour, nor other natural parts, nor qualities.

Q. But do we not speak of His hands, eyes, arms, and other parts?

A. Yes; it is because we are able to think and speak of Him only in human figurative terms.

Q. If, then, you had to speak or think of the colour of God, how would you describe it?

A. As black; since we are created in his image and likeness.

Q. On what would you base your assumption that God is black?

A. On the same basis as that taken by white people when they assume that God is of their colour.[97]

Though it was affirmed here that God was Black, this affirmation did not aim to make any exclusive claim. God's identification with humanity was not dependent on race. Further supporting Garvey's contention, Blacks were co-equal with all other races. However, while the color of God was 'non-specific,' God does have a color concerning the perception and articulation of human realities.

In his *Dissertation on Man*, Garvey asserted that "when God breathed into the nostrils of man the breath of life, made him a living soul, and bestowed upon him the authority of "Lord of Creation," God never intended for that individual to descend to the level of a peon, a serf, or a slave. Rather, he should always be a man in the fullest possession of his senses and with the truest knowledge of himself..." In other words, wherever ranks were established in human relationships and potential was stifled, these were human inventions that contradicted God's creative purposes. Thus, the place of Blacks in the world could never be a subordinate one.

Garvey was so deeply engaged with his understanding of God's creative purpose for humanity that this insight even transformed into the passion narrative. In an Easter sermon delivered at Liberty Hall in New York City on April 16, 1922, Garvey proclaimed:

[97] Robert A. Hill, (ed.), **The Marcus Garvey and UNIA Papers**, Berkeley: University of California Press, 1983-1985, Vol.111. pp. 302-303

The work of the UNIA for the past four and a half years has been that of guiding us to realise that there should be a resurrection in us, and if at no other time I trust that at this Easter-tide we will realise that there is great need for a resurrection- a resurrection from the lethargy of the past – from that feeling that made us accept the idea and opinion that God intended that we should occupy an inferior place in the world.[98]

Garvey's religion had clear political goals. He founded the UNIA (Universal Negro Improvement Association) in Kingston, Jamaica, on July 20, 1914, as a benevolent or fraternal reform association focused on racial uplift and the creation of educational and industrial opportunities for Blacks[99]. **This dedication to racial uplift ensured** that the UNIA's efforts aimed at the welfare and well-being of the entire individual.

Through its activities and programs, it was intended that Blacks would view themselves as equals to any race and capable of defining their identity and shaping their future.

Moreover, self-determination was not the privilege of a single race, specifically the White race. For Garvey, the power bestowed by God upon humanity to govern social affairs and seek fulfillment was not exclusive to one race. In his *Dissertation on Man*, Garvey wrote:

After the creation and after man [sic] was given possession of the world, the Creator relinquished all authority to his Lord, except that which was spiritual. All that authority which meant the regulation of human affairs, human society, and human happiness was given to man [sic] by the Creator, and man [sic], therefore,

---

[98] Jacques-Garvey (ed.), **Philosophy and Opinions** *Easter Sunday Sermon*, Liberty Hall, New York City, April 16, 1922, p. 67
[99] Hill (ed.), **Garvey and UNIA Papers**, p. 435

became master of his own destiny and architect of his own fate...In the process of time we find that only a certain type of man [sic] has been able to make good in God's creation.[100]

As a result, Garvey urged Black people to take charge of their liberation and dismiss the idea that God had predetermined their situation. For Garvey, it was essential for Black individuals to be accountable to themselves. Moreover, the key biblical text for Garvey's vision of God's fulfillment of history was Psalm 68:31 *(Princes shall come out of Egypt; Ethiopia shall soon stretch out her hands unto God).* In the 1929 editorial of his newspaper, the Blackman, Garvey noted that Ethiopia symbolized God's special concern for Africa and the people of African descent. He further observed that *'stretch out her hands'* referred to the redemption of Africa from foreign domination, as well as the emancipation of all descendants of Africa from the structural and systemic bondage that prevented them from realizing their full potential as human beings. Garvey articulated his vision of the future in this way:

The redemption of Africa is a great commission, not only to

recover Africa for Africans, but to rescue the souls of Africa's sons and daughters from social, political, economic and spiritual bondage, and place them on a ground of vantage to secure the true uplift of the race, and the general good of the human family. …. Where they (Negroes) find themselves, they can be absolutely loyal citizens and at the same time absolutely loyal to the cause of Africa redeemed. They may build up the nation and government just where they are with great success. They may build up their social, intellectual, political and economic dependence, a common consciousness

---

[100] Jacques-Garvey (ed.), **Philosophy and Opinions**, p. 24.

and a great confraternity of all Negroes all over the
world.[101]

In other words, God's fulfillment of history had tangible goals.
The hope of Blacks for self-definition and self-determination was not
relegated to the not-yet, but also to the here-and-now. Hope was
fundamentally a reality within history. Even so, Garvey struggled to
balance the understanding of the kingdom of God as already realized
in Jesus Christ but not yet fulfilled in its final consummation at the end
of time. Additionally, while Garvey made appropriate references and
utilized his society's ideological interests and social practices, he largely
overlooked the socio- historic context of the biblical text.

Intercultural hermeneutics

Philip Potter

Philip Potter's particular interest and most engaging work is in
a universal dialogue of cultures. Potter's signal contribution to the
ecumenical movement through the World Council of Churches
(WCC)[102] which he served from 1967 to 1983, is the promotion and
embodiment of a dialogue of civilizations. Potter's concept of a dialogue
of cultures arises from his diverse cultural heritage, his international
engagement, the call for unity among churches worldwide, and his
vision of the oikoumene (the whole inhabited earth), a vision grounded
in his interpretation of the biblical narrative of the Tower of Babel
(Genesis 11) and the New Jerusalem (Revelation 21). The interpretive
perspective that emerges from Potter's exploration of a universal
dialogue of cultures is an *intercultural hermeneutic.*

Potter is a native of the Creole and English-speaking Caribbean

---

[101] Ibid., p. 140
[102] **Cultures in Dialogue**, Documents From a Symposium in Honour of Philip
A. Potter, Cartigny, Switzerland, October 3-7, 1984, p. vi

island of Dominica, which was colonized by both France and Britain. Therefore, Potter hails from a region that experienced some of the earliest and most intense encounters between cultures.[103] This tumultuous meeting of cultures marked the era of European exploration and domination of the New World, during which culture was equated with civilization, leading to the shaping of the peoples of the New World and their cultures in the image of Europeans.

Due to his origins, Potter acknowledges that he carries many cultures within himself—Caribbean, African, Irish, and French—encompassing both the oppressed and the oppressors, as well as individuals of various races, including white, black, and Asian. This rich cultural heritage signifies that Potter embodies this cultural dialogue as both an intrinsic and extrinsic aspect of his experience.[104] In other words, the dialogue of civilizations is not merely an abstract concept but a concrete reality.

From 1948 to 1990, Potter encountered many world cultures through his international involvement.[105] However, for Potter, although "encounters with people from other cultures entail shocks, mistakes, making a fool of oneself, and incomprehension," these experiences did not pose a threat. Instead, they provided opportunities for human understanding and enrichment to reach its full potential. Through his

---

[103] **Cultures in Dialogue**, p. 86

[104] Philip Potter, **Life in All Its Fullness**, Geneva, World Council of Churches, 1981, p. 142

[105] 1948-1950 mission secretary of the British Student Christian Movement (SCM); 1950-1954 missionary/Methodist minister in Haiti; 1954-1960 secretary of the Youth Department of the WCC; 1960-66 overseas secretary for West Africa and the Caribbean with the Methodist Missionary Society (MMS); 1967-72 director of Commission on World Mission and Evangelism WCC; 1972-83 General Secretary of WCC; 1984-90 lecturer and chaplain at the United Theological College of the West Indies (UTCWI) and University of the West Indies (UWI), Mona Campus, Jamaica. See Michael Jagessar who wrote a book on the life, work and theology of Philip Potter, **Full Life For All**, Uitgeverij Boekencentrum, Zoetermeer, 1997

international involvement, Potter served as a voice from the 'two-thirds world,' shaping and guiding ecumenical thinking and work.

Additionally, the dialogue among cultures stems from the ecumenical effort to unite the divided churches of the world in response to Jesus' high priestly prayer that "They all may be One" (John 17). What Potter discovered from this call was that we cannot discuss the unity of the church without simultaneously addressing God's oikonomia (God's economy) or His design for the unity of humanity. The unity and mission of the church are inseparable. What became essential for Potter in the effort to concretize the oikonomia was a dialogue between the world's cultures, requiring a clearer understanding of the meanings of dialogue and culture.

The individual who most significantly influenced Potter's understanding of dialogue was Martin Buber.[106] Potter summarizes Buber's ideas as follows:

> Real life is meeting. The history of the world is the dialogue between human beings and God. The fundamental fact of human existence is person-with-person dialogue. Where there is no dialogue, no sharing, there is no reality. The basic movement of dialogue is the turning toward the other. The limit of the possibility of dialogue is the limit of our awareness.[107]

Additionally, Potter derives his understanding of dialogue from the Latin word *conversari* (conversation), which translates to "to turn to another in the sense of living with, engaging with, or keeping company with someone."[108] Conversation embodies a relationship; thus, dialogue

---

[106] Potter, **Life in All Its Fullness**, p. 162
[107] Ibid, p. 162
[108] Philip Potter, *"Towards a Universal Dialogue of Cultures"* in **A Vision For Man, Essays on Faith, Theology and Society in honour of Joshua Russell**

is not a meaningless or unrelated discourse but rather a conversation that encompasses the environment, culture, and other individuals.[109] In this context, culture, for Potter, refers to "the many ways in which people connect with nature and with one another, as well as how they express these relationships."[110] Here, culture is inherently political, as it involves decisions and judgments about how life is lived and organized to ensure a good quality of life.[111] Fundamentally, therefore, dialogue is relational, serving as a mode of existence (interpersonal), while culture reflects the interconnections of life within a community (interdependence).

Potter envisions this dialogue of cultures as a city. A city serves as a space for a plurality of cultures, experienced as threat, violence, and promise, whose viability hinges on its ability to maintain an open dialogue among civilizations.[112] Potter roots this understanding of the city in the biblical story of the Tower of Babel (Genesis 11) and the vision of the New Jerusalem (Revelation 21). He interprets the story of the Tower of Babel as one of the empires striving to homogenize life, which suggests expansionism and domination.[113] Yet, the failed attempts at homogeneity by Empires do not represent the outcome. The narrative continues with the call of Abraham, shifting from punishment to the promise of blessing (Genesis 12: 1-3). Potter views the Hebrew term for "to bless" (*barak*) as "to share one's strength, one's essence with another, to be present with the other."[114] This implies that "all families of the earth will, through their faith in Abraham's God, be empowered to share their cultures, languages, and identities in all their

---

Chandran, ed. Samuel Amirtham (Madras: Christian Literature Society, 1978, p. 323.

[109] Ibid.

[110] Philip Potter, *"Culture and the City"*, Whither Ecumenism? ed. by Thomas Wieser (Geneva, 1986), p. 9

[111] Philip Potter, **Towards a Universal Dialogue of Cultures**, p. 325

[112] **Cultures in Dialogue**, pp. 68-69

[113] Ibid. p. 70

[114] Philip Potter, **Towards a Universal Dialogue of Cultures**, p. 318

rich variety."[115] Thus, in contrast to imperial aspirations for expansion and domination, the call of Abraham embodies vulnerability and powerlessness as pathways to share life with others.[116] The dialogue of cultures is not about alienating or dominating others but rather about empowerment, freedom, and self-identity.

In Revelation 21, the vision for the New Jerusalem emerges as a counterpoint to the Roman Empire, which embodies alienation and domination, and speaks not only of a new creation but also of a new city[117] that encompasses all cultures. Unlike the gate of God in the Tower of Babel story, the gates in the New Jerusalem are always open. Babel is not merely a gate or fortress of involuntary submission. In the New Jerusalem, access is free and open to the full diversity of all peoples, thus embodying the space for universal dialogue among cultures.

This universal dialogue of cultures serves at least two purposes. First, it is the most effective way to understand the world's cultures.[118] Second, it avoids the totalizing tendencies of any culture and makes irrelevant binary distinctions or molds of exploiter/exploited, oppressor/oppressed, subject/object, identity/non–identity; and, in contrast, promotes a community and respect in which human life is valued for its diversity.[119]

In summary, Potter's multicultural Caribbean origins, along with his freedom from the securities and privileges of traditional institutional structures of the church,[120] his encounters with various world cultures,

---

[115] Ibid.

[116] **Cultures in Dialogue**, p. 71

[117] **Cultures in Dialogue**, p. 71

[118] Philip Potter, **Towards a Universal Dialogue of Cultures**, p. 316; see also Potter, **Life in All Its Fullness**, p. 154f

[119] cf. Jagessar, Michael N., **Full Life For All: The Work and Theology of Philip A. Potter – A Historical Survey and Systematic Analysis of Major Themes** (Uitgeverij Boekencentrum, Zoetermeer, 1997), pp. 227-247

[120] Konrad Raiser *"Celebrating and ecumenical pilgrimage: and address to honour Philip Potter on the occasion of his 80th birthday"*, **Ecumenical Review**, October 2001, p. 523

and his understanding of the city contributed to his intercultural hermeneutics. Potter's intercultural hermeneutics includes at least two movements. One is the awareness and exposure to issues that dehumanize and violate life, both in the context of biblical texts and the contexts of interpreters. The second is a dialogue concerning the judgments and decisions needed to ensure a full life for everyone.

Outcome: quest for self-identity and self-determination

Hermeneutic of authentic self-affirmation

One of the concrete consequences of the post-emancipation era, which typified the struggle for self-definition and self-determination, was the emergence of *Rastafarianism* in the Caribbean. Rastafarianism emerged and flourished out of a complex of circumstances. One, the harsh economic circumstances in Jamaica in the 1930s that widened the economic gap between the upper and middle and peasant classes[121]; two, the prophecy and call of Marcus Garvey that Black people should look to Africa where a black king shall arise and such will be the day of their deliverance[122]; three, the colonial legacy of colour prejudice where light skin tone was determinative of value and a guarantee to be spared the humiliations and hopelessness of those of a darker hue[123]; four, the foreign control of the decision- making processes and the productive forces of Caribbean territories; and five, the economic and racial stratification that were in sharp relief to the flourishing tourist industry with American tourists flocking to the English-speaking

---

[121] Leonard E. Barrett, **Soul Force** (New York: Anchor Press, 1974), pp. 182-83
[122] Horace Campbell, **Rasta and Resistance From Marcus Garvey to Walter Rodney** (London: Hansib Publishing Limited, 1985), p. 48
[123] Noel Erskine *"Biblical Hermeneutics in Modern Caribbean Experience: Paradigms and Prospects"* in Gossai and Murrell, **Religion, Culture and Tradition in the Caribbean**, p. 223.

countries in the wake of the Cuban revolution. With the economic and racial landscape dominated and controlled by Whites, Rastafarians reasoned that the roots of Caribbean oppression, exploitation, and alienation were in the system of white supremacy,[124] or what Rasta call Babylon. Babylon was an aged and oppressive socio-economic and political system that needed to be dismantled, not simply surmounted.

Thus, race and class consciousness, pan-Africanism, and foreign domination not only provide the complex origins of Rastafarianism but also shape its epistemological lens in the struggle for identity, cultural freedom, and dignity, as well as in the quest to make sense of life and biblical faith. Through these epistemological lenses, Rastafarians reject the idea of God as transcendent—unreal and unrelated to their harsh lived experiences. A God who is immanent, present amid the challenges of their existence, carries far more significance. God as immanent offers both distance and connection. Therefore, experience is definitive of the truth about God for Rasta.

Additionally, Rastafarians link their struggle to the biblical existential metaphor of Babylon and Exodus. Babylon represents a life of alienation and symbolizes everything that seeks to denigrate African origins and suppress the desire for freedom. Essentially, Babylon embodies cultural slavery. The path to liberation from cultural slavery is through Exodus, the quest for free cultural identity, dignity, and freedom.

Moreover, for Rasta, salvation is not found in 'another world' but in Ethiopia, a specific earthly location identified as the Promised Land. Ethiopia holds significance not only for its role in the biblical narrative as the fulfillment of Psalm 68:31— *"Princes shall come out of Egypt; Ethiopia stretches forth her hands unto God"*—but also for its revolutionary implications. In 1896 at Adwa, the Abyssinians, or Ethiopians, defeated the Italians, a foreign white Western power. The defeat of a white army

---

[124] Catherine A. Sunshine, **The Caribbean: Survival, Struggle and Sovereignty** (An EPICA Publication, 1985), p. 53

by a black king symbolized the potential for social and political change, not just for Africa, but for the entire black race. This victory also led to a new form of deification. Not only was a foreign ruler and system overthrown, but so was their God. In its place were a black king and a God experienced through the lived realities of the people, as this historical knowledge became a tool of resistance against the cultural imposition of white foreign values and customs.[125]

Consequently, we have the bold outline of Rasta hermeneutics of authentic self-affirmation, which begins with the existential realities that degrade, denigrate, alienate, and disempower humans and then turns to the biblical texts. However, when Rastafarians engage with the biblical texts, they do not limit themselves to any sustained interpretation of any passage or book. Instead, Rastafarians "cite up" or proofread biblical passages to suit their purposes.[126] In Rasta hermeneutics of authentic self-affirmation, therefore, the agents of meaning are experience, immanence, and historical knowledge, rather than the biblical texts.

Eisegetics and Exegetics

Biblical interpretation from the nineteenth century to the mid-twentieth century primarily focused on analyzing a biblical text within its context and understanding its historical and cultural origins. Scholars explored questions such as: What did the text mean? What does it mean? How did the text convey its message? Figures like Bogle, Garvey, Potter, and the Rastafarians raised different questions.

Their inquiries reflected a greater concern with applying biblical faith than with exegeting biblical texts. In other words, they were much

---

[125] Robert Beckford, **Dread and Pentecostal (London: SPCK, 2000)**, pp. 114-15

[126] Noel Erskine *"Biblical Hermeneutics in Modern Caribbean Experience: Paradigms and Prospects"*, pp. 221-24, and Nathaniel Samuel Murrell *"Dangerous Memories, Underdevelopment, and the Bible in Colonial Caribbean Experience"*, pp. 28-32 in Gossai and Murrell, **Religion, Culture and Tradition in the Caribbean.**

more focused on addressing the question: what sense and meaning did the material realities of inferiority and political and economic exploitation hold for a biblical faith that professed a just and impartial God? Consequently, their interest was not only historical but also examined how biblical faith supported emancipation from conditions of enslavement.

Additionally, by beginning with the human condition, Bogle, Garvey, Potter, and Rastafarianism were able to uncover and highlight the inherent contradictions within the constructed views or interpretations of the dominant culture. In doing so, they established a theological perspective where the concept of God was not alien to one's socio-geographic context. In contrast, a distinctly different understanding and vision of God's intentions for the well-being of creation also emerged.

Furthermore, Bogle, Garvey, Potter, and Rastafarianism assigned a formative role to the Bible rather than a normative one in their method of biblical interpretation. In their interpretive approach, biblical revelation is not intended for all times, places, and people; thus, it remains confined to the Bible. While it is true that God spoke, it is also true that God continues to speak. Additionally, individuals are challenged to re-envision their world by considering the analysis of the Biblical text, thus making sense of and finding meaning in their daily existence. This interpretive approach is, therefore, perspectival, as the biblical text is read in a way that allows existential realities to inform and shape its interpretation. In this way, the meaning of texts is understood to reside in lived experiences. Consequently, individuals can envision and develop alternative forms of existence, especially when the prevailing experiences of social systems and practices are oppressive.

However, the above also clarifies that for Bogle, Garvey, and Potter, the focus on socio-ideological interest and social practices was more on the material context and less on the biblical text. This is not to undermine the effectiveness of the work of Bogle, Garvey, Potter, and Rastafarianism. History will reveal otherwise. Instead, it supports my claim that placing biblical texts back into their socio-historic environment merely exposes the socio-ideological interests and social practices that created them, as well as the conflict and tension among the social forces in that inhabited world.

Even so, the elements of how and why resistance in biblical hermeneutics develops are evident in the biblical interpretive strategies of Bogle, Garvey, and Potter. First, their way of knowing, which penetrated the biblical texts, was through the materiality of their contexts, which were oppressive; second, through religious symbol – the chapel for Bogle, the biblical story of creation in the case of Garvey, and cultural heritage for Potter- they articulated an alternative social order. Third, camps of interests in conflict were formed. Besides, Bogle, Garvey, and Potter came to the biblical texts out of a concrete commitment to the struggle for social justice.

Table 1: 3

Biblical reading strategies during the post-'emancipation' Period 1838 –1959

Reader/ Interpreter	Social location	Biblical Texts	Socio-historical Realities	Reading strategy	Location of meaning	Understanding of Bible	Consequences
Paul Bogle	Male, Black slave, Baptist Deacon	The Psalms, Ephesians 2:14	Economic exploitation, racially stratified society, inculcation of	A resistant reading strategy			Rebellion against oppression, frontal attack on the system
Marcus Garvey	Male, Black, social & political activist	The biblical Creation story, the Passion Narrative	English values, formation and failure of West Indian Federation, industrialisation	A resistant reading strategy	Interaction between biblical texts and reader	Formative	Concrete socio-economic transformation, emergence of Rastafarianism,
Rastafarianism	Middle class, proletariat		by invitation, invasion of the Dominican	Hermeneutic of authentic self-affirmation			Challenging the status quo

Philip Potter	Male, middle class, trained theologian, Serving the church outside conventional institutional structures	Liberation: full life for all/life in all its fullness	Republic by USA, Cuban revolution 1959, formation of CADEC 1973	Intercultural hermeneutics	Relation between faith & active engagement with the Biblical texts	Advocacy for the liberation of all oppressed people

Post-"independence" era: 1959 onwards
Socio-historical and political realities and forces

Dependency syndrome

The post-"independence" era was one of political and economic self- determination in which Caribbean governments and peoples sought to build their communities by and for themselves. The efforts fell on hard times. Political self- determination was not matched by economic independence or regional unity. A dependency process was set in train that did more to enforce political and economic dependence for Caribbean countries than to foster the ability to determine their future. The Puerto Rican model of industrialization by invitation during the 1960s was colonialism warmed all over again. With this model, the Caribbean countries' economies were shaped to meet the needs of the industrialised countries, low-wage labour and cheap raw materials were demanded, profits were repatriated to imperial metropolis, and expatriates performed all the technically skilled jobs. With an emphasis on creating the right environment for foreign investment (road networks, holiday resorts, the construction of air and seaports that met international standards, repression of workers' rights), agriculture and agro-based industries were virtually ignored or undeveloped.

Models of economic development

Furthermore, the alternative development models, except the Cuban revolution, encountered failures or self-destruction in the revolutions of Nicaragua and Grenada in 1979 and the democratic socialism of the Michael Manley-led PNP (People's National Party) in Jamaica, often influenced by foreign geopolitical factors. The collapse of these development models was hastened and exacerbated by capital flight to foreign banks, the pullback of foreign investments, and the harsh measures imposed by the IMF (International Monetary Fund), requiring

49

cuts in public spending and employment. Consequently, the economies of these territories weakened as they lacked the socio-economic and political power to fulfil the aspirations of complete human development and liberation, or self-definition and self- determination, which emerged from emancipation in 1838 and the liberation movements of the 1960s to the late 1970s. The period was marked by despair.

Right-wing evangelical religion

Adding to these despairing times was the rise of American-inspired right-wing evangelical religion, which emphasizes personal salvation and triumph over earthly struggles and injustices in the hereafter.

Natural and man-made disasters

Despairing times became even more dismal with natural and "man-made" disasters. Hurricanes grew more frequent, powerful, and destructive, while volcanoes dormant for centuries suddenly erupted. On the human front, political tribalism, nepotism, and the lucrative drug trade emerged as means of survival.

The post-"independence" era, then, is one of economic dependence on foreign investments, stagnation, and powerlessness. It was also characterised by the search for alternative development models and the Caribbean peoples' deep search for freedom, wholeness, and authenticity. The character of the times has led one Caribbean theologian, Kortright Davis, to conclude that 'emancipation still comin'.[127]

Biblical Interpretive approaches

In these changing and challenging times, the Caribbean Conference of Churches became involved in the process of self-determination and

---

[127] Emancipation still comin' is also the title of Kortright Davis's book *Emancipation still comin', Explorations in Caribbean Emancipatory Theology* (Maryknoll, New York: Orbis Books, 1990.

self-definition by advocating for a development model aimed at human liberation and social transformation. In 1971, a historic ecumenical consultation occurred in Chaguaramas, Trinidad, culminating two years later with the formation of the CCC (Caribbean Conference of Churches) in 1973. The Caribbean Conference of Churches declared its intention "to promote the human liberation of our people and commit to achieving social justice and the dignity of man in our society."[128] Biblical events, motifs, traditions, and personalities were primarily used to challenge and critique the social order and to provide the basis and impetus for a model of human development and social transformation.

Critical re-reading of the biblical texts

The Exodus event was utilized by Idris Hamid, one of the leading advocates for the decolonization of theology in the Caribbean, William Watty, the sharpest of Caribbean theologians, and Bishop Clive Abdullah, a bishop in the Catholic Church of Trinidad. In their interpretation of the Exodus event, both Hamid and Watty recognized that God liberates the oppressed and that salvation equates to liberation. Hamid asserted that the churches were bound by the ethos of colonialism— domination and subjugation, unreality and disconnection—and thus could not appropriately employ the Exodus motif with its implications for deliverance without questioning that ethos[129] or condemning themselves. For Hamid, the God of the Biblical tradition, from the Exodus to the Resurrection, is a God who liberates from all forms of bondage, both external and internal, including the bondage of death. This God remains absent in the religious imagination, in the everyday experience of Caribbean peoples; God is perceived as an outsider.[130]

---

[128] **Called To Be**, pp. 23-24, 33-34
[129] David I Mitchell ed., **With Eyes Wide Open** (Kingston, Jamaica: 1973), pp. 123-126
[130] Ibid p. 122

For his part, Watty challenged the idea that divine sovereignty was related to power, dominance, and privilege. For Watty, the God who liberated from Egypt's power "was on the side of the weak and oppressed and against the power, dominance, and privileges that oppressed and dehumanized people."[131] However, Watty was eager to emphasize that "liberation theology comes not from a situation of oppression but from a community under God."[132] In fact, for Watty, the Exodus story was revisited *only after* they had been formed into a community under God... in ways that influenced their relationships—how they harvest their crops, collect their dues, write off their debts, and care for the weak, vulnerable, and stranger."[133] Thus, a theology of liberation is grounded in God's purposes as creator and within creation,[134] not solely based on the Exodus event.

In his interpretation of the said Exodus event but emphasizing the role of Moses, Bishop Abdullah saw that the church in the Caribbean must agitate for the transformation of unjust and inhumane societal structures. He saw the demand that God gave Moses to deliver to Pharoah, "Let my people go," as the same self- authenticating requirement that was demanded of the Caribbean church to all oppressive powers.[135]

Robert Cuthbert, one of the founders of CADEC (Christian Action for Development in the Eastern Caribbean) in 1969, drew on the prophetic tradition (Isaiah 65:20-22; Amos 8:4-6; Micah 4:3-4; Luke 4:16-18). He cultivated the idea that development is liberation based on his understanding of the prophetic tradition.[136] For Cuthbert, the church must advocate for and create conditions that foster full human development.

---

[131] Idris Hamid ed., **Troubling of the Waters** (San Fernando, Trinidad: 1973), pp. 70-71
[132] William Watty, **From Shore to Shore: Soundings in Caribbean Theology** (Barbados: CEDAR Press, 1981) p. 45
[133] Ibid. pp. 44 – 45
[134] Ibid.. p. 45
[135] Ibid. p. 17
[136] Mitchell, **With Eyes Wide Open,** p. 111

Allan Kirton, a former General Secretary of the CCC, and Leslie Lett, an Anglican priest and key figure in the CCC's work, also used the prophetic tradition. Kirton turned to the prophet Jeremiah (Jeremiah 33),[137] drawing on the image of disaster to encourage making "an investment in hope"[138] despite the despairing times in the Caribbean. The senses provided the way into the text, in this case, seeing. Hope, for Kirton, is an act of faith, the substance of things not seen.

Critical reflection on praxis

While utilizing the Exodus and prophetic tradition, Leslie Lett, one of the Regional Officers of the Caribbean Conference of Churches, advocated for a different hermeneutical approach. Lett began the interpretive process with critical reflection on praxis. Analysis of socio-political realities and commitment to, as well as involvement in, the struggle for social justice came first, providing the context for interpretation and meaning; then, the analysis of the biblical text followed, informed by an understanding of the social realities.[139] This meant that a process of conscientization of existential realities was integrated into the interpretive process.

This reading strategy – critical reflection on praxis followed by an analysis of Biblical texts – is recognized in the works of several Caribbean hermeneuticians throughout and beyond the 1970s: Ashley Smith, Burchell Taylor, Noel Erskine, John Holder, Joyce Bailey, Leslie James, Marjorie Lewis Cooper, Nathaniel Samuel Murrell, and others.[140] For instance, John Holder, former principal of the Codrington

---

[137] Allan Kirton and William Watty eds., **Consultation for Ministry in a New Decade** (Barbados: CADEC, 1985), p. 5

[138] Kirton and Watty, **Consultation for ministry**, p. 6

[139] Leslie Lett, *"Working for Peace in the Caribbean"* in **Peace: A Challenge to the Caribbean**, ed. Allan Kirton (Barbados: CADEC, 1982), p. 27

[140] See Hemchand Gossai & Nathaniel Samuel Murrell, **Religion, Culture and Tradition in the Caribbean** (New York: St. Marin's Press, 2000)

Theological College in Barbados, noted that the hermeneutical approach of Caribbean theologians in the 1970s and 1980s involved using the Bible to address and illuminate the experiences of Caribbean people.[141] In his hermeneutical method, Holder first contextualized issues of land, identity, and leadership within a Deuteronomical framework, then analyzed and applied their relevance to the Caribbean.[142]

The American-inspired right-wing evangelicals adopt an interpretive approach that focuses primarily on the literal meaning of biblical texts. They extract value from these texts for personal salvation, piety, spiritual formation, and an otherworldly hope, thereby avoiding socio-political issues. For these fundamentalists, humanity is evil, the current world is beyond redemption, and hope rests in the promise of salvation in the afterlife. This creates a disconnect between understanding the material realities of the people, the reader's context, and the biblical text.

What the above shows is that regardless of the reading strategy employed— whether text to context or context to text—it is the reader's ideological interest and social practice that prevail, not those of the text, except for Watty.

Reading into the biblical texts

A distinctly different hermeneutical approach is evident in the work of George Mulrain, a noted Caribbean theologian and former tutor at the UTCWI (United Theological College of the West Indies), Winston Persaud, a Caribbean diaspora theologian from the USA, and Joseph Nicholas, another former UTCWI tutor, along with Michael Jagessar, a Caribbean diaspora theologian, J. Michael Middleton, yet another Caribbean diaspora theologian, and Althea Spencer Miller, a female

---

[141] John Holder, *"Is This the Word of the Lord?"* in Hemchand Gossai and Nathaniel Samuel Murrell eds. **Religion, Culture and Tradition in the Caribbean** (London: Macmillan, 2000), p. 136
[142] Ibid. p. 136

Caribbean diaspora theologian. All six theologians utilized aspects of Caribbean culture as "texts" for interpreting and deriving meaning in biblical hermeneutics. Mulrain drew from calypso, Nicholas and Gossai referenced cricket, Jagessar highlighted literature, and Middleton incorporated reggae music.

For Mulrain, a calypso is a narrative folk song.[143] A calypso encompasses methodology (how it conveys its message), culture (the way of life of a particular people), and communication (the use of voice as a medium of expression that covers the entire spectrum of human experience). The foundation of Mulrain's interpretive approach is the belief in the existence of spirits and demons, or Jumbie stories, as they are called in some Caribbean countries, along with laughter. For instance, concerning communication between the living and the dead, Mulrain cites an occasion narrated in a calypso when two lovers visited a cemetery for private reasons and were startled by a voice that claimed they were courageous for consorting in his "abode." After a hasty retreat to civilization, they recounted the incident to the first person they encountered in the street. His reply did little to calm their racing hearts:

He said: 'I can understan' You're a wild young man But you are not to be blame

When I was alive I was jus' de same.[144]

Mulrain then made the hermeneutical shift to Colossians 2:9 and Ephesians 6:11-13. While not denying the possibility that issues of the living communicating with the dead are viewed as cases for psychologists and psychiatrists, calypso exegesis allowed for the text to be interpreted without being demythologized.

---

[143] See George M. Mulrain *"Is There a Calypso Exegesis"?* In R.S. Sugirtharajah ed. **Voices From The Margin, Interpreting the Bible in the Third World** (Maryknoll, New York: 1995), p. 39

[144] Ibid. p. 43

Another example mentioned by Mulrain is laughter. One characteristic of Caribbean people is their ability to laugh even when times are tough or to pick up the pieces, smile, and move on. Mulrain stated that the ability to laugh in dire situations reflects a theological concept: Despite what happens, all things will ultimately work for good.[145] Additionally, laughter is liberating[146] as it shows a refusal to give in or give up when the going gets tough.

In establishing the parameters for his interpretive approach, Persaud begins with a socio-cultural analysis of cricket as a "text," using Rohan Kanhai, an Indo- Guyanese cricketer, as an example, and then transitioning to an exegesis of the biblical book of Ruth.[147] Essentially, Persaud focuses on the theme of identity in the book of Ruth. By doing so, Persaud attributes to cricket the religious or sacred designation of "text" that informs and interprets the lives of people in the English- speaking Caribbean, even as the Bible remains the primary religious text. Among the eleven players on a cricket team, it is crucial to note where each player fielded and who served as captain, as these were primary indicators of power and authority, subservience, and deference.[148]

Persaud claimed that a cricket match is more than just a game or a pastime. He referenced Frank Birbalsingh, a writer on 'West Indian' cricket, who asserts that cricket is "a spectacle that can galvanize a people's spiritual resources, stimulate their national self-esteem, and remind them of their place in the world... it recognizes West Indian resistance to an oppressive colonial legacy, for it acknowledges test cricket as the first opportunity for West Indians to demonstrate their

---

[145] Ibid. p. 42
[146] Ibid. p. 44
[147] See Winston Persaud, *"Hermeneutics of the Bible and 'Cricket as Text': Reading as an Exile"* in Fernando F. Segovia, **Interpreting Beyond Borders** (Sheffield, England: Sheffield Academic Press, 2000), p. 175-188
[148] Ibid. p. 176

abilities on the international stage."[149] For Caribbean people, cricket is more than a game; it reflects our identity and how we live our lives. Thus, Persaud's framing of cricket as 'text' debunks stereotypes, showing that the people of the Caribbean, with their history of slavery, are not as marginalized, powerless, or inherently inferior as that experience might suggest.[150]

With Rohan Kanhai, an Indo-Guyanese cricketer, his inclusion in the team for the tour of India in 1958-1959 meant that more than just cricket was at stake.

Kanhai's selection was laden with symbolic significance because it represented an allegorical journey back 'home' for all Indo-Guyanese. In Kanhai, there was a sense of communal identity. The test match to be played in Calcutta was anticipated with great interest. Calcutta was the port from which Indians were transported to the West Indies between 1838 and 1917 to work on sugar plantations. Thus, Calcutta was evocative, serving as a metaphor for dislocation, separation, and the loss of traditional certainties[151]. Kanhai ultimately did not disappoint. His 256 in the third test match in Calcutta was hailed as a "gift of newfound identity to a people who were not disgraced in returning 'home'."

Kanhai, though, was significant not only for Indo-Guyanese but also for all Caribbean people. Notwithstanding ethnicity, all Caribbean people share a history of slavery, subjugation, and exploitation. His further success in Australia during the 1960-61 series and the unbridled and favourable comments on Khanhai's batting skills and dominance made all Caribbean people feel that they were somebody and mattered[152].

Persaud's next hermeneutical move was to consider the question: How does cricket as a 'text' assist in reading and interpreting the

---

[149] Ibid. p. 177
[150] Ibid. p. 178
[151] Ibid. p. 181
[152] Ibid. p. 182

book of Ruth? In other words, how will his socio-cultural analysis of cricket inform and shape his exegesis of the book of Ruth? For Persaud, "Ruth the 'foreigner' *(Rohan Kanhai)* became a symbol of courage and inclusiveness, even to the 'exiled' people *(Indo-Guyanese)* of Israel who had to come to terms with their new 'home' *(Guyana)." (Emphasis mine)*

Unlike Persaud, Nicholas made three hermeneutical moves in his work. He began with a historical-critical analysis of the invincibility of Zion in its ancient context. Then, he compared the historical circumstances of West Indies cricket and Zion to demonstrate that their invincibility was not primarily due to the strength of their batting defenses or superior skills but to their faith in God. Lastly, an analysis of the socio-cultural significance of West Indies cricket will be provided, considering the theological insights gained from the exegesis of the text.

Jagessar and Middleton have noted that some Caribbean cultural artists work from a distinctly biblical-theological perspective. Christianity is so deeply woven into the life and institutions of Caribbean societies that reflecting on biblical and theological matters has significantly influenced their work, rather than remaining entirely outside their interests or abilities. Therefore, both Jagessar and Middleton have demonstrated how Caribbean cultural artists have drawn on biblical theological allusions, concepts, and constructs and have engaged with biblical texts as part of their framework for meaning, analysis, and critique.

For example, one way Jagessar approaches the biblical text is through Caribbean literature. In his work, Jagessar[153] has keenly observed how Derek Walcott, a St. Lucian and Nobel laureate, engages with the Exodus tradition. In his book *'What the Twilight Says – Essays,'* and specifically in a chapter titled 'The Muse of History,' Walcott comments

---

[153] Unpublished master's Thesis entitled **"A Theological Evaluation of Wilson Harris' Understanding of Community as reflected in the 'Guiana Quartet', An Interdisciplinary Study of Theology and Caribbean Literature"** (Jamaica: University of the West Indies, 1992)

on the Middle Passage: 'the passage over our Red Sea was not from bondage to freedom but its opposite (from freedom to bondage) so the tribes arrived at their new Canaan chained.'[154] Jagessar uses this inversion of the Exodus narrative to interpret the Caribbean historical experience of bondage. He further suggests that by doing this, Walcott opens new vistas for Caribbean hermeneuts to critically and authentically re-read the biblical narrative, rather than adopting the liberation theologians' interpretation of the Exodus paradigm.

Even more tellingly, however, Jagessar employs Anansi, an elusive trickster and anti-establishment figure from Afro-Caribbean folklore, as a cultural and discursive partner to deconstruct totalizing tendencies and practices regarding perspectives on Christianity and the Bible within a Caribbean context. For Jagessar, in a diverse socio-religious, ethnic, and cultural landscape like the Caribbean, Anansi serves as a practical conversation partner "through which to engage biblical texts from a multiplicity of views rather than a single[155] view." Anansi traverses and intertwines cultures, defying categories and embodying the "manifoldness of what is."[156] Therefore, there exists a multitude of ways, through the lens of Anansi, to understand and interpret social realities.

Therefore, in Jagessar's multiverse hermeneutics, Anansi represents a sub- type of the underdog and trickster who serves to disrupt and challenge the status quo while hinting at counter-hegemony, oppression, and pride. For Jagessar, multiverse hermeneutics encompasses four movements:

---

[154] Derek Walcott, **What the Twilight Says – Essays** (London: Faber & Faber, 1998), pp. 36-64
[155] Michael Jagessar & Anthony Reddie, **Postcolonial Black British Theology – New Textures and Themes** (Peterborough: Epworth, 2007), p. 126
[156] Ibid. p. 129

1. Alternative God-talk in the context of 'space' rather than 'place.' The focus here is not on physical dimensions and conditions, but on liberating the mind and its faculties, daring to dream, and envisioning a preferred future.[157]

2. Reflecting the preferred future in resistance art practice. This resistance practice involves the dramatic use of jokes, speech, calypso, carnival, and gossip as acts of retelling and re-envisioning lived realities to create a new reality that cannot be easily subdued[158], and

3. A search and exploration of biblical texts from the viewpoint of the underdog and trickster, aiming to illuminate and broaden the relevance of these texts in real-life situations.[159]

4. The indeterminacy of texts and interpretation punctures any tendency to confine texts and their interpretations to exactitude. The hermeneut's task is to unravel interpretation since no interpretation is fixed.[160] Interpretation is dynamic. In other words, all conclusions are subject to challenge and scrutiny.

Middleton's entry point into the biblical texts, particularly biblical creation theology centered around Genesis 1:26-27, is through the lyrics of reggae music by Bob Marley and the Wailers. Middleton's reading strategy draws on historical memory and God's intent from the creation of the world as an alternative to the status quo.[161] This approach highlights how Bob Marley and the Wailers contemporize and expand the biblical narrative to encompass the Black struggle against

---

[157] Ibid. p. 177
[158] Ibid. pp. 136-138
[159] Ibid. pp. 137-138
[160] Michael Jagessar, **"Unending the Bible: The Book of Revelation Through the Optics of Anancy and Rastafari"**; unpublished paper presented at the Black Theology Annual Conference on Reading and Re-reading the Bible, July 27, 2006 Queens College, Birmingham, p. 12
[161] Gossai & Murrell, **Religion, Culture and Tradition** p. 182

dehumanization and degradation. Consequently, the biblical story of redemption extends from the Exodus to Marcus Garvey and beyond:

> I'll never forget, no way
> They crucified Jess-us Christ I'll never forget, no way
> They stole Marcus for rights I'll never forget, no way
> They turned their backs on Paul Bogle
> So don't you forget, no youth Who you are
> And where you stand in the struggle.[162]

The appeal to God's purposes as Creator and within creation challenges the oppressive social relations in the world, aiming for reconciliation before the Eschaton. In the song "One Love," Marley and the Wailers make a call.

> Let's get together to fight this
> Holy Armagiddyon (One Love)
> So when the Man comes there will be no,
> No doom (One Song)
> Have pity on those whose chances grow thinner
> There ain't no hiding place from the Father of Creation.[163]

Through this reading strategy, Middleton interprets Genesis 1:26-27 as a gift of human dignity and a call to responsible action for justice and blessing in a world belonging to Jah.[164] Therefore, the purpose of Genesis 1:26-27 is to 'resist the system', affirming human identity and dignity as the *Imago Dei* in the face of degradation, oppression, and domination.

Spencer Miller engages in an act of prophetic imagination by

---

[162] From the *Exodus* album by Bob Marley and Wailers (Island Records, 1977)
[163] Ibid.
[164] Gossai & Murrell, p. 183

conscripting Lucy Bailey to recognise the trajectory of struggle, survival, creativity and resourcefulness of Caribbean peoples.[165] For Spencer Miller, Lucy Bailey is an icon of Caribbean peoples and their religion.[166] What Spencer goes on to do, by way of example, is to represent Lucy Bailey in a popular Jamaican aphorism – likkle but Tallawah – in her appropriation of Luke 21:1-4. "Likkle but Tallawah" means "small but strong, effective and great" or "we bigger than our size".[167] Though Lucy Bailey was "likkle", small of stature, and despite the violent neighbourhood in which she lives, residents and gangsters respect her. So, Lucy Bailey is "tallawah" in mi(gh)te.[168] In comparison, the widow's mite represented her straightforward and faithful existence, revealing the complexities of the insincerity and guile of the scribes and the temple system.[169] Furthermore, the widow's mite served as her allegiance to a system that exploited her.[170] Spencer Miller's objective in this context is to identify and analyze power relationships within the text. She achieves this by centering her reading strategy on a socio-structural text analysis.

Outcome: economic dependency versus human liberation& Social Transformation

In the post-independence period, natives engaged in the interpretive process. Despite a strong reliance on the Eurocentric historical critical method, the starting point rooted in existential realities made the interpretive approaches primarily perspectival and illuminating. As a result, they critiqued and challenged the social order to foster social

---

[165] Kathleen O'Brien Wicker, Althea Spencer Miller & Musa W. Dube eds. **Feminist New Testament Studies, Global and Future Perspectives** (New York: Palgrave MacMillan, 2005), pp. 211-214

[166] Ibid. p. 213

[167] Ibid. p. 214

[168] Ibid. p. 234

[169] Ibid. p. 234

[170] Ibid. p. 234

transformation for the sake of social justice, even amid American-inspired evangelicals who emphasized "veriticalism" or a futuristic and triumphal view of Christianity.

Eisegetics and Exegetics

Three reading strategies are discernible from the foregoing:

- Analysis of the biblical text in its contexts and then analysis of the context of the reader considering biblical texts,
- Critical reflection on praxis and/or analysis of the context of the reader and then analysis of biblical text in its context,
- Culture is "text," and then the analysis of the biblical text in its context is considered "text" or the culture.

One commendable aspect of these reading strategies is the sustained emphasis on the material dimensions of both text and context. However, it is observable that the nature of social relationships, systems, and structures is increasingly exposed in the context and culture and less so in the biblical text.

Interestingly, as in the case of Sam Sharpe and the slaves, Bogle and Garvey discussed above, resistance does not occur with the same social effects due to the interpretive strategies of those cited in the post-independence period. And this is not because they do not give agency to the materiality of the biblical texts and their contexts. Instead, it is because they are doing their interpretive work from within an institutionalised system, not from without, and therefore, their praxis is more oppositional than resistant. It is a praxis of resistance conjoined with an interpretive strategy that gives agency to the materiality of both biblical texts and the context of the interpreter, which results in resistance. Such a praxis will lead to a critique and exposure of and challenge to oppressive systems and practices in society.

Table 1: 4

Biblical hermeneutics during the post-'Independence' period: 1959 onwards

Reader/Interpreter	Social location	Biblical Texts	Socio-historical Realities	Reading strategy	Location of meaning	Understanding of Bible	Consequences
Idris Hamid, William Watty, Bishop Clive Abdullah	Male, Indian, Black, middle class, trained theologian	Exodus tradition	Enforced economic	Critical re-reading of Biblical texts			
Robert Cuthbert, Allan Kirton	Male, Brown, black, middle class, trained theologian	Prophetic tradition	& political dependence, undeveloped agriculture & agro-based	Critical re-reading of Biblical texts			
Leslie Lett, Ashley Smith, Burchell Taylor, Noel Erskine, John Holder, Joyce Bailey, Leslie James, Marjorie Lewis-cooper, Nathaniel Samuel Murrell	Male, female, black, middle class, trained theologian	Liberation tradition	industries, Nicaragua & Grenada revolutions 1979, withdrawal of foreign investments, IMF demands	Critical reflection on praxis	In existential realities/in the text	Formative	Advocacy for human liberation and social transformation

George Mulrain, Winston Persaud, Michael Jagessar, J. Michael Middleton, Althea Spencer Miller	Male, female, black, middle class, trained theologian	Culture as "text"	cut public expenditure and employment, democratic socialism, American-inspired evangelicalism, formation of CCC	A reading into the Biblical texts	In socio-cultural realities
Oral Thomas	Male, black, middle class, trained theologian			Cultural Historical-materialist	In socio-historic environment of both text and context.

Analysis and Conclusion

As we have seen above, the biblical resistant reading strategy of Sharpe, Bogle, and Garvey resulted in concrete socio-economic transformations of oppressive social systems and practices. The critical constitutive elements of this reading strategy were the interpretation of biblical texts stemming from a concrete commitment to and involvement in the struggle for social justice, alongside an awareness of the specific socio-economic and historical realities of the context.

While other reading strategies did not lead to complicity with the status quo (such as uncritical retelling of the biblical story, scriptural allusions, and quotations), they often advocated for liberation and social change (including citing biblical texts, cultural dialogue, critical re-reading of biblical texts, critical reflection on praxis, and readings into biblical texts). The key difference between the resistant strategy and the others is praxis. Additionally, what is lacking in all the reading strategies is that agency is not attributed to the socio-ideological interests and social practices that produced the biblical texts. Effectively, what we observe here in biblical hermeneutical practice within a Caribbean context is a fluid reading strategy that shifts between the universal (the Bible as the word of God) and the socio-economic and historical realities of the context, and vice versa.

Mulrain's analysis of hermeneutics within a Caribbean context reflects the fluidity between the universal and the particular. By situating Caribbean biblical hermeneutics within Black theology, Mulrain asserts that the context of readers is crucial in hermeneutics.[171] This context serves as an epistemological lens that influences the interpretation of biblical texts, likely leading to radical opposition to and confrontation

---

[171] George Mulrain *"Hermeneutics within a Caribbean Context"* in R.S. Sugirtharajah ed. **Vernacular Hermeneutics** (Sheffield: Sheffield Academic Press, 1999), p. 122

with, though not resistance to, political and economic powers.[172] Presented here is a biblical reading strategy that moves from the specific to the universal. In the preceding analysis, this reading strategy, moving from the specific to the universal, is characteristic of a critical rereading of biblical texts, critical reflection on praxis, and interpretation of these texts.

However, Mulrain argues that we should not assume the authors of biblical books were purely objective. They had their own perspectives and understood God in unique ways.[173] Since biblical texts are shaped by biases and written from specific perspectives and contexts, it is essential to consider these factors in the hermeneutical process. This biblical reading strategy starts from the universal while acknowledging the material conditions that led to the creation of the texts. It maintains flexibility within the Caribbean biblical hermeneutical practice. The critical point is that regardless of the starting point in the hermeneutical process, one must exegete biblical texts in a way that analyzes the material conditions that produced them. It matters little at which stage of the hermeneutical process this analysis occurs; what is essential is that it is performed.

Therefore, the fluidity of reading strategies in this study is not the critical issue in biblical hermeneutical practice within a Caribbean context. Instead, how the Bible is understood and "read" are the decisive factors. This does not imply that one's social location or epistemology is insignificant. On the contrary, as this study acknowledges and will continue to acknowledge, the cultural significance of one's social location is crucial in the biblical hermeneutical process. Rather, it emphasizes the study's preference for moving from the particular (context) to the universal (biblical text). Nonetheless, regardless of where the biblical text fits into the hermeneutical process, exegesis of that text concerning

---

[172] Ibid., P. 122
[173] Ibid. p. 127

its ideological interests and the resulting socio-structural formations and practices cannot be omitted. Neglecting this dimension may lead the interpreter to unwittingly align with oppressive systems and practices.

In the Caribbean today, self-definition is still unclear, and self-determination is still manipulated and controlled by foreign influences and forces. Resisting these influences and forces is still the primary challenge. The challenge is to develop a biblical hermeneutic as a weapon of struggle to resist, not just oppose, and eventually overthrow them.

However, first, it is necessary to demonstrate that biblical texts are produced and that their compositions involve a socio-ideological agenda and social practices. The letter to Philemon provides ample evidence to support this perspective.

Another task arising from this analysis is to examine whether that agenda and those practices influence hermeneutical practice outside of the Caribbean. By doing so, the specificities of biblical hermeneutics within a Caribbean context are highlighted against the broader backdrop of hermeneutics. Completing the tasks of illustrating that biblical texts are products and placing biblical hermeneutical practice within a Caribbean context on the broader framework will position this study to propose biblical hermeneutics within a Caribbean context and draw implications from it.

CHAPTER 2

BIBLICAL HERMENEUTICAL PRACTICES WITHIN THE CARIBBEAN

Introduction

In the context of weekday Bible study sessions, Sunday school classes, roadside preaching, and home devotions, biblical hermeneutics in a Caribbean setting is primarily a leader-centered activity. While reading the Bible is valuable during private home devotions, it is within worship experiences, weekday Bible study sessions, and Sunday school classes that the Bible is interpreted. In these experiences and sessions, both reading and interpreting aim to nurture faith and cultivate "a faith that is relevant to what people confront every day of their lives."[174] Consequently, biblical hermeneutics is pursued in a Caribbean context to serve both ecclesiological and personal purposes.

What happens, therefore, is that in biblical hermeneutics, the Bible is not read and interpreted mainly by a community of interests or from the perspective of community interests. Mulrain acknowledges the necessity, relevance, and consequences of reading biblical texts as a community by emphasizing that

---

[174] George Mulrain *"Hermeneutics Within a Caribbean Context"* in R.S. Sugirtharajah ed., **Vernacular Hermeneutics** (Sheffield: Sheffield Academic Press, 1999), p. 119

Maybe it is 'safer' to apply the Bible to individual situations. In so doing, you address individual sins and shortcomings and point to the need for individuals to be saved. Once you read it through the eyes of the community or society or nation, then you find yourself radically opposed to and confronting political and economic powers.[175]

The point is that reading biblical texts from the interests of the community, and as a community of interest rather than as a leader-centered activity, carries the potential for societal and systemic transformation, not just fostering faith and cultivating a relevant belief. Additionally, merely reading the Bible to promote faith and to maintain a relevant belief, while failing to critique, transform, and challenge oppressive societal realities, dulls the Bible's effectiveness as a cultural tool for social change.

My contention in this study is not to assert that the Bible is not read within a Caribbean context; it is read. Instead, my argument concerns how it is read. In other words, what beliefs, assumptions, and practices influence the reading process? What role do social location, gender, ethnicity, hybridity, lived realities, and history play in interpreting biblical texts? Is there an awareness in the reading or listening strategies that biblical texts are intertwined with dominant interests and the silencing of the oppressed? Which voice do Caribbean people hear and act upon? The fact is that "the strategies one employs in reading a text will depend largely on one's overall disposition toward the act of reading itself... texts are read not only within contexts; a text's meaning also depends on the pretext(s) of its readers."[176] Contextual realities condition

---

[175] Ibid. p. 122

[176] Renita J. Weems "*Reading Her Way through the struggle: African American Women and the Bible*" in Norman K. Gottwald & Richard A. Horsley eds. **The Bible**

reading and are just as critical as the social realities from which biblical texts emerged.

In what follows, I will first share the findings of an empirical study I conducted in six Caribbean islands: Antigua, Dominica, St. Lucia, Barbados, St. Kitts, and St. Thomas (United States Virgin Islands), along with a reflective summary of the results. Next, I will outline and discuss the issues that arise from the reading strategies and their consequences during the three periods of Caribbean social history mentioned earlier. In doing so, I will develop a clearer understanding of biblical hermeneutical practices that are prevalent 'on the ground' within a Caribbean context.

Findings of Empirical Study

Three reading strategies emerged from the exercises in response to the question, How would you interpret Philemon? Which reading strategy would you use to analyze this letter? The strategies that emerged focus on the text itself, the text as it stands, and an interest in universal concepts. I will discuss each one in turn.

On The Text

First, regarding *the text*, the significance of the text for lived realities emerged as the primary reading strategy identified. Participants examined verses within a paragraph for insights into how the text communicates its messages. This method of exploring mainly grammatical structure, keywords, word meanings, and characterization led participants to concentrate more on the rhetorical features of the letter and less on the material circumstances that influenced its creation. Below, I present a glimpse of the hermeneutical practices, by way of example, from the transcript of an ecumenical study group of about twenty-five individuals

---

and Liberation, Political and Social hermeneutics, rev. ed. (SPCK: Orbis Books, 1993), p. 35

in Antigua, sharing their reading strategies, insights, and comments on the verses:

vv.1-3   Paul states that he is a prisoner of Christ; the church gathers in Philemon's house; nature of prison life in Rome; letter is written to Philemon and not the house meeting in his house;

vv. 4-7   thanksgiving

vv. 8-16   humility of Paul; appeal based on love; Onesimus as Paul's convert
Onesimus went to prison to seek Paul's help (divine purpose); Onesimus ran away because he desired freedom; no one wants to be a slave.
At that time, it was common for people to own slaves, and runaway slaves faced death or other severe consequences. Paul appealed to Philemon's Christian beliefs and practices to convince him to pardon Onesimus. Utilizing his influence as a close friend, Paul urged Philemon to accept his former slave as both a friend and a fellow Christian, as Onesimus had come to faith during his imprisonment and had become a valuable help to Paul in spreading the good news. Paul sought to soften Philemon's heart and encourage his forgiveness.

These passages speak of forgiveness, accepting each other, breaking social barriers of status, and self-acceptance. They also discuss faith and the quality of the Christian faith.
It seems that Paul was presumptuous without persuading Philemon.
Philemon must forgive Onesimus because Onesimus was a converted man and now a brother in Christ.

Onesimus is to return not as a slave, but as a mission partner; his role has changed, but his status remains the same.

Slavery is unacceptable; however, the path to freedom should be the proclamation of the Gospel, rather than the killing of the slave master or the indirect overthrow of the system.
Onesimus's freedom was physical, not spiritual, and the change of ownership was not physical but spiritual.

Did Onesimus' changed life relate to his running away? Was his life altered prior to his escape? Who holds the power when someone flees? Did Onesimus' conversion take place in prison? There exists a freedom that binds and a bondage that liberates.

The right belongs to Philemon to free Onesimus.

v. 17–25   Paul's willingness to take responsibility;
            Radical Paul: They ought to accept Onesimus because of their debt to Paul.
            Paul's call for a new loving relationship;
            This makes spiritual fellowship possible. This is what it means for Philemon and Onesimus to be brothers.

As may be observed from this reading strategy, which does not engage with the material circumstances from which biblical texts emerged, it allows for the spiritualizing of insights. For example, some participants acknowledged that slavery is unacceptable and that genuine repentance leads to social activism. Yet these same participants suggested that the means of achieving freedom should be the proclamation of the Gospel rather than confronting the exploitative and oppressive system of slavery based on their interpretation of the Gospel. Thus, freedom is spiritualized as deliverance from oppressive habits rather than oppressive structures and systems.

Text As It Stands

Second, an approach focused on the text itself was rarely employed. Considering that all the participants had backgrounds connected to slavery, it's understandable to assume that slavery could serve as the epistemological lens. However, participants interpreted the *text as it stands*. When I suggested using slavery as a lens, there was widespread agreement that it would have helped to contextualize the interpretation. Below is a commentary from one group that appreciates reading the text as it is:

> Paul wrote to specific individuals while imprisoned. He asked for forgiveness for Onesimus, who had run away from his master. Paul converted Onesimus to Christianity, considered him his son, and sent him back to his master as a brother in Christ. He used strong arguments to appeal for love and acceptance for Onesimus. Once a person accepts Christ, forgiveness becomes critical in their life. Sin enslaves us; we can become slaves to sin by continuing to engage in wrongdoing. Christ died to free us from this bondage. Even though Paul was in prison, he still demonstrated love and compassion for Onesimus. We, too, should show love and kindness to our fallen brothers and sisters through our prayers and actions.

This commentary shows no interest in addressing the social structures, practices, and systems that shaped the relationship between

Philemon and Onesimus and the society in which they lived. Instead, it perceives the personal and emotional aspects of their relationship as the key issues, focusing on forgiveness, love, and compassion. Nevertheless, a material understanding of love and compassion involves the willingness to take risks or care for the other in a way that makes the other's fate impact one's own, or to give to the other at the genuine cost of one's life.

Interest in Universalities

Third, more *interest was shown in universalities than in casual particularities.* In other words, participants were less inclined to address the social implications of their exegetical results. One might have expected that, given the context of the letter to Philemon, which speaks to issues of social inequality and distinction, participants would consider this aspect more seriously. This reluctance reflected their response to the question of *what the letter to Philemon pertains to.* For participants, the letter is primarily about reconciliation, understood as the forgiveness of past wrongs committed against others. Additionally, participants identified various socio- historical, economic, and theological issues that do have social implications, but they did not view these as the focus of the letter:

- Asked what defines a brother.
- If Onesimus hadn't been converted, would he still be considered a brother?
- Philemon and Onesimus are brothers in Christ due to a transformation in their identity that transcends social distinctions, rather than focusing on material circumstances.
- How should we understand freedom in and through Christ?

Possible Reasons For Reading Strategies

Not Seeing Texts As Products

One reason for the reading strategies emphasized in the findings of the empirical study is the failure to view texts as products. When biblical texts are not examined concerning their socio-historical foundations, it becomes challenging for subsequent exegesis to explore the issues arising from the biblical text regarding their social implications. As Norman Gottwald notes, "an unstructural understanding of the Bible, that is, the history of social forms and ideas from biblical times to the present, leads to or reinforces or confirms an unstructural understanding of the present."[177]

This approach of not viewing biblical texts as products facilitates a spiritual interpretation. Such a spiritual interpretation lacks consideration of the social implications of its exegesis, leaving the unjust system unchanged. For example, some participants interpreted the letter's purpose to Philemon as a call for reconciliation between Philemon and Onesimus. Thus, Onesimus returns to his master, Philemon, as a brother in Christ, indicating that social distinctions are eliminated while social inequality remains intact. Consequently, the system stays unaffected. For biblical hermeneutics to be meaningful and serve as a tool in the fight for social justice, it must prioritize social transformation over mere personal morality.

Reading Out Of The Text

Even more significant is the fact that all the participants had a history of slavery, and since reading the text was the predominant

---

[177] Norman K. Gottwald, *"Socio-historical Precision in the Biblical Grounding of Liberation Theologies"*, address to the Catholic Biblical Association of America at its annual meeting, San Francisco, August 1985

strategy, some issues went unaddressed and questions that were never posed. Little attention was given to the problems surrounding the denial of Onesimus' personhood, his silence in the letter, or to questions such as whether running away was an act of resistance and hope. What kind of values or belief systems did the letter promote? How did the power dynamics affect the livelihoods of the members of the house church and household mentioned in the letter? This disinterest raises an important question: Why did individuals with a history of subjugation and exploitation, living in an underdeveloped society, navigate Paul's letter to Philemon without viewing it through the lens of marginalization, domination, resistance, ideology, and power? One possible explanation is that participants concentrated more on the text's inherent meaning rather than its social implications. In other words, they aimed to *read from the text* rather than into it.

Tradition

Another reason is *tradition*. By tradition, I refer to the accepted method for many years in which confessional bodies teach and study the Bible. In fact, for about fifteen years as a Christian minister in the Methodist church, and I am not alone in this, I conducted Bible study using what Paulo Freire, a former professor of philosophy of education in Brazil known for his works on literacy as a tool for social change[178], describes as the banking system of education. The banking system of education assumes that learners are empty vessels to be filled.[179] This traditional approach requires me to stand before ten or fifteen people and explain the chosen book or passage verse by verse, or by paragraphs of a chapter, or chapter by chapter, with occasional questions or comments

---

[178] See **Education for Critical Consciousness, Pedagogy in Process (The Letters to Guinea- Bissau)**, and **Pedagogy of Hope**.

[179] Paulo Freire **Pedagogy of the Oppressed** (Middlesex: Penguin Books, 1972), pp. 45-59

from the group. In other words, the minister or leader serves as the source of knowledge, or the 'expert' from whom participants must learn. This unchanging traditional method of teaching and studying the Bible represents only the provision of a predetermined interpretation that leads to merely applying what is "taught." Essentially, the content is what the traditional reading strategy adopts as a method. What is needed is for the 'expert' to facilitate learning rather than simply impart knowledge.

What is often little observed and questioned is that the social position of the 'expert' is frequently more privileged and elitist than that of the members he or she teaches. After the Bible study session, the pastor typically drives to the suburbs, while those who attended go to their rural homes. This stark contrast in social position poses slim possibilities for examining and exploring biblical texts through socio-structural analysis, starting with a socio-structural examination of social realities. Such a hermeneutical endeavor challenges privilege and undermines it. Simultaneously, it is implicitly complicit with the status quo, no matter how oppressive.

Trust Invested in the Trained Interpreters of the Bible

This method of studying and teaching the Bible impacts the authority and trust placed in those trained to interpret it and lead congregations.[180] However, this raises the question of how those granted authority acquire it to interpret the Bible. In other words, who determines the meaning of biblical texts, since they cannot interpret themselves? Who generates meaning? Who holds the authority – the text or the 'expert'? Thus, what becomes the role of the reader or the interpretive community.

---

[180] Kathleen C. Boone, **The Bible Tells Them So – The Discourse of Protestant Fundamentalism** (London: SCM Press, 1990), p. 19

Hermeneutical Presupposition

Moreover, the *presupposition* that participants brought to the letter to Philemon is another crucial factor. Their willingness to spiritualize interpretive results suggests a belief that justice and grace, politics and religion, in relation to social power dynamics, should remain distinct. Thus, for the participants, reconciliation lacks socio- economic dimensions.

Despite this, even if your position is compromised or penetrated, that is where you stand. And that social position still determines what you see. While they may not approach the letter to Philemon – their epistemology, or way of understanding the text – through the lens of their social history, this does not detach them from where they are situated. For all one knows, they may be standing in a place where they have been brainwashed, colonized, and are suffering from mental slavery, but that is still a place. What you see does depend on where you stand. The challenge is getting them to "stand" in a space where they can "see."

Cultural Illiteracy

The failure to grapple with the socio-ideological dimensions of biblical texts, along with the lack of political awareness evident in the reading strategies of participants, may indicate that they were not adequately attuned to hermeneutical suspicion or sufficiently aware of the critical importance of social location in biblical hermeneutics. Nevertheless, there is no impartial reader of biblical texts. A hermeneutical suspicion that questions what factors contributed to the dynamics of master and slave in society and the understanding that our identities, beliefs, and origins shape us represents vital aspects of the interpretive process that could have led to a different experience and interpretation of Philemon. This failure to be attuned and aware reflects the consequences of a compromised social location due to cultural imperialism or penetration, where individuals adopt foreign values, customs, language, and ideologies. This situation illustrates a harsh reality, exposing one of the enduring legacies of slavery and how Christianity has been employed to enslave people mentally.

Reflective Summary

In summary, the research experience highlights the need for biblical hermeneutics within a Caribbean context to focus on the reader— who reads intentionally, what they read, and how they interpret it. In other words, it emphasizes examining the Caribbean reader of biblical texts, considering both psychosocial dimensions and socio-geographic context. Caribbean social commentator and critic Ralph Gonsalves asserted, "Our geographic space has been more influential in determining our being than our history...our geography and history collide."[181] Caribbean biblical hermeneuts must incorporate the cultural meanings of existence, recognizing the reader's socially and historically conditioned context—such as sexuality, ethnicity, gender, class, ideology, and religion—into the hermeneutical experience. No one approaches the text as a blank slate. Every reader engages with the biblical text already positioned and invested.[182] Each interpreter has a specific context and belongs to a particular class in society.

Moreover, the research experience indicates that participants are much more interested in deepening their understanding of the biblical texts than in using those texts as cultural weapons in the fight for social change and transformation. It appears that the aim of Bible study is to "indwell" the insights of the biblical text rather than "embody" its lessons. When "indwelling" takes precedence over "embodying" in

---

[181] Ralph E. Gonsalves, *"Our Caribbean civilisation: Retrospect and Prospect"*, **Caribbean Quarterly Vol. 44, Nos. 3 & 4, September – December, 1998**, p. 132
[182] Ibid.

biblical study, the texts are diminished, and there is no impetus to act or take a stance.

Reading Strategies From Caribbean Social History

Furthermore, from the reading strategies I have derived from Caribbean biblical hermeneutical practice, I observe a lack of homogeneity in these approaches. Below, I outline the reading strategies corresponding to different periods of Caribbean social history and conclude there.

Table 2:1

Reading strategies the missionaries during the colonial period

Period	Reading Strategy		
Colonial	reader (missionaries)	text as text	context
	male, middle, class	a reading out of the text proof-texting	
	privileged		
	slavery as natural to socio-economic and political order		
	Consequence: Uncritical support for the establishment.		

Reading from the text was the reading strategy mainly utilized by the missionaries, particularly Zinzendorf, Bishop Coleridge, and Liele. Although Knibbs was also a missionary, he aligned himself with the natives to read the text in opposition to the colonizers, the class he belonged to. Thus, Knibbs was a dissident and engaged in a dissident reading strategy, which led to solidarity with the victims of the system.

Conclusions:

- The identity of the reader and the way the biblical text is interpreted matter.

- Regardless of the social context, the reader is always engaged and interested.

- An uncritical retelling of the biblical text fosters escapism, passivity, and docility, thereby reinforcing the status quo.

Therefore, if no agency is granted to the materiality of biblical texts and if interpreters do not engage with those texts critically in relation to their social contexts and concrete commitments to social struggles, then there can be no resistance to oppressive systems and structures. Furthermore, one cannot separate oneself or the church from the oppressive plantocracy system while denouncing it as contrary to God's just purposes in creation.

Table 2:2

Reading Strategy of the Slaves During the Colonial Period

Period	Reading Strategy			
Colonial	reader (enslaved Africans) male, oppressed, discriminated against fighting for freedom, justice and a vindication of rights	praxis/experience	context	text as message a reading into the text a resistant reading
	Consequence: Socio-economic and political reconstruction.			

The reading strategy of enslaved Africans was significantly different from that of the missionaries, even though it occurred during the same period and both groups were reading from the same Bible.

Conclusions:

- A resistant perspective arises from those whom the system marginalizes.

- A resistant reading leads to a restructuring of the social system.

- A resistant reading strongly leans toward being revolutionary but not necessarily toward a revolution. According to Chris Mullard, resistance has both negative and positive dimensions. On the negative side, Mullard argues that resistance targets the ruling class while justifying its actions through alternative and utopian beliefs and values.[183] Positively, resistance seeks to construct and gain power, replacing the ruling class's ideology and systems with its own, grounded in alternative and utopian beliefs and values.[184] Thus, resistance focuses on the quality of the change it brings about (revolutionary), not the method of that change (revolution).

- When your socio-economic status is not shaped by birth or by participation in the economy's commanding heights, your access to power and privilege, as well as your human dignity, is hindered. Consequently, your social position remains subordinate. Whenever this barrier arises, it leads to feelings of outrage, rage, and alienation,[185] which collectively inspire a vision for an alternative reality. A transformation of the social system that facilitates partnership and participation can grant the marginalized access to power and privilege, fostering human dignity.

Resistance became both probable and unavoidable due to the ruling elite's exploitation and oppression, as well as the church's failure to protect the vulnerable. The reading of biblical texts through a commitment to social justice provided a vision and hope for an alternative social order. Furthermore, the enslaved individuals distanced themselves from

---

[183] Chris Mullard, *Race, Power and Resistance* (London, Boston, Melbourne: Routledge & Kegan Paul, 1985), p. 35
[184] Ibid. p. 35
[185] Segovia & Tolbert eds., *Reading From This Place*, pp. 312-313

the oppressive system, condemned it as unjust, and worked towards establishing God's rule on earth as it is in Heaven.

Table 2:3

Reading strategies during the post-"emancipation" period

Period	Reading Strategy		
Post-"emancipation"	reader praxis context	text as message	
Bogle	hope:	a conflict between	a reading
	Reality	courthouse (justice)	into the
	Within	and chapel (grace)	text History
	a resistant		
	questioned		reading
	the status quo oppressed/deprivileged		
	Consequence: Rebellion against and a frontal attack on the system		
Garvey	racism,	struggle against	a reading Into the text
	Despoils		(a resistant
	God's		Reading)
	purposes as Creator and in The creation		
	Consequence: Organisational attack on the system		
Rastafarianism	Oppressed/	struggle against	a reading
	Deprivileged	downpression.	into the
	And for self-		text
	Determination		(a resistant
	And self-definition		reading)
	Consequence: Challenge to reconstruct the system		
Potter	middle-class	struggle against	an
	Questioned the	domination and	inter
	establishment	for fullness of.	cultural
	within a system	life	reading
	(church & academy)		
	Consequence: advocacy for the transformation of unjust systems		

Conclusions:

- Those whom the system deprives develop a resistant reading of biblical texts, which leads to an attack on or challenge to oppressive social systems and practices; whereas those privileged by the social system and structure, who thereby struggle from within the system, lead to advocacy.

- A resistant interpretation of biblical texts reveals the socio-ideological agenda and practices embedded in the social system and structure.

- Using a resistant reading strategy to view biblical texts as products signifies that the class, economic, cultural, political, theological, and ideological interests, values, beliefs, and ideas in these texts are intertwined with those of the reader. This connection between the biblical text and the interpreter's context allows for critique and examination of the social systems present in both the text and its context, with the expressed goal of creating a new individual and transforming the socio-economic order.

- Additionally, resistant reading guarantees that the reader not only uncovers the voice of the oppressed hidden in the biblical text but also remains independent of the ruling class's ideas and interests.

- Biblical texts were read out of a concrete commitment and involvement or struggle and from the perspective of the marginalized, dispossessed, and underdeveloped or in contexts of underdeveloped societies. For Bogle, it was the courthouse and chapel; Garvey emphasised racism and humanity as created in God's image; Potter stressed domination and selfhood; and Rastafarianism highlighted downpression, self-definition, and self- determination.

Table 2:4
Reading Strategies During the Post-"Independence Period

Period	reading strategy		
Post-*"Independence"*	reader praxis context text as means		
Idris Hamid et al	middle-class Female	struggle for development And self-determination	a contextual reading
	Questioned the status quo	but from within a system (church and academy)	
	Consequence: advocacy for the transformation of unjust systems		

Inevitably, because oppression was seen as stemming from the social system, the dominant voice in biblical texts, read through a lens of concrete social commitment and involvement, acted as both the foundation and motivation for an alternative social order, leading to resistance. Furthermore, resistance emerged as the exegetes positioned themselves outside the social system, denouncing it as harmful to the community's well-being and in conflict with God's rule.

Conclusions:

- A contextual reading of biblical texts encourages advocacy rather than a complete overhaul of social systems.
- Individuals within institutions find themselves trapped between their ideological commitments and perspectives. They seek to remain loyal to traditions while also wishing to dismantle the hegemonic and oppressive systems tied to those traditions.

Consequently, the interpreter may have questionable practices and thus is not entirely free from co-option by or complicity with the status quo. Similarly, the social system is being challenged from within rather than from outside, resulting in resistance losing its revolutionary edge. In other words, while the proclamation of God's rule was celebrated, its authenticity and integrity were dubious, as the separation from the social system and its condemnation by those complicit with the status quo was not wholly convincing.

Table 2:5

Reading strategy by the Fundamentalists

(Fundamentalists)	reader	text as text	life (eternal)
	middle class	a reading out of the text	
	proletariat		
	divorce between		
	religion and politics		
	Consequence: an otherworldly orientation		

Conclusions:

- Social location, hermeneutical suspicion, and contextual realities appear to neither influence nor condition the hermeneutical process. Social experiences do not shape the interpretation of biblical texts. This occurs because the movement is fundamentally about survival amid life's marginalities. This viewpoint has led Pentecostal pastor Garnet Roper to assert, "While Pentecostalism and Evangelicalism connect with the masses, they simultaneously do not advocate *for* the poor...they speak *from* the perspective of the underclass without speaking *for* them." Conceptually, the Bible is the infallible word of God and the source of irrefutable truths. It is the Spirit that grants agency, not social circumstances.
- Justice is delayed for the sake of raw Adventism;[186] individuals are so captivated by the gratification of their charismatic experiences, their connection to the Holy Spirit, and their

---

[186] Ibid. p. 39

confidence in the outcome of history that they exhibit little concern for worldly matters.

- Meaning exists within the biblical text and is, therefore, determinate.

As a result, there is a lack of interest in recognizing the dominant voices within biblical texts or the systemic inequities and inequalities, along with a disconnect between faith and practice. Resistance fails to occur, and the ethic of resistance is upended. However, this separation from the oppressive social system is not meant to showcase a different ideological perspective or commitment. Instead, it serves as a public and vigorous critique of an unjust social system by advocating for God's justice.

Table 2:6
Reading strategies during the Post-"Independence" period

Mulrain, Persaud,	reader	praxis	culture as "text"	text as product
Jagessar,	middle class	struggle for	a reading into text	
	Male, question the	identity hybridity multi-logues,	a cultural reading	
Spencer Miller, Middleton		inclusiveness,		
	Question the status quo	embrace of of Indigenous culture but from within a system (church & academy)		
Consequence: advocacy for cultural relevance				

Conclusions:

- Meaning occurs in the interaction between "worlds."
- Regardless of the reader's analysis, how the text is interpreted, or the approach taken, when the practice exists within a system, the outcome is advocacy, not a revolutionary change to the socio-economic structure.

Here, the goal is not to resist but to remain relevant in culturally diverse and evolving contexts. Nevertheless, being relevant requires aligning oneself with social systems and practices that promote well-being while condemning unjust ones.

Overall Conclusion

In summary, what I have argued and discovered is that, both in practice and throughout Caribbean social history, biblical hermeneutical practices in a Caribbean context are more influenced by the need to contextualize biblical texts than by examining them as socio-ideological productions and products of social practice. The resistant reading strategy also impacts resistance and challenges oppressive systems and practices. The resistant reading strategies of Sharpe, Bogle, Garvey, and Rastafarianism do not aim to overcome the system; instead, they encompass comprehensive efforts to transform the system into a framework of liberation.

Transforming socio-economic systems into a realm of liberation is indeed the historic mission of enslaved Africans and their descendants in the Caribbean: *to acquire and reconstruct power so that Caribbean people own and control the socio- political and cultural economy.* This mission reflects a reversal of the biblical liberation/Exodus tradition, as identified by Derek Walcott. Walcott noted that, in the Bible, the emancipatory movement transitions *from* bondage in *Pharaoh's Egypt to freedom in the promised land, via the Sea of Reeds. However,* for Africans who were captured and brought against their will to the Caribbean and the Americas, the movement, much to the contrary of emancipation, was *from freedom and civilization to bondage and Christianization, across the Atlantic Sea.*[187] Emancipation remains the enduring historic mission and social project. A resistant biblical hermeneutic within a Caribbean context is a cultural weapon in that mission and project.

---

[187] Derek Walcott, *What The Twilight Says, Essays* (London: Faber & Faber, 1998), pp. 44-48

PART TWO

PHILEMON AS TEXT CASE

CHAPTER 3

PUTTING PHILEMON IN ITS PLACE

Introduction

The task here is not merely to paint a possible picture of Imperial Graeco- Roman society but to uncover the socio-ideological agenda and social practices at work in Philemon that are deeply influenced by its imperial context. The socio- historical backdrop of Philemon is the colonial occupation of Palestine by Imperial Rome. Essentially, my aim here is to determine the role of (the shadow of) empire in shaping biblical texts. Dube warns that "failure to keep the empire in view as a central player unwittingly preserves the structures of oppression in both the past and the present."[188] I will not restrict the discussion to the supposed internal conflict between Onesimus, Philemon, and Paul to maintain a focus on the Roman Empire. Such a limited discussion would only serve to obscure the exploitation and oppression of the Roman Empire present in Philemon. By reconstructing the material conditions of Philemon (using a historical-materialist reading strategy), the ideological influence of empire (via a postcolonial reading strategy) is revealed.

Since this study aims to place biblical texts back into their

---

[188] Musa W. Dube, *"Saviour of the World But not of This World: Postcolonial Reading of Spatial Construction in John"*, in Sugirtharajah ed., **The Post Colonial Bible**, p. 131

socio-historic context as a valid aspect of the historical-materialist hermeneutical process, three tasks must be performed. First, identify the structural elements or signified forms of the mode of production from which Philemon emerged, thereby highlighting the forces of production in first-century C.E. Palestine. Second, distinguish the social relations of production within the letter to Philemon and, consequently, within first-century Palestine. Third, connect the class structure formation of Philemon or the social structure formation/social division of labor in Palestine (and the resulting tension between the social forces within social relationships in the structures and systems or the opposing social relations of production, exchange, and distribution[189]) with the mode of production and social relations to production.

My interest here, therefore, is not so much in those socio-historical issues – such as recovering the original audience, message, and intention of the author – but rather in the kinds of situations, social struggles, social experiences, socio-ideological and theological interests, and social practices that shape the letter to Philemon. In other words, what is the social class perspective from which Philemon is written and interpreted? What ideology influenced the production of Philemon? How are power relationships constituted? How is the social system developed and maintained?

Mode of Production

In first-century Palestine, the primary forces of production were land and waterways, including lakes, seas, and rivers.[190] Land ownership was characterized by the principle of 'land by the spear.' According[191] to this principle, private land ownership was supplanted by latifundia,

---

[189] Mosala, **Biblical Hermeneutics**, p. 115

[190] G.E.M. de Ste Croix, **The Class Struggle in The Ancient Greek World** (London: Duckworth, 1981), p. 120

[191] Sean Freyne, **Galilee: From Alexander to Hadrian** (Notre Dame, Indiana: University of Indiana Press, 1980), p. 156

where extensive land holdings were owned by the royal house.[192] These latifundia, or large estates, were overseen by managers appointed by the ruling class, who were responsible for collecting rents and taxes from the people living on the land.[193] Essentially, latifundia functioned as household economies. Philemon was a member of the ruling class and operated in its interest. The house church that gathered in Philemon's home, and thus was part of the household economy, is significant to this study.

However, the war industry fueled the economy's productive and technological bases and benefited the interests and needs of the ruling class more than the populace.[194] The war industry was funded by exacting tributes from the populace in land taxes, animal taxes, and tithes from resident alien armies and the populace.[195B]

Therefore, the production mode was tributary, primarily designed to supply the Roman imperial administration with tributes. However, regardless of a country's raw materials, they alone cannot generate wealth. In addition to raw materials, human labor is necessary to create wealth. Human involvement and input introduce the issue of social relations concerning the means of production.

Social Relationships to Production

The Roman tributary social formation represented a dead end for the populace. None of the tribute collected was reinvested into projects benefiting the people. In effect, they were funding the habits and interests of the ruling class. The tributary social formation had several defining characteristics.

---

[192] Ibid.
[193] Freyne, **Galilee**, p. 158
[194] Martin Hengel, **Judaism and Hellenism** (London: SCM Press, 1974), p. 13
[195] Mosala, **Biblical hermeneutics**, p. 157

Hierarchical Social Structure and System

Pre-industrial advanced agrarian societies, such as Imperial Graeco-Rome, had a *hierarchical social structure*[196]. At the top were the politically powerful urban elites, or the imperial upper classes of Senators and Knights. At the bottom were the peasant class, including tenants, rootless day laborers, and artisans, who were "far removed from the vast possessions and power of the imperial upper classes."[197] There was no middle class. Income came from taxation and the productive output of the peasant class. As a result, the wealth and power of the urban elites stemmed from their relationship to the production of essential goods in society. These[198] relationships to the mode of production fundamentally shaped the hierarchical social structure.[199]

Pyramid Economic Structure

This hierarchical social structure and system resulted directly from a *pyramid economic structure*. The status and livelihood of a select few urban elites depended on the many. Individuals were born into privilege, wealth, and status, as well as into poverty. Thus, birth—not income or lifestyles—determined one's livelihood.[200]

---

[196] Carolyn Osiek, R.S.C.J., *What are They Saying About the Social Setting of The New Testament* (New York: Paulist Press, 1992), p. 41

[197] Gerd Theissen, *"The Social Structure of Pauline Communities: Some Critical Remarks on J.J. Meggit – Paul, Poverty, Survival"*, in *Journal For The Study of the New Testament* 84 (2001), p. 73

[198] Norman K. Gottwald, *"Social Classes as an Analytical and Hermeneutical Category in Biblical Studies"* in *Journal of Biblical Literature* Vol. 112 No. 1 Spring 1993, p. 4

[199] Itumeleng Mosala, *Biblical Hermeneutics and Black Theology in South Africa* (Michigan: William B. Eerdmans Publishing Co., 1990), p. 103

[200] Osiek, *What are They Saying About the Social Setting*, p. 41

Structure of Households

Similarly, the *structure of households* also reflected the hierarchy within the social structure and system. For instance, a typical household was made up of family members, domestic workers, and subordinates, all united under the authority of a male head.[201] This male-led household was known as a Paterfamilias. Several Paterfamilia combined to form a Village, and multiple villages constituted the Politea. This standard household economy involved routine agrarian or trade activities. The subordinates within the households were slaves, who managed the administrative and practical aspects of the home, while the male head met their material and social needs. The household economy emphasized collectivist values such as obligation, duty, obedience to authority, subordination, acquiescence, dependency, and respect for tradition.[202] Consequently, households mirrored *dominant-subordinate relationships*, which fostered a servile culture.

Common Religion

Additionally, households were united by a shared *religion*. Essentially, the household and the house church were made up of the same individuals. Religion was intertwined with the economics of the household and the house Church. The dilemma was that while the house church offered social equality regarding status and dignity, social inequality was present regarding material resources and power. Nonetheless, the co-equality within the house church did little to disguise the fact that true social equality exists *only before God*.[203]

---

[201] Derek Tidball, *The Social Context of the New Testament* (Exeter: The Paternoster Press, 1983), p. 79

[202] Craig S. de Vos, "*Once a Slave Always a Slave – Manumission and Relational Patterns in Paul's Letter to Philemon*" in *Journal For The Study of the New Testament* Issue 82/2001, p. 95

[203] Dimitris J. Kyrtatas, *The Social Structure of Early Christian Communities* (London, New York: 1987), p. 30

Agrarian Based

Furthermore, the Imperial Graeco-Roman society was primarily agrarian. For the imperial classes to maximize their economic benefit from the system, they required labor that was not only manual but also free of charge. Here, the problem— or perhaps the challenge—was the Free person's recognition that they were not obligated to follow the dictates of the imperial classes or to work for their economic advantage. This refusal by the Free person created tension and strain within society. The situation was further worsened by the fact that the wealth of free individuals outstripped their power, and their power exceeded their status, leading to additional strain and tension in the social system.[204]

Slave as Property

In Roman law, whether one was a captive turned slave or already a slave in a household, *a slave was considered property.*[205] Interestingly, it was not the labor of the slave that became a commodity but rather the slave himself or herself.[206] The law granted slave owners total control over their slave property—a "right" that extended to the slave's person and personality.[207] As Patterson puts it, 'a slave was a slave not because he was the object of property but because he was the subject of property.'[208] Thus, the relationship between master and slave was one in which the master held absolute power over the slave as property.

[204] John Dominic Crossan, **The Birth of Christianity** (Edinburgh: T & T Clark, 1998), p. 181

[205] Orlando Patterson, **Slavery and Social Death** (Cambridge, Massachusetts: Harvard University Press, 1982), p. 28; Richard A. Horsley, *"The Slave Systems of Classical Antiquity and their Reluctant Recognition by Modern Scholars" pp. 19-59* and Dexter E. Callender, Jr., *"Servants of God(s) and Servants as Kings in Israel and the Ancient Near East" pp. 67-80* in **Semeia** 83/84 Slavery in Text and Interpretation, pp; Moses I. Finley, **Ancient Slavery,** p. 97

[206] Moses I. Finley, **Ancient Slavery**, pp. 74-75

[207] Ibid.

[208] Orlando Patterson, **Slavery and Social Death**, p. 28

Consequently, like property and unlike free individuals, slaves were subject to the will, if not the mercy, of their "owners." Since society was agrarian, it relied on free manual labor to yield sufficient returns. However, this labor was only considered free if it was coerced and beaten into submission. Thus, slaves were governed by fear, which led to *servile loyalty*. Slavery originated in violence and was sustained through domination and exploitation.

The climate of fear stemmed from the fact that those taken into slavery lost all formal, legal, and enforceable connections of blood.[209] Not only were they uprooted, but families could also be separated at the pleasure and in the manner decided by the slave owner. This power to sever ties from native origins granted slave masters a peculiar status within the dynamic of domination and submission.[210] Essentially, the slave became the ultimate human commodity, *socially dead*[211] and devoid of connections to their native roots.

Nevertheless, in whatever way the slave was perceived and treated, it was undeniable that the slave was a human being. To do violence to and to humiliate the slave was to violate and degrade the slave's humanity. Despite this, the intention was to so "undermine and degrade the slave's humanity as to distinguish the slave from human beings who are not property".[212] Corporal punishment, physical torture, sexual exploitation, branding, beatings, and demeaning grown male slaves by referring to them as boys were some of the procedures used to achieve this end. The whip became the symbol of degradation and humiliation.[213]

---

[209] Orlando *Patterson, Slavery and Social Death*, p. 7

[210] Ibid.

[211] Ibid.

[212] Finley, *Ancient Slavery*, pp. 95-96

[213] Patterson, *Slavery as Social Death*, p. 74; See also Jennifer A. Glancy, *"Slaves and Slavery in the Matthean Parables"* in *Journal of Biblical Literature*, Vol. 119, No. 1 Spring 2000, pp. 67-90 who has emphasized the vulnerability of the enslaved body to violence and showed the kind of abuses suffered by slaves in the first century.

While few succeeded, the system did allow some slaves to regain their "freedom." Manumission and the use of the peculium were two of those allowances.

Manumission

In theory, manumission aimed to redeem the slave's humanity through the owner's grace or the payment of a fee by the slave. However, manumission was never a guarantee of freedom. To maintain the balance between supply and demand, manumission was granted based on the number of individuals brought into the system. The number of enslaved people depended on how many individuals were given their "freedom."[214] When manumission was eventually granted, the slave was no longer considered property or a commodity and was allowed to reclaim kinship ties, own property, and claim citizenship. However, since the slave could not, by law, own property, the fee paid for manumission was viewed as a gift to the slave owner. The slave could never adequately compensate for the master's right to and over his slave- property, as 'whatever the slave gives already belongs to the master.'[215] The amount required for manumission was set at a figure that allowed the slave owner to purchase the bondage of another slave. Thus, in effect, manumission functioned as a commercial transaction that reinforced the institution of slavery and perpetuated the system.[216] Therefore, manumission served as an incentive for obedient servitude and a recapitalization of the slave's value.

To redeem the humanity of slaves, Orlando Patterson, a Jamaican historical sociologist and professor at Harvard University, observes that a double negation occurs in manumission. Patterson is uniquely qualified to discuss the institution of slavery, given his lifelong academic interest in

---

[214] Patterson, *Slavery as Social Death*, pp. 209-14
[215] Patterson, *Slavery as Social Death*, p. 211
[216] Kyrtatas, *The Social Structure*, p.61

slavery, freedom, and ethnic inequality worldwide, particularly among people of African descent. His focus is on the sociology of slave societies as a system of total domination. He compares enslavement to an act of taking life and views manumission as a life-giving or life-creating process. Thus, in manumission, there is a negation of the negation of social death, where the slave was cut off from native origins and lacked an independent social life during enslavement.[217] As a "freedman," the individual now reconnected with all formal ties of "blood" and could reside in locations of their choosing.

However, under Roman law, manumission was only permitted *at* the age of thirty, not *before*.[218] This restriction indicated the law's ineffectiveness in aiding the slave. In those times, people were not expected to live beyond thirty years. By the time one reached thirty, they would have already spent their most productive years. Therefore, the "freedom" reluctantly granted in the twilight of one's life was hardly a cause for celebration or a renewed sense of ambition.

As a result, in theory, "freedom" was bestowed. In practice, however, "freedom" was never truly felt. Liberty came at a cost. Even after manumission was granted, the *obsequium*—*showing* respect to masters—and the *operae*—obligation to work specific hours for masters—remained[219] commonplace and were the norm. In fact, "freed slaves" were consistently recognized as "freed" rather than freeborn and were always expected to owe their benefactor loyalty.[220]

Peculium

The peculium was another way that "freedom" was granted to slaves. It was a system of "perks" available to them. Slaves were allowed

---

[217] See Patterson, *Slavery and Social Death*, pp. 209-14
[218] Callahan, *The Slavery of New Testament Studies*, p. 6
[219] Horsley, *The Slave System of Classical Antiquity*, p. 50
[220] Crossan, *The Birth of Christianity*, p. 181

to possess and enjoy a range of goods – cash, food, livestock, other slaves, and grazing rights – at the master's discretion. However, the fact that, by law, a slave could not own property meant that he or she could never dispose of or transact any of the peculium without the master's permission. The peculium was also what the slave used to pay for his or her manumission. In this sense, it served as a motivating tool. The master had no obligation to make any deals with the slave. Yet, in these situations, carrots work better than sticks.[221] **Ultimately, like manumission, it was merely a capital investment by the master since the money was used to purchase another slave's bondage. The possibility of self-redemption was what made the system function, thereby** reinforcing the institution of slavery.

Overall, neither manumission nor the peculium truly changed the oppressive social systems and structures of imperial Graeco-Roman societies. The system consistently condemned the enslaved to bondage, oppression, and exploitation, ensuring that masters or oppressors maintained firm control over the reins of power. Manumission served merely as a recapitalization scheme for slave owners and an incentive for obedient servitude among slaves. Although the peculium appeared to be a motivating device, the lack of binding commitment from slave owners to honor obligations meant it demotivated more than it inspired. Worse yet, at the age when manumission was bestowed, individuals no longer possessed the physical strength and youthful ambition needed to pursue their goals. It effectively allowed old, worn- out slaves to purchase the freedom of new ones.

Even so, slaves did not always operate within the system, an impossible mission, nor did they rely on the system to grant them freedom. For those slaves who faced long waits for manumission, the desperate yet subversive choice was to run away.[222] By fleeing, slaves

---

[221] Crossan, *The Birth of Christianity*, p. 181
[222] See Daube, *Saviour of the World,* p. 131

resisted domination and alienation while undermining the system, fighting for their inalienable rights and birth claims. When conditions became unbearably inhumane and crossed the limits of civility, running away should be viewed not as escape but as a rebellion against the system.[223]

One aspect of subverting the system is evident in the fact that running away is economically disadvantageous for slave owners.[224] Running away resembled removing a cog from the wheel of the productive forces. On a mass scale, running away had significant social and revolutionary implications, as it could cause production to grind to a halt, undermine the socio-economic base of society, and dismantle the power structure. Hence, there were draconian measures to limit or discourage its occurrence.

Formation of Social Class Structure

While slavery was already established, the concept of slavery 'in the form of labor for others'[225] represented a new development. People providing free labor had to come from somewhere. Captives taken as slaves in war were one solution. When the existing supply of slaves was insufficient, this prompted new wars to acquire captives for free labor. Regardless of how one views the argument, the roots of slavery were tied to commercial interests: private land ownership that necessitated free manual labor. Commercial interests either transformed captives into slaves or created the conditions that led to slavery. Therefore, the economic framework of imperial Graeco-Roman society was founded on domination and exploitation.

---

[223] Callender, Jr., *Servants of God(s) and Servants as Kings*, p. 78

[224] Moses I. Finley ed. *Slavery in Classical Antiquity – Views and Controversies* (Cambridge: Heffer, 1968), pp. 68-69

[225] Moses I. Finley, *Ancient Slavery and Modern Ideology* (London: Chatto & Windus, 1980), p. 90

Socially Stratified Society of Two Classes

Essentially, the socio-economic structure and system of imperial Graeco- Roman society reflected a *socially stratified society divided into two classes: the dominant and the dominated.* In fact, Richard Horsley argued that Roman society was split between the rulers and the ruled.[226] Each estate essentially functioned as its own economy, making the societies agglomerates[227] governed and exploited by a more resourceful estate. This division carries several social implications. First, there was no "social ladder"[228] or middle class, leading to a lack of hope for upward social mobility or participation in the decision-making process for the ruled. Second, people's identities were shaped not by the accident of birth but by their resources and status. Third, a significant divide existed between religion and economics. Although, in theory, there was co-equality between the ruler and the ruled within the house- church, social inequality persisted in the household. Lastly, the peasant class and slaves had no control over their lives; they were valued primarily for their utility.

For Mosala, this peasant or slave class represented the underclass—a distinct third class that was politically, economically, and ideologically exploitable.[229] Supporting evidence from New Testament texts highlights that this underclass was vulnerable in all three of these areas: politically, as they were used for mercenary activities that served others' interests (Mark 14: 10-11); economically, as they were tricked into fighting each

---

[226] Richard A. Horsley, *Sociology and the Jesus Movement* (New York: Continuum, 1989), p. 69

[227] John H. Kautsky, *The Politics of Aristocratic Empires* (New Brunswick, London: Transaction Publishers, 1997, rev. ed.), p. 72

[228] Allan Callahan, *"The Slavery of New Testament Studies"* in **Semeia** 83/84 Slavery in Text and Interpretation, p. 5

[229] Mosala, **Biblical Hermeneutics**, pp. 159-60

other over wages (Matthew 20:1-16); and ideologically, as they faced moral and religious double standards (John 8: 1-11).[230]

Mosala's identification of this underclass finds support—albeit from a different ideological stance, without calculated malicious intent, and lacking a hermeneutical purpose—in the derogatory characterization of Onesimus by J.B. Lightfoot, a well- known biblical scholar. Lightfoot states,

> Onesimus represents the least respectable type of the least respectable class in the social scale. He was regarded by philosophers as a 'live chattel', a 'live implement';...He was treated by the law as having no rights; and he had carried the principles of the law to their logical consequences. He had declined to entertain any responsibilities. There was absolutely nothing to recommend him. He was a slave, and what was worse, a Phrygian slave; and he had confirmed the popular estimate of his class and nation by his own conduct. He was a thief and runaway. His offence did not differ in any way, so far as we know, from the vulgar type of slavish offences. He seems to have done just what the representative slave in Roman comedy threatens to do, when he gets in trouble. He had 'packed up some goods and taken to his heels'. Rome was the natural cesspool for those offscourings of humanity. In the thronging crowd of the metropolis was his best hope of secrecy. In the dregs of the city rabble he would find the society of congenial spirits.[231]

---

[230] Ibid.
[231] J.B. Lightfoot, **Saint Paul's Epistles to the Colossians and to Philemon** (London: Macmillan & Co. Ltd., 1912), pp. 309-10

For this study, such a characterization of Onesimus is outlandish and appears to be rooted in ruling class ideology. It also reflects the era in which it was written. When Philemon is read from the perspective of Onesimus or the underclass, completely contrasting conclusions are reached, as this study will demonstrate (see chapter 5). Nevertheless, this representation of Onesimus aligns with the conclusion that the socio-economic and political domination of Palestine by Imperial Rome resulted in three social classes: ruling, dominated, and underclass.

In summary, economic interests shaped how the humanity of enslaved people was defined and treated. The slave was commandeered, violated, and degraded, indiscriminately and brutally, without any sense of conscience, as profit appeared to outweigh morality. Essentially, ideology became one of humanity's commodifications. For Philemon's household—both a house church and a home—this emphasis on economic profit over respect for the humanity of others turned Onesimus into a living testament to the contradiction between faith and practice, as well as the conflict between the sacred and the secular.

What, then, did this socio-economic structure signify for Philemon's household? In Philemon's household, on one hand, Onesimus led a marginalized existence as a slave; his identity was defined by his utility value rather than the content of his character, and he stood as a living witness to the contradiction between faith and practice. On the other hand, Philemon, as head of the household and owner of the estate, faced the responsibility of ensuring the economic viability and profitability of his estate while also practicing the Christian faith. Thus, the letter to Philemon emerged from the interplay of the socio-religious implications of the master-slave relationship within the context of the house church in a household economy, which was inherently a model of an egalitarian system and structure.

The foregoing demonstrates that social forces and struggles in imperial Graeco-Roman society between the dominant and the dominated clashed due to their vested interests in the system, showing that social inequality has its roots in casual relationships. While the dominant aimed to maximize economic profit and benefit at the expense of the dominated, the dominated sought to define themselves and control their destiny. In other words, social inequality produces social conflict. Thus, there is a causal relationship between the means of production and the quality of life in a society.[232] Onesimus's running away raises the issue of whether Paul prioritizes reconciliation over social justice.

We must now focus on how religion interacted with social inequality and conflict, along with the socio-ideological interests and social practices in imperial Graeco-Roman society. Specifically, we will examine how the empire or the political economy limited, influenced, and shaped the theology, thinking, and version of reality presented by the writer of the biblical text, in this case, Paul.

Pauline Theopolitics and Slavery

Brothers But Master and Slave

In discussing Onesimus' status upon his return to Philemon's household and the question of whether Philemon should accept him, Paul addresses the concepts of equality and freedom within the context of the empire. Considering that the house church and the household members are the same group of people, the reality is this: in the house church, Philemon and Onesimus are co-equals, but within the household, they are socially unequal. The moral question that needs clarity is whether Onesimus can be both brother and slave, and whether Philemon can be both slave master and brother. Philemon accepting Onesimus as a co-equal would signify freedom for Onesimus. While equality would bring about freedom, freedom does not necessarily

---

[232] Leonardo Boff, O.F.M., *Faith On the Edge – Religion and Marginalized Existence* (San Francisco: Harper & Row Publishers, 1989), p. 7

ensure equality. One can be free but not equal; however, one cannot be equal without also being free. Therefore, the issues of equality and freedom are central to Paul's moral guidance, revealing his perspective on slavery in the Roman Empire.

However, with slavery having three levels according to Patterson, one must have clarity about the level at which to assess Paul's moral stance.[233] According to Patterson, the levels of slavery are personal, institutional, and systemic[234]. At the personal level, one is dealing with a dominated, oppressed, and natally alienated individual.[235] At the institutional level, mechanisms such as laws, violence, manumission, and peculium were employed to uphold a relation of absolute domination over individuals considered natally alienated. At the systemic level, there was a structural dependence on the institution of slavery.[236]

For Patterson, Paul dealt personally and sought all legal means for manumission.[237] But is not the individual part of the web of social relationships, that no man is an island? The personal cannot be separated from the institutional and systemic. Any attempt to do so leads to accommodation and complicity with the status quo. However, as Paul asked Philemon to do more than what was requested, that is, to accept Onesimus not merely as a slave but as a beloved brother, and addressing the letter not only to Philemon himself, indicates that Paul's view on slavery influences both Patterson's institutional and systemic levels. Patterson's conclusion, therefore, is not without challenge.

Paul's perspective on slavery is a topic of significant debate. Arguments vary from whether he endorses slavery as an institution[238]

---

[233] Orlando Patterson, *"Paul, Slavery and Freedom: Personal and Social-historical Reflections"*, **Semeia** 83/84 1998, Slavery in Text and Interpretation, p. 267
[234] Ibid.
[235] Ibid.
[236] Ibid.
[237] Ibid.
[238] Views here have taken into consideration the disputed Pauline letters of Colossians, Ephesians, Titus, Peter; John Knox, *"Paul Among the "Liberals"* in

to the ambiguity of his advice in 1 Corinthians 7:20-24.[239] Also part of these discussions is whether moral judgment is confined to the personal, institutional, or systemic levels, and[240] whether his apparent indifference reflects "sheer pragmatic realism"[241] or a belief in the Parousia[242].

This study, however, derives its understanding of Paul's view on slavery from Galatians 3:23-29, 1 Corinthians 7:20-24, and Philemon, among the seven authentic or undisputed Pauline letters (the others being 1 Thessalonians, 1 & 2 Corinthians, Romans, Philippians). This implies that the study accepts the viewpoint that the Deutero-Pauline Epistles (Colossians, Ephesians, Peter, Titus, 1 & 2 Timothy), written after 70 C.E., reflect efforts to restore patriarchy and promote the idea that Christianity was not a threat to the status quo.[243] Consequently, these Deutero-Pauline Epistles do not impact the perspective articulated here. Galatians 3:26-28, 1 Corinthians 7:20-24, and Philemon highlight social equality, co-equality, and freedom. Given these emphases, one must conclude that Philemon and Onesimus are brothers, not master and slave. In contrast, the Deutero-Pauline Epistles, which emphasize

---

Religion In Life 49 Wint 1980 pp. 416-421.

[239] Will Deming, *"A Diatribe Pattern in 1 Corinthians 7:21-22: A New Perspective on Paul's Direction to Slaves"*, in **Novum Testamentum**, Vol. XXXVII, FASC. 2 April 1995, pp. 131-137

[240] Patterson, *Paul, Slavery and Freedom*, pp. 263-279

[241] C.J. Cadoux, **The Early Church and the World** (Edinburgh: T & T Clark, 1st ed. 1925 reprinted 1955), pp 132-133; Burchell Taylor, *"Onesimus: The Voiceless, Powerless Initiator of the Liberating Process"*, in Howard Gregory ed. **Caribbean Theology – Preparing for the Challenges Ahead** (Barbados: Cedar Press, 1995), p. 18; Biot ed. 1840, pp. 125-126, 140-141

[242] Christian Beker, **Paul's Apocalyptic Gospel – The Coming Triumph of God** (Philadelphia: Fortress Press, 1982), pp. 111-15; J. Paul Samply, **Walking Between the Times – Paul's Moral Reasoning** (Minneapolis: Fortress Press, 1991), p. 9

[243] Clarice J. Martin, *"The Haustafeln (Household codes) in African American Biblical Interpretation: "Free Slaves" and "Subordinate Women"* in Cain Hope Felder ed. **Stony the Road We Trod: African American Biblical Interpretation** (Minneapolis: Fortress Press, 1991), pp. 207-210; see also Richard A. Horsley, **Paul and Empire: Religion and Power in Roman Imperial Society** (Pennsylvania: Trinity Press International, 1997), pp.228-231

submission, obedience, patience, and endurance, suggest that it is neither irreconcilable nor incompatible for master and slave to be brothers.

Nonetheless, below is a further analysis of scholarly thinking concerning Paul's perspective on slavery in relation to his counsel in the letter to Philemon. Care is taken to discern how the issues of equality and freedom are adjudged and on what level— personal, institutional, and systemic—the discussion takes place.

Socio-Political Ethics of God's Reign

For Patterson, Pauline Christianity is fundamentally dualistic, separating the two modes of existence: the house church and the household.[244] In this separation, the house church's focus on the interior and the otherworldly remains distinct from the social realities and forces of the household. What the slaves lost in society was recovered in the church. The cause of this separation lies in the dualistic ethic of judgment and the justified sinner within the conception of Jesus as Messiah and Savior[245] This manifests in two ways. First, regarding the ethic of judgment, Jesus Christ is seen as the Messiah who punishes the wicked and rewards the righteous. Jesus Christ as Messiah saves through divine enslavement rather than by eliminating social injustice.[246] Second, the demands of Jesus Christ as Messiah call for vigilance, obedience, and stoic acceptance of the status quo. Thus, concerning the ethic of the justified sinner, Jesus serves as the liberator from enslavement to sin. Consequently, both master and slave can attain justification through the same crucified Jesus who died for all.[247] Therefore, reconciliation between master and slave involves right relationships (righteousness), not merely right relations (justice). It is not that Patterson endorses this

---

[244] Patterson, **Slavery and Social Death**, pp. 75-76
[245] Ibid.
[246] Ibid.
[247] Ibid.

dualism in Pauline Christianity; rather, he argues that "Christianity, after Paul, had already constructed an extraordinarily shrewd creed with a built-in flexibility that allowed both emperor and slave to worship the same god without threatening the system, while preserving the dignity of the oppressed."[248]

Patterson's dualistic view of Christianity is challenged by the view taken by David Bosch who was brought up in a Nationalist Afrikaner home in Apartheid South Africa. As such, Bosch was schooled in the ways of racial, economic, cultural, linguistic and religious distinctiveness. Bosch contends that in Paul's day, there was no dualistic distinction between a conception of political and religious hopes as "all reality was of a piece".[249] The issue for Bosch is that Paul is read through the prism of Augustine and Martin Luther. He contends that Augustine is responding to Pelagianism and Donatism and thereby, on the one hand, individualized salvation and, on the other, centred salvation in the church or sacristy. Martin Luther saw Paul as stressing that salvation comes through justification by grace through faith, hence the view of Paul's disinterest in secular activities. For Bosch, Paul needs reading through the lens of the reconciling work of Jesus Christ who destroyed all barriers that divide humankind.[250] In the reconciling work of Jesus Christ, there is no polarity, and racial, ethnic, social, and economic distinctions are wiped out.[251] While Bosch advocates for reconciliation to be the alternative vision of reality that the church must incarnate, Bosch fails to advance the political implications of reconciliation in Apartheid South Africa. Even so, reading Paul this way makes it possible

---

[248] Ibid. p. 76

[249] David Bosch, *"Paul on Human Hopes"* in **Journal of Theology for Southern Africa**, No. 67, June 1989, p. 4

[250] David Bosch, *"Mission and the Alternative Community: How My Mind Changed"* in **Journal of Theology For Southern Africa** 41 (December 1982), p. 9

[251] David Bosch, *"The Churches as the Alternative Community"* in **Journal of Theology For Southern Africa** 13 (December 1975): 3-11

to relate to the same person as both inferior and one's equal,[252] that brothers and sisters can still exist as master and slave.

In sum, this dualistic ethic allows Christianity to play a complicit and accommodating role in society, ensuring that institutionalised injustice is never challenged. Equality and freedom are dealt with on the personal level, not the institutional and systemic.

However, while Patterson and Bosch view the dualistic ethic as reinforcing the status quo, Derek Tidball, who teaches pastoral theology at the London School of Theology and has training in sociology, sees it as manipulative: a reinterpretation of the world that suggests things are not as bad as they appear, thus providing a means to cope. Tidball states it this way:

> *What Paul offers to Christian slaves is a totally new appreciation of their value as persons.* They are no longer "things" but people who have standing and status before God (1 Corinthians 7:20-24). In Christ, the slave is a freeman. God has demonstrated their worth by forfeiting the life of his son through crucifixion. If only, Paul argues, they grasped this greater fact, slavery itself *becomes inconsequential. A slave can remain happily a slave and still serve the Lord inspite of his social limitations.* Such a view affects not only the slave's self esteem but the actual pattern of relationships which exist between Christian masters and slaves...[253]

This perspective merely encourages submissive obedience. How can slavery be viewed as inconsequential when it is a daily reality? For Tidball, despite his sociology training, religion serves more as an opiate than as a tool for social change. Tidball's pastoral instincts and

---

[252] Bosch, *Paul on Human Hopes*, p. 8
[253] Tidball, **The Social Context of the New Testament**, p. 116

tendencies seem to outweigh his sociological viewpoint. Essentially, it is acceptable for a brother to be a slave and for the slave master to be a brother, regardless of the social boundaries.

Furthermore, some commentators believe that Paul's belief in the Parousia, the coming reign of God, will bring about social justice, which makes the abolition of slavery comparatively unimportant.[254] However, J. Christian Beker, a professor of biblical theology at Princeton Theological Seminary, argues that those who interpret Paul's understanding of the Parousia as an invitation to ethical passivity, quietism, ethical irresponsibility, fatalism, or withdrawal from the world have misunderstood him. Becker advocates that for Paul, the Parousia motivates and challenges believers "to move God's creation toward that future triumph of God."[255] Therefore, bringing the future into the present cannot happen through passivity, quietism, irresponsibility, or withdrawal.

On the contrary, social activism is expected of those who believe in the Parousia. Social activism redeems God's coming triumph from the bleak theology of speculation and an escapist view of salvation. This implies that issues of equality and social injustice must be addressed in this present life. Addressing social justice issues between master and slave in this life is a sign of the presence of God's kingdom here. Likewise, in understanding Parousia as a present reality, J. Paul Sampley, professor of New Testament at Boston University School of Theology, examines the issue from another angle. Through Christ's death and resurrection, God has destroyed the forces of death and evil and "already has begun the new creation amid the old (Romans 8:21; 2 Corinthians 5:17, 15:14-28; Galatians 6:15)." Even so, what is now or already is also not yet. To be in Christ means to already share in the fullness of life, which is still to come in all its fullness. In other words, what we hope for is already

---

[254] Cadoux, *The Early Church and the World*, p. 133
[255] Ibid

possessed. Thus, disciples must become who they already are or strive for their destined goal.[256] In reality, the issues of co-equality and social inequality should not even arise. Social inequality has no place in the kingdom of God.

However, the reign of God is yet to come. Bosch suggests that Christ's arrival signifies the start of a new era, a unique historical period that, while not the final age, is distinct from the previous one.[257] This new era is neither the end nor the fulfillment of the present. Instead, the death and resurrection of Christ act as tangible evidence of God's ultimate victory over history.[258] The time between the ages encourages hopeful engagement with historical realities. By developing systems and structures of social justice, both masters and enslaved individuals, who were regarded as brothers, remained hopeful in their current lives.

In contrast, while Becker and Sampley advocate for social activism, John Knox, a Scottish religious reformer along Calvinist lines, **promo**ted patience. Drawing from Romans 13:1-7, Knox believed that "the power of the state, soon to be superseded, was to be patiently accepted, even by the deprived."[259] Furthermore, Knox argued that conforming to the status quo, no matter how oppressive, helps maintain a tolerable order and peace, while the alternative could lead to civil war.[260] Knox's Calvinist beliefs in the sovereignty of God in all things were evident here. Calvinists hold a belief in predestination, whereby God's infallible foresight determines one's fate in advance. Knox's argument for patience serves as a thinly veiled justification for the status quo, whether oppressive or not. While the reign of God is anticipated, mere obedience will never transform exploitation into justice and domination

---

[256] Frank C. Porter, *"The Place of Apocalyptic conceptions in the Thought of Paul"* in **Journal of Biblical Literature** Vol. XLI, 1992, p. 204

[257] Bosch, *Paul on Human Hopes*, p. 6

[258] Ibid.

[259] John Knox, *"Paul and the "Liberals"* **Religion In Life** 49 Wint 1980, p. 418

[260] Ibid.

into liberation. Instead, it is the act of humanizing oppressive and exploitative systems that will achieve that. Therefore, if the brother patiently practices servile obedience, he will forever remain a slave; and if the slave master fervently encourages compliant servitude, he will never attain equality with his brother.

The views on the Parousia expressed by Beker and Sampley represent a realized eschatological perspective.[261] Horsley argues that this perspective depoliticizes Paul or "pulls Paul's political punches" and advocates for a theory of functionalism.[262] Functionalism ensures that groups adapt to fit the system, embracing the status quo and reinforcing group solidarity.[263] Its goal is to reform and perfect the social system. The situation in which Philemon and Onesimus are brothers yet also master and slave reflects tension and conflict due to their differing interests and relationships to the means of production. Relations of domination and submission arise from conflicting relationships to social production. Therefore, any changes that aim toward social justice and equality must be structural. However, to accept the theory of functionalism is to view the slave and the slaveholder as brothers.

Another interpretation views Paul's attitude toward the issues of equality and freedom inherent in slavery as pragmatic, tactical, and commonsensical. Taylor and Patterson argue that there is nothing an infant community of faith could effectively or emotionally do to revolutionize a system and structure so deeply entrenched in imperial

---

[261] C.H. Dodd took the lead in the development of the realised eschatological perspective. Dodd held that the Christ-event is the realisation of the rule of God in this present world. As such, every aspect of the age to come is fulfilled in the present. 1 Thessalonians, 1 Corinthians 10, 2 Corinthians 5:17, Mathew 13:37-43 and 25:31-46 are key texts for Dodd. See C.H. Dodd **New Testament Studies** (Manchester: University of Manchester, 1953), pp. 54-57, 108-118; and **The Meaning of Paul for Today** (Cleveland: World Publishing Co., 1957)
[262] Horsley, *Paul and Empire*, p. 142
[263] Horsley, Paul *and Empire*, p. 143

Graeco-Roman society.[264] B. Gerhardsson perceives Paul's socio-political liberation program as tactical and commonsensical given the circumstances. It is tactical because provoking the authorities might lead to even greater hardships for the enslaved, and commonsensical since slaves were not in the position of power needed to effect social change[265].

Nevertheless, one cannot accept that Paul's letter to Philemon is entirely personal, as it was also addressed to Apphia, Archippus, and the church that met in Philemon's house. On the contrary, a close reading reveals that Paul's personal letter carries broader social implications beyond an individual household economy. Therefore, since the household economy serves as the foundation or microcosm of the state, addressing, if not redressing, the issues of equality and freedom in relation to the Philemon household economy implicitly pertains to the larger polity of the Graeco-Roman Empire.

One should add to the argument that liberation must be integral for both the master and the slave to be genuine brothers in this life. Integral liberation refers to the freedom of the whole person and all individuals in all the oppressed and subjected dimensions of their lives.[266] In other words, economic liberation (from material poverty), political liberation (from social oppression), and religious liberation (from sin) do not occur one after the other in different stages and times, but rather all at once. As Boff contends, the struggle for economic liberation is also a struggle for political and religious liberation,[267] as "justice and grace are affairs of economics too."[268] What the preceding analysis of the social structures and systems of imperial Graeco-Roman society, Pauline theopolitics,

---

[264] Taylor, *Onesimus*, p. 18; Patterson, *Paul, Slavery and Freedom*, p. 266
[265] Berger Gerhardsson, *Eleutheria (Freedom) in the Bible*, in Barry P. Thompson ed. *Scripture: Method and Meaning, Essays Presented to Anthony Tyrell Hanson on his 70th Birthday* (Hull: Hull University Press, 1987), pp. 3-23
[266] Boff, O.F.M., *Faith On The Edge,* p. 60
[267] Ibid.
[268] Ibid.

and slavery demonstrates is the impossibility of addressing slavery or issues of equality and freedom on a purely individual level. The individual is also a social being, a member of a community. Addressing the mechanisms that regulate that individual's life within the community requires engaging with the structures and systems that make up that community. In other words, reconciling master and slave as brothers is not merely about eliminating social distinctions or returning the slave to his or her place of origin. Rather, it is essential to transform the relations to production so that the mechanisms, structures, and systems of that society facilitate self-definition and self-determination. After all, what value do rights hold without social power or the means to empower?

Socio-historic Environment of Philemon

From the foregoing, the portrayal of life in imperial Graeco-Roman society suggests that households were more political than mere domestic units or economies; it was more a matter of industry than morality, and the social system was the reverse of what it had been.

Household Economy, More Political Than Domestic

In the socio-economic hierarchy of imperial Graeco-Roman society, an individual was defined, determined, and characterized by their relationship to social forces and production processes. This relationship was unlikely to change, as the circumstances of birth primarily dictated it. In these power dynamics, the rulers' main concern was maximizing productivity and profitability while minimizing benefits for the ruled. The outcome was a delicate balancing act between enforcing submission and managing corresponding resistance, especially in the absence of a middle class. With limited opportunities for social mobility and no chance for economic advancement for the ruled, not only were interests clearly defined, but the likelihood of redefining relationships to production was virtually nonexistent.

Industry and Morality

Moreover, in imperial Graeco-Roman society, slaves were defined as property.[269] As property, they were priced and displaced—bought, sold, traded, leased, bequeathed, given as gifts, and pledged for debt.[270] Slaves, therefore, had no independent social existence.[271] What cannot be denied is that, regardless of the definition of a slave, the slave was still a person, a human being, possessing human capacities and therefore in need of protection against indignity, injustice, and dishonor. This makes it impossible, if not incongruent, to regard the slave as both a person and a thing simultaneously. Yet, this was the case in Paul's day. The understanding of the slave as both a person and a thing suggests that, during that era, slavery was more a matter of industry than morality.[272] In any era, isn't industry a moral issue as well? Can the two exist separately?

In his letter to Philemon, Paul addresses the issue of industry and morality through Onesimus' name, which means "useful." Paul is contemplating the most industrious (practical) use for Onesimus. In other words, is the best industrious (practical) use of Onesimus to stay with Paul as a mission partner, for which Paul needs Philemon's consent (vv. 13-14)? Or should Onesimus return to Philemon, no longer as a slave but as more than a slave—a beloved brother (v. 16)? What's at stake here is that Onesimus is a person, not a mere object or item of trade. Therefore, the issue involves the morality of industry rather than being limited to a question of industry alone. When addressing this moral dilemma, the problem centers on Onesimus's right to self-definition and self-determination.

---

[269] Finley, *Ancient Slavery*, pp. 73-75; Patterson, *Slavery and Social Death*, p. 28
[270] David Brion Davis, *The Problem of Slavery in Western Culture* (New York, Oxford: Oxford University Press, 1966), p. 10
[271] Patterson, *Slavery and Social Death*, p. 5
[272] Finley, *Ancient Slavery*, p.32

Opposites In The Society

Despite the ruler's dominance, several aspects of imperial Graeco-Roman society's socio-economic and political structure reveal that, in many ways, the system appeared to be the opposite of what it truly was. To begin with, the slave master's claim to independence and power was simultaneously a point of dependence.[273] The authority of slave owners rested on something uncertain: the submission of the slave, which still relied on the use of force. Onesimus's act of running away illustrates the fragility of the slave master's dominance. Governors can only rule with the consent of the governed.

Furthermore, bondage gives way to freedom. Ironically, without slavery, freedom was never conceived. It was the promise of redemption or eventual freedom that was used to keep the slave in bondage.[274] Thus, freedom as a motivating force was more powerful than the whip. In other words, "slavery was a self-correcting institution: what it denied the slave, it utilized as a means of motivating him."[275] If Onesimus had never been enslaved, he would not have needed to escape.

Lastly, within imperial Graeco-Roman society, as previously noted by Patterson, three levels of freedom were at play. Firstly, there was personal freedom, which manifested in both negative and positive ways.[276] Negatively, it refers to the refusal to exercise absolute power over another. Conversely, positively, it involves the implicit recognition and acceptance of one's liberty to live as one chooses "as far as one can."[277] On another level, freedom is sovereign.[278] This represents the authority to suppress and control the expression of another's will,

---

[273] Patterson, *Slavery and Social Death*, p. 98

[274] Patterson, *Slavery and Social Death*, p. 101

[275] Ibid.

[276] Orlando Patterson, *Freedom Vol. 1 Freedom in the Making of Western Culture* (London: I.B. Tauris & Co. Ltd., 1991), p.3

[277] Ibid.

[278] Patterson, *Freedom in the Making*, p. 4

whether through print or speech.[279] Finally, civic freedom exists when adult community members participate in the decision-making processes of their birth community or one in which they are recognized.[280] Thus, in civic liberty, it is acknowledged that everyone has rights and obligations.

In Philemon, viewing the master and slave as brothers highlights that these levels of freedom indicate a struggle for personal freedom amid the overarching dominance of sovereign freedom necessary *for* the complete realization of civic liberty. This struggle is not limited to Onesimus alone, but extends to all slaves in the imperial Graeco-Roman society as well as to oppressed people everywhere who resist domination and exploitation.

Eisegetics and Exegetics

Hermeneutic of Domination-Resistance

The fundamental question that arises from the issue of "brothers" versus master and slave is: how does the structural and systemic character (mutuality, egalitarianism, liberation, social justice) of the house church challenge, redefine, and revolutionize the structural and systemic character (authoritarianism, oppression, exploitation, profit orientation) of the household?[281] The dilemma is that the structural and systemic characteristics of the household and house church are fundamentally different. The challenge presented by this dilemma is how to radically turn the vision of a new creation into reality or build

---

[279] Ibid.

[280] Ibid.

[281] John Dominic Crossan & Jonathan L. Reed, *In search of Paul – How Jesus' Apostle Opposed Rome's Empire with God's Kingdom* (London: SPCK, 2004), p. 12

a liberated community,[282] using the Bible as the hermeneutical tool, specifically Philemon.

In the letter to Philemon, a clash of interests arises, representing a social struggle between Philemon as the oppressor and Onesimus as the oppressed. This situation evolves into social relationships marked by inequality and exploitation. The solution requires structural and systemic change within the household, which serves as the locus of oppression and the root cause of injustice. A new kind of relationship must emerge, prioritizing social justice and the socialization of power, so that life in the household is defined by partnership and participation.[283] Onesimus becomes a brother when he shares in the ownership of the means of production and actively participates in the household's decision-making process. It is this egalitarian system and structure of social relations—free from existing social distinctions—that is already present in the house church (v.1). In the absence of such partnership and participation, there will always be a need for resistance or a desire to "run away," as in the case of Philemon (v. 12).

Therefore, I recommend that we examine the phrase 'run away' from a different perspective. The term "sending back" (v. 12) should not be interpreted as "run away."[284] To run away suggests that Onesimus was "on the run" from the law or justice. However, if Onesimus was fleeing, he was escaping from injustice in search of justice rather than from justice itself. Onesimus's flight positioned him as an activist in his

---

[282] Crossan & Reed, *In Search of Paul*, p. xi

[283] Boff, **Faith On The Edge**, p. 73

[284] See J.B. Lightfoot, **Saint Paul's Epistles to the Colossians and to Philemon** (London: Macmillan & Co. Ltd., 1912); John M.G. Barclay *"Paul, Philemon and the Dilemma of Christian Slave-ownership"* in **New Testament Studies** Vol. 37 No. 2 April 1991; Joseph A. Fitzmyer, S.J. **The Anchor Bible: The Letter to Philemon, A New Translation with Introduction and Commentary** (New York: Doubleday, 2000); Norman K. Petersen, **Rediscovering Paul, Philemon and the Sociology of Paul's Narrative World** (Philadelphia: Fortress Press, 1985); John D. *Nordling "Onesimus Fugitivus: A Defence of the Runaway Slave Hypothesis in Philemon"* in **Journal for the Study of the New Testament** No. 41 February 1991

own liberation, an agent of his destiny; he was not merely represented but actively represented himself.[285] In other words, Onesimus was not in Philemon's house executing one tactical manoeuvre after another against the slave system, opposing the system of slavery from within. Instead, by running away, Onesimus stood outside the system of slavery, thereby resisting it. Richard D.E. Barton, a professor of African and Asian studies at the University of Sussex, England, emphasizes that "Resistance requires an 'elsewhere' from which the system may be perceived and understood as a whole, and from which a coherent strategy may be developed."[286] Running away constituted Onesimus's "elsewhere," acting in his interest toward a new kind of household.

Conclusion

In imperial Graeco-Roman society, relationships with the forces and systems of production define and determine connections and quality of life. Focusing on the personal nature and character of these relationships means adjusting and accommodating the status quo. However, emphasizing the systemic and structural aspects, the causal relationships, reveals the need to eliminate social injustices and inequalities, leading to a new and transformed social order where the right to self- definition and self-determination is restored. Since the letter to Philemon was not addressed solely to him, Paul does not expect the restoration of Onesimus to be resolved between Philemon and Onesimus alone.

Any appeal to Philemon personalizes the unequal relationships between the oppressor (the ruling class of imperial Rome and its appointees) and the oppressed (Onesimus and all the dominated). Calling on Philemon to act kindly without initiating social transformation is

---

[285] *Fan The Flame* by Tim Hector, in **Outlet Newspaper** January 19, 2001, p. 5
[286] Richard D.E. Barton, **Afro-Creole, Power, Opposition and Play in the Caribbean** (Inthaca and London: Cornell University Press, 1997), p. 50

to appeal to his moral convictions, thereby attempting to change the system from within. Appeals to moral convictions often result in good individuals with pure intentions who tolerate oppressive institutions and permit power structures to remain unchanged. The struggle does not seem to be against structures but rather within[287] oneself. Essentially, the appeal to Philemon asks for the impossible—requesting that he oppose resist, the system from which he benefits. Moreover, it highlights that resistance is not merely about protecting the weak but also a protest against the social system perpetuating injustice and inequality.[288]

More precisely, Philemon's role is to establish a liberating praxis for justice and effective change in a society marked by domination and oppression. However, whether Paul intended for the full social implications of the (casual) relationship between Philemon and Onesimus to be recognized is up for debate, as Paul's letter lacks specificity.[289]

This study now turns to an examination of how Philemon is interpreted. The aim of this examination is to determine whether interpreters perceive Philemon as a site of struggle or as a product of social forces, ideologies, and conflicts occurring in its context (behind the text); whether they focus on the rhetorical features of the text/letter (on/in the text); or whether they let their contextual experiences and influences shape their interpretations (in front of the text). In other words, I am interested in exploring what grants agency to their "readings" of Philemon and where they identify resistance as present in the letter.

---

[287] R.S. Sugirtharajah, **Postcolonial Criticism and Biblical Interpretation** (Oxford: Oxford University Press, 2000), p. 90

[288] Ibid. p. 91

[289] John M.G. Barclay *"Paul, Philemon and the Dilemma of Christian Slave-ownership"* in **New Testament Studies** Vol. 37 No. 2 April 1991, p. 183

CHAPTER 4

"READINGS" OF PHILEMON

Introduction

Any analysis or interpretation of biblical texts that fails to consider the socio- historical context of the Bible reveals more about the interpreter than the interpretation itself. As C.L.R. James, a world-renowned social commentator from the Caribbean, observes, "Any extended cricket analysis that is not based on historical facts... reveals more about the writer than the subject he is discussing." James supports this viewpoint: "Whoever writes a biography of Sir Donald Bradman must be able to write the history of Australia during the same period."[290] Essentially, in any effort to "read" biblical texts, one cannot overlook the socio-historical praxis of those who composed them. Such an oversight highlights the context, presupposition, hermeneutical suspicion, and social location of the interpreter more than the biblical text itself. This is not to suggest that the interpreter is more significant than the text. No. Rather, interpretive strategies are shaped by the interpreter's context, influences, and experiences. A truly disinterested reader of biblical texts does not exist. Nonetheless, if one is interpreting historical phenomena, the circumstances surrounding those phenomena cannot be disregarded.

---

[290] C.L.R. James, *Beyond A Boundary* (London: Stanley Paul & Co., 1963), p.182

Thus, the task is to determine whether the interpretations of Philemon were influenced by the material conditions surrounding its creation or by the context of the interpreter. I will examine both the era of slavery and the modern day to analyze Philemon. My goal is to identify the sophisticated arguments and reveal the prevalent interpretive practices of these periods. Ultimately, I aim to understand what grants agency in interpreting Philemon during both slavery and today.

The Era of Slavery

Thus, examining the nature of the discourses surrounding the letter to Philemon is essential. To facilitate this examination, I will evaluate the work of three pro-slavery proponents: bishops N. S. Wheaton, Protestant Episcopalian bishop of Connecticut; John Henry Hopkins, Protestant Episcopal bishop of Vermont; and Rev. Raymund Harris, a Spanish-born Jesuit priest. Additionally, I will assess three anti- slavery advocates: Rev. Thomas Atkins, an ordained Baptist minister who served in Pennsylvania, Virginia, and Philadelphia, and was secretary of the Eastern Baptists of Pennsylvania Colored Relief Protective Association; Olaudah Equiano, a native African and former slave; and Frederick Douglass, an outspoken abolitionist born into slavery in 1818, who escaped in 1838 and was legally emancipated in 1846. I will determine how they used and understood Philemon in their advocacy for or against slavery. In doing so, I will uncover whether the interpreter influenced their interpretation of Philemon more than the biblical text itself, meaning whether Philemon was taken out of its socio-historical context. Misusing Philemon by ignoring its socio-historical origins and failing to acknowledge the socio-ideological and theological agenda evident in its composition constitutes a misapplication of its meaning.

Racism signifies the dominance of one race over another. During the seventeenth and eighteenth centuries, the Caribbean and the Americas' socio-political, cultural, and economic systems were structured around slavery. According to Patterson, a prominent Caribbean sociologist at Harvard University, slavery is defined as "the permanent, violent domination of natally alienated and generally dishonored[291] people." The native Caribs, Arawaks, and Mestizos, followed by Africans who were forcibly brought in to provide free labor, bore the harshest impacts of this system of violent domination and dishonor. These exploitative, dominating, and discriminatory conditions established the socio-historical, economic, cultural, and political backdrop that both pro- and anti-slavery advocates, as well as the enslaved, navigated. Acknowledging this context is crucial, as it enables us to comprehend the agency involved in using or misusing the letter concerning the previously outlined socio-historical context of Philemon.

I will present several arguments put forth by pro-slavery advocates.

The Black Race As A Curse

To begin with, pro-slavery advocates argued that social equality between black and white races was impossible because Africans were believed to be destined to be subservient to whites by divine order. One such proponent was Bishop N.S. Wheaton, whose perspectives were based on Genesis 9.

In a context of natal alienation, violent domination and the dishonouring of humanity, Wheaton stated *"the inferior race must, by a law which we cannot control, remain under the same kind of subordination to the higher intellect of the Anglo Saxon, till it shall please God to lift up the curse, pronounced four thousand and five hundred years ago".*[292] Similarly, Wheaton divided the human race into two groups, the sons of Ham, the Africans

---

[291] Orlando Patterson, **Slavery and Social Death** (Cambridge, Massachusetts: Harvard University Press, 1982), p. 13

[292] N.S. Wheaton, *Discourse on St. Paul's Epistle to Philemon* (Hartford: Press of Case, Tiffany and Company, 1851), p. 23

and the sons of Japheth, the Whites. So, Wheaton claimed *"wherever the sons of Ham and the sons of Japheth have been brought into juxtaposition, the original of servitude, in some of its forms, has universally prevailed: a servant of servants shall be unto his brethren. I do not understand this in the light of a command that it should be so, as of a prophecy, it would be so".[293]* Thus, the sons of Ham are deemed to be inferior and fated to slavery. Bondage in slavery is their divinely ordained destiny. In short, Genesis 9 is used to justify relations of domination- submission.

Furthermore, Wheaton cited Pauline practices in Ephesians, Colossians, Titus, and 1 Peter to advocate for servile obedience. He summarized his argument as follows: *"Divine master never taught Paul that the purchasing of slaves, servitude, or bondage was an unnatural, iniquitous pursuit contrary to the spirit and practice of faith in God. If that were the case, Paul would have fervently condemned the unjustifiable conduct of Philemon in detaining Onesimus in criminal bondage."[294]* Wheaton then asked, *"Is not obedience in the slave, according to the Apostolic standard, made a duty as sacred as any other, whether sacred or moral?"* Therefore, for him, there was nothing morally wrong with slavery because Paul condoned the system of slavery and its practices. Wheaton is willing to rely on Paul's authority despite the disputed authorship of Ephesians and Colossians. Titus and 1 Peter were composed in a context where the church accommodated the status quo.

Wheaton accepted that the relationships of domination and submission between master and slave were legitimate. Nonetheless, there is also a remarkable and surprising acknowledgment by Wheaton, considering his earlier views on race, that suggests no power can halt the quest for freedom: *"When bondage becomes more stringent and oppressive, and when it is understood that, in the event of their escape, there will be no hope of recovery, the aggrieved party is left with a lingering sense of unaddressed*

---

[293] Ibid.
[294] Op. cit. p. 12

wrongs — of intolerable insults and a broken covenant – all of which tend to provoke and nurture a desire to separate forever from, and cease all interactions with, a people who cannot or will not adhere to any compact, however sacred."[295]
In other words, no power or system can stop the quest for freedom.

Giving support to the view that the Black race is a curse was Bishop John Henry Hopkins. For bishop Hopkins, in the relations between master and slave, there is no sin.[296] Sin was only committed in the treatment of slaves. If the slave masters treat the slaves with 'justice' and 'kindness', there are no sinners and sinned against. Treating slaves with 'justice' and 'kindness' is but to do what is scriptural and constitutional.[297] Bishop Hopkins believed slavery was a physical evil rather than a moral evil. He claimed that Genesis 9:25, 11:14, and 6:9 showed that the Almighty God ordained slaves to servitude because *"he judged it to be their fittest condition and all history proves how accurate the prediction has been accomplished, even to the present day".[298]* Additionally, Bishop Hopkins dismissed Deuteronomy 23:15-16 as referring to a foreign heathen master rather than Israelite slaves.[299] He further developed his argument by interpreting Genesis 16:9 as the angel instructing the fugitive Hagar to return to her mistress and submit herself[300]. He suggested that the Mosaic law (Exodus 20:17, Leviticus 25:10) sanctioned persons' ownership as property.[301] In other words, the domination of one race over another is considered divinely ordained.

Building on this interpretation, Hopkins viewed Philemon as Paul

---

[295] Ibid. p. 28
[296] Bishop John Henry Hopkins, **The Bible View of Slavery: A Letter From the Bishop of Vermont, New England to the Bishop of Pennsylvania** (London: Saunders, Ottley & Co., 1863), p. 7
[297] Ibid. p. 8
[298] Bishop John Henry Hopkins, *Scriptural, Ecclesiastical and Historical View of Slavery: From the Days of Patriarch Abraham to the Nineteenth Century* (New York: Pooley & Co., 1864), p. 7
[299] Ibid. p. 11
[300] 11 Ibid.
[301] Ibid.

returning a fugitive who had converted to Christianity and sought forgiveness.[302] In doing so, Paul did not act against the principles of Christianity.

Rev. Thomas Atkins, however, challenged Hopkins's interpretations and offered alternative scriptural evidence. Atkins questioned Hopkins' exegesis of Genesis 9, arguing that at that time *"whatever servitude existed was mild; families were not separated and only able-bodied men were appointed to be hewers of wood and drawers of water for service of the Temple".*[303] Still slaves, bro!! Additionally, the bondservants in Abraham's house *"were the confidential and faithful domestics of Pharaoh's household and trained for defensive warfare by their masters".*[304] In comparison, Atkins noted, slave masters did not instruct their slaves in the principles of Christian religion or the use of arms. It was a penal offence to instruct slaves in reading and writing.[305] Also, Atkins observed that Hagar's condition and circumstances were different in degree and nature to American slaves. Hagar and her son Ishmael were not sold to strangers; they were granted personal liberty and supplies for the journey.[306] Atkins considered the separation of families as an act of violence and a violation of the principles of natural justice.[307] As such, he was standing against the legitimization of domination by one race over another on the authority of the Bible, arguing that, in Bible times, servitude was benign, slaves were in positions to exercise authority, and the character of slavery in the New World was different.

Furthermore, Atkins argued that while in a Graeco-Roman legal context wives, children, and servants were considered the property of husbands, fathers, and masters, *they are not merely things, chattels, or articles*

---

[302] Op. cit. p. 14
[303] Atkins, *American Slavery...A Reply*, p. 4
[304] Atkins, *American Slavery...A Reply*, p. 6
[305] Atkins, *American Slavery...A Reply*, p. 7
[306] Ibid.
[307] Atkins, *American Slavery...A Reply*, p. 8

of lawful merchandising; they are individuals and, by the law of revelation and nature, are rightfully entitled to civil and religious rights and privileges.[308] In summary, for Atkins, denying another person's humanity cannot be justified by reference to the Bible or nature.

In summary, Wheaton contended that the domination-submission relations between master and slave were legitimate; Hopkins acknowledged that while slavery was a physical evil, it was not morally offensive and viewed Onesimus as an outlaw. In contrast to both Wheaton and Hopkins, Atkins argued that it is difficult to find any moral justification for slavery in the Bible and the natural order. However, all three interpreters have completely overlooked the text of Philemon, neglecting the socio- historic context in which the letter was produced while forming their interpretation. They have not given agency to the socio-ideological interests and social practices that influenced Philemon's emergence. The question now becomes: what reading strategy did they employ to arrive at this domination-submission theory?

Blame The Victim

Another position put forth by pro-slavery advocates was to blame the victim. This idea stemmed from an interpretation of Philemon that viewed Onesimus as the wrongdoer, rather than the wronged one. Rev. Raymund Harris held this perspective. Harris expressed several views on slavery that highlighted the racial undertones of his argument. For Harris, the 'rights' of masters over slaves were considered *"sacred*[309] and inviolable," which implied that slaves held no 'rights' concerning their masters. This 'right' of masters over slaves is evidenced by Paul sending

---

[308] Atkins, *American Slavery...A Reply*, p. 9

[309] Raymund Harris, *Scriptural Research on the Licitness of the Slave Trade* (London: 1788), p. 69

Onesimus back to Philemon, as he never had Philemon's "*express approbation and consent*" to keep Onesimus.[310] Harris furthered this argument by observing that Paul's refusal to acknowledge Philemon's 'right' was because Jesus never condemned slavery as unjust. God established the relationship of Philemon as master and Onesimus as slave. The race- and class-based discrimination espoused by Harris remains indefensible.

Consequently, he regarded Philemon as a Christian of "*distinguished merit,*" Onesimus was charged with "*defrauding his master of some part of his master's property and eloped.*"[311] As such, Paul wrote "*to effect a reconciliation between Onesimus and Philemon and to obtain from the master the re-admission of his fugitive slave into his house and service,*"[312] that is, a return to servile fidelity. However, as James G. Birney, who was secretary of the American Antislavery Society in 1837-38 and struggled to bring an end to slavery through constitutional and political means[313], asked, "How could Onesimus wrong Philemon or be indebted to him when Philemon had absolute power over him?" In other words, Onesimus did not have the means to wrong Philemon, except by running away.

Seemingly, Harris attempted to find scriptural evidence to dissemble his own arguments. He posited "*all things whatsoever he would that men would do to you do the same for them*" and thereby saw in this that "*no person should reduce another to the condition of a slave and that every type of subordination ought to be suffered to continue in the world*". And pointed out further that masters should behave to their slaves "*with the same tenderness, justice and humanity as he desired his slave to him*". Yet he argued that the golden maxim "*ferves to enforce masters and slaves reciprocal duties in*

---

[310] Ibid.
[311] p. 65
[312] Harris, *Scriptural Researches*, p. 66
[313] See **Dictionary of American Biography** (London: Oxford University Press, 1929, Vol. 2), p, 293

their spheres of life.". In other words, he does not condemn slavery. Slaves would never find themselves in a position to reciprocate.

Nonetheless, Olaudah Equiano, in a robust response to Harris, rejected the idea that Paul encouraged servile fidelity For Harris, bondage was compatible with Christianity; what was needed was patience under servitude. Equiano, in reply, based his challenge on the argument that the brotherly love Paul spoke of when urging Onesimus to return to Philemon was subversive of slavery. To Equiano, slavery was incompatible with the values of dignity, compassion, and equality found in Christ's kingdom. Therefore, for Paul to have condemned slavery equated to advocating for revolution rather than personal reform. As a[314] result, slaves would have preferred to be freed from material bondage rather than to seek redemption from personal sin.

Furthermore, Equiano also challenged the domination-submission theory. He believed that slavery was inconsistent with Christianity, asserting that it was unacceptable in Christ's kingdom for one human being to hold another in bondage. Equiano stated, *"slavery was derogatory to the honor of Christianity, for it was wrong that persons whom Christ redeemed be regarded as slaves and property."*[315] Thus, slavery contradicted the doctrine of atonement—human beings could only be redeemed through the sacrificial death of Christ at Calvary. Therefore, the situation between Philemon and Onesimus, and by extension within the imperial Graeco-Roman world in general, was untenable for Equiano.

Human Person As Property

Another argument made by pro-slavery advocates in their interpretation of Philemon was the view of the human being as property. In this context, the individual was seen as a commodity, rather than valued for their skills or labor. This perspective made it possible to

[314] Ibid.
[315] Equiano, *The Interesting Narrative*, p. 336

buy and thus own a person, which ultimately stripped any rights the "possessed" individual had.

Nevertheless, Rev. David Young, a Presbyterian minister who converted to Methodism in 1859 in Harrisburg, Ohio, objected to this argument. His objection focused on the reality or extent of one person's power over another. For him, it was simply wrong and evil for one individual to wield such power.[316] Thus, Philemon's ownership of Onesimus as property was incorrect. In this context, Young interpreted v.16 as Onesimus's chance to restore relationships with relatives, fellow beings,[317] and Christians, asserting that "in the flesh" and "in the Lord" pertained to equality in personal and social relations.[318]

Hermeneutics Of Plain Sense

The arguments and counterarguments reveal the interpreters' reading strategies or epistemologies and their understanding of the text or letter. Both Wheaton and Hopkins arrived at their interpretation of Philemon through an understanding of Old Testament passages that seemingly legitimize the domination of one race over another. They based their arguments on the Old Testament story of Ham in Genesis 9 while dismissing Deuteronomy 23:15-16, as well as the disputed Pauline letters of Ephesians, Colossians, Titus, and 1 Peter, all during a time when the nascent New Testament church was accommodating to the status quo. For instance, Wheaton believes that the essential facts of Paul's letter to Philemon are that Philemon is an exemplary Christian and that Onesimus, as a converted fugitive, wants to return to his master.[319] From these "facts," Wheaton concluded that Paul never criticized Philemon, made no appeal to Philemon's conscience, and

---

[316] Rev. David Young, *Slavery Forbidden by the Word of God* (Aberdeen: G & R King, 1847), p. 5

[317] Young, *Slavery Forbidden*, p. 10

[318] Ibid

[319] Wheaton, **Discourse on St. Paul**, p. 8

returned Onesimus to bondage even though Onesimus was already free.[320] Thus, slavery is justified, and Onesimus's absolute freedom was his adoption into the house church that met in Philemon's home.

Bishop Hopkins argued that the Bible does not contain anything morally objectionable regarding slavery, thus rejecting the belief that a fugitive slave should not be returned to his former master. He noted that Paul acted correctly in returning Onesimus to Philemon. In other words, slavery is deemed acceptable.

Consequently, while reading biblical texts, or eisegesis, is valid, both Wheaton and Hopkins employed proof-texting in their interpretation of Philemon through the Old Testament. However, proof-texting is distinct from eisegesis. Eisegesis occurs when the interpreter applies their socio-historical and contextual realities as an epistemological lens to interpret biblical texts. Neither Hopkins nor Wheaton approached the abhorrence of slavery as an epistemological lens. They also did not engage, even from a safe distance, with the socio-ideological theological agenda present in Philemon. As a result, by approaching Philemon without considering their contextual realities or the circumstances that led to its creation, they abstracted Philemon from its historical and social context.

Hermeneutic Of Human Rights

Approaching the issue from a different perspective and drawing more from experience than from angle, Frederick Douglass employed mockery and ridicule in at least three of his speeches to challenge the domination-submission theory as an interpretive tool. In the eulogy he delivered on April 14, 1858, in New York for William Jay, he praised the tenth clause of William Jay's last will and testament as the first bequest to a. The clause states in part, *"I bequeath to my son one thousand dollars to be applied by him at his discretion in promoting the safety and comfort*

---

[320] Ibid.

of fugitive slaves."[321] This bequest was not disguised support for resisting the system of slavery and its practices; rather, it provided tangible and open encouragement for resistance. It is hard to overlook the apparent reference to Philemon 10–19 used by conservative clergymen as a call to obey the fugitive slave law of 1850. Onesimus did not run away as an outlaw; being "away," he stood outside the system of slavery to challenge it. Douglass regarded attempts to control and intimidate others through inhumane laws as futile and blasphemous,[322] labelling wrong as right and right as wrong.

Similarly, in a speech titled 'The American Constitution and the Slave," delivered in Glasgow, Scotland, on March 26, 1860, Douglass challenged the idea that both the American Constitution and the letter of Philemon in the Bible legitimized slavery. While the American Constitution is often viewed as pro-slavery, the Bible is considered to oppose liberty. However, with some exaggeration and irony, Douglass rhetorically asks, *"So, you declare something is bad because it has been misused, abused, and exploited? Do you discard it for that reason? No! You hold it even closer to your heart; you study it more thoroughly and demonstrate from its pages that it supports liberty—not slavery. So let's treat the Constitution of the United States the*[323] *same way."* Essentially, the harmful way the Bible has been used to justify slavery does not render it deficient. The damaging misuse is dangerous, yet the essence of the Bible remains intact. Thus, for Douglass, just as the Constitution of the United States should not be cast aside even when viewed as misused in ways that contradict liberty, neither should the Bible be ignored.

In his speech on the Proclamation and the Negro Army on February 6, 1863, in New York, Douglass similarly challenged the belief that

---

[321] John W. Blassingame, ed., ***Frederick Douglass Papers, Series on: Speeches, Debates, Interviews, Vol. 3, 1855-63*** (New Haven: Yale University Press, 1985), p. 258

[322] Ibid.

[323] Blassingame, ed., ***Frederick Douglass Papers***, p. 363

slavery was divinely ordained. He pointed out that in the churches, it was taught that Jesus and the Apostles, fully aware of Roman slavery, never condemned it and instead encouraged slaves to obey their masters. Douglass mockingly remarked, *"even catching and returning runaway slaves was by Apostolic example, and the main feature of the Fugitive Slave Bill was in line with Paul's Epistle to Philemon (laughter)."*[324] For Douglass and his audience, no slave would be foolish enough to return voluntarily to his master after successfully escaping.

In summary, through satire, Douglass exposed and criticized the misuse and abuse of Paul's letter to Philemon as legitimizing slavery. However, even Douglass did not attribute agency to the socio-ideological and theological agenda present in the letter to Philemon. Instead, he granted agency to his experience of deprivation and dishonor, providing the epistemological lens through which he interpreted Philemon. To sum up, Wheaton and Hopkins engaged in *proof-texting*; Douglass and Equiano relied on their personal *experiences* of the harsh realities of slavery and spoke with righteous indignation; Harris employed *reverse psychology,* wherein Onesimus ought to have felt guilty for running away; and Young used the *material conditions* of the letter's composition. Each strategy served the interest of the interpreter. None was neutral.

Nonetheless, aside from the responses of Harris, Young, and Equiano, the reading strategies of Wheaton, Hopkins, and Douglass failed to engage with the socio- historical context of the text or letter. Although Wheaton and Hopkins acknowledged the material conditions surrounding the composition of the letter, their intent was not to effect social transformation in their society but rather to maintain the status quo and reinforce servile fidelity. In contrast, Equiano, who had experienced slavery in all its harsh and dehumanizing aspects, adopted a different perspective on the letter. This perspective acknowledged both the contextual realities and the socio-ideological and theological

---

[324] Blassingame, ed., ***Frederick Douglass Papers***, p. 559

agendas present in the letter, thus advocating for a social order of liberation. The question is, why?

Exegetics and Eisegetics

The preceding raises two contradictory questions. First, how can Christians use the Bible as an authority to support slavery while simultaneously disregarding its teachings that those redeemed by Christ cannot be considered slaves or property? Second, how is it that Christians reading the exact biblical text can arrive at conflicting conclusions about slavery?

To begin with, Wheaton and Hopkins occupied privileged positions within the establishment and can thus be seen as defenders of the status quo. Their social standing within the socio-political structure was indeed privileged. Therefore, unlike Atkins, Douglas, Equiano, and Young, they were not inclined to question the causes of oppression, exploitation, and inequality in society. While Young's social standing was also privileged, he was willing to challenge the status quo, which stemmed from the agency he afforded the letter as a product of the socio-ideological practices and systems of its context. This elevated his critical awareness of the oppressive nature of the social system and its practices.

However, the personal experience of slavery provided the context from which the reading strategies of Douglass and Equiano emerged. Both were slaves, meaning they came from a culture where forbidding slaves to learn to read served as a tool of oppression. In slave societies, the Bible was inevitably taught through the lens of the ruling class's ideas and vested interests. Slaves had to depend on listening and memory, relying on the aural tradition. The reading strategy held authority for slaves, not just the biblical text itself. This resulted in slaves having no loyalty to any official text, translation, or interpretation, allowing them the freedom to remember, repeat, retell, and resist any narratives or portions of scripture that aligned with their interests or resonated with their struggles.[325] Thus, slave hermeneutics began with their lived experience of oppression, enabling them to measure what they were told against their actual experiences and self-perceptions.[326] Social location—who we are and where we come from—along with hermeneutical suspicion, influences interpretation.

In addition to social location and hermeneutical suspicion, which can complicate our beliefs about God and how we interpret the Bible, understanding biblical texts as products of their environment is also critical in exposing oppressive systems and practices within the context from which one interprets and in which biblical texts were created. When interpretation does not privilege the underclass, it reinforces the status quo. Young and Equiano granted such privilege to the underclass in the interpretive process. However, it is not always true that the oppressed and exploited will question, let alone challenge, the status quo.

The answer to the first contradictory question, then, is that where the materiality of the Bible – the socio-economic, political, cultural, and ideological dimensions of the text - does not influence interpretation, a disjuncture arises between the material conditions of the interpreter and the biblical texts. The material conditions of the biblical text do not significantly impact interpreting the context, leading to a disjuncture between faith and praxis. Thus, it is this disjuncture between the materiality of the interpreter and biblical texts that characterizes Caribbean biblical hermeneutical practice.

The second contradiction mentioned above receives the same response: a failure to grant agency to the materiality of the Bible. Harris blamed the victim, not the systems and structures, for society's

---

[325] Renita J. Weems, *"Reading Her Way Through the Struggle: African American Women and the Bible"* in Norman K. Gottwald & Richard A. Horsley, **The Bible and Liberation – Political and Social Hermeneutics**, revised edition (Maryknoll, N.Y: Orbis Books, 1993), p. 34
[326] Ibid. p. 38

upheaval, dislocation, and struggle. Through his reverse psychological reading strategy, Harris depicted Onesimus as the sinner instead of as the one who was sinned against. Viewing Onesimus as the sinner obscures the violation he faced from societal systems and structures. These systems and structures have infringed upon Onesimus's rights as an individual. Structural violence occurs when a few benefit from the labor of the many. Simultaneously, resources and power are used for the self-satisfaction of the few rather than for the self-actualization of the many.[327] Structural violence initiates a spiral of violence in three stages: oppression, resistance, and repression.[328] In Philemon, all three stages are present. How Onesimus's return is primarily interpreted depends on whether he is viewed as the one who committed a wrong or as the one who was wronged, requiring an epistemology capable of identifying the actual victim and interpreting the letter from the victim's perspective.

However, while the question of whether Onesimus was wronged or he wronged others does not remove Philemon from its life context, interpreting the letter from the perspective of the privileged Philemon reinforces the status quo and structural violence.

Furthermore, following J. Albert Harrill's argument, while antislavery advocates viewed slavery from a moral perspective—right versus wrong, justice versus injustice—the pro-slavery supporters considered it from a political angle. For antislavery advocates, the appeal to Christian morality emphasizes conscience over biblical authority,[329] leading to a more critical reading of Scripture.

According to Harrill, anti-slavery proponents read Scripture through three hermeneutical movements. The first step is the development of the

---

[327] See Thomas Merton, *Faith and Violence* (Notre Dame: University of Notre Dame Press, 1968), pp. 7-8; and the Report on the Consultation on *"Violence, Non-Violence and the Struggle for Social Justice"* (Geneva: World Council of Churches, 1972), p. 6

[328] Richard A. Horsley, *Jesus and the Spiral of Violence – Popular Jewish Resistance in Roman Palestine* (Minneapolis: Fortress Press, 1933), p. 22

[329] Harrill, p. 149

hermeneutic of immutable principles, which is an egalitarian reading of Jesus' golden rule as opposed to a patriarchal reading.[330] Matthew 7:12 and Luke 6:31 are taken as the core principles of this epistemology.

The second step involves the argument from conscience regarding biblical authority.[331] One might misinterpret a text while still upholding a cause's morality. For Harrill, "the moral norms of the Bible were conditioned by the social arrangements and cultural assumptions of a specific age and people."[332] Thus, it is essential to distinguish between the "word of God" and the "word of writers."

The third step involves the hermeneutic of typology (Revelation 6:15-16, 19:11-13) and apocalyptic theology, which incorporates the actual use of force to achieve freedom.[333]

On the other hand, for proponents of pro-slavery, the political imperative is biblicism—a literal interpretation of Scripture. This approach to engaging with the text is driven by the belief that the New Testament does not condemn slavery. Thus, it suggests an acceptance of an organic model of society in which subjection is deemed essential.[334]

Harrill, therefore, contributes two key points to the discussion on the contradictory conclusions reached by Christians regarding the material conditions of slavery: first, that these contradictions stem from Christians' understanding of morality and politics; and second, a literal reading strategy rather than an egalitarian, typological, or conscientious one. However, in addition to overlooking the issues of social location and hermeneutical suspicion, Harrill fails to acknowledge the agency of the material conditions that shaped the development of the text.

In summary, the reading strategies—proof-texting, experience, reverse psychology, and reasoning—of the interpreters mentioned above

---

[330] Harrill, p. 174
[331] Ibid.
[332] Ibid.
[333] Ibid.
[334] Ibid

resulted in an interpretation of Philemon through Genesis 9 and disputed Pauline letters from a time when the church was accommodating the status quo. Furthermore, these interpreters focused on the struggles occurring in their context. While these reading strategies and the focus on the existential realities of the context are not dismissed, I argue that in Philemon, a profound social struggle is occurring for social control or transformation. Essentially, a socio-ideological and theological agenda was at play in Philemon. This agenda was overlooked, meaning the ruling class's ideas and interests embedded in the letter were not recognized.

Notably, no challenge to the status quo arises when the materiality of both biblical texts and the interpreter's context is disregarded. A disconnection between faith and practice emerges, as there is neither foundation nor motivation for an alternative social order, largely due to their personal experiences of the brutal realities of slavery while also connecting those experiences to the dehumanizing conditions in Philemon. Only Douglass and Equiano resisted the oppressive slave system. If there is no vision or hope for an alternative social order stemming from practice and the unjust and repressive nature of the status quo, then resistance does not take place.

The discussion here underscores the critique I am making in this study regarding biblical hermeneutical practice in the Caribbean. It becomes evident in the interpretations of Young, Equiano, and Douglass that it is essential to do more than just apply biblical interpretations to contextual realities in order to expose, challenge, and resist oppressive systems and practices. Both the social forces and struggles of the readers' context, as well as the environment from which biblical texts originated, must be acknowledged to create any meaningful and practical challenge to the status quo based on the authority of the Bible. Attempts to contextualize biblical texts without considering their materiality merely serve as a pretext for social action, lacking any real power to resist oppressive systems and practices.

The Contemporary Era

One could argue or even attempt to excuse both the anti- and pro-slavery advocates, as well as the slaves themselves, for allowing contextual and existential realities to influence their biblical reading practices. However, while the harsh, dehumanizing, and exploitative conditions rooted in oppressive intent have evolved since the era of slavery, the essence and purpose of that oppressive intent have remained unchanged. The "leopard" of oppression has not altered its spots. Leopards of any kind do not change their spots. The question is, have biblical reading practices taken on a different form or have they retained the same character and intent from the days of slavery to the present? In other words, what empowers biblical reading practices in today's context? Below, I explore this question through the lenses of liberal, liberationist, and postcolonial biblical reading strategies from 1980 to the present.

Liberal Hermeneutics

Using the liberal reading strategy, I aim to identify the site of struggle, whether in the material conditions of the letter to Philemon or within the social context and hermeneutical assumptions of the referenced interpreters. These explorations seek to reveal what provides agency and where resistance arises. I define a liberal as someone who upholds and emphasizes the expression of individual 'rights,' freedom, enterprise, and the rule of law in society. Therefore, within a liberal reading strategy, I am interested in examining which individualistic, abstract, and subjective aspects of the letter to Philemon are highlighted, considering the socio-ideological, theological interests, and social practices evident in the text.

In New Testament studies, several scholars, including Gillian Feeley-Harnick, Norman K. Petersen, John M. Barclay, and Chris Frilingos, focused on the site of struggle in the letter, emphasizing the significant influence that Philemon and Paul held within the household and house church, as well as the necessity for Philemon and Onesimus to resolve their conflicts. Others who share this perspective include B.M. Rapske, Ralph P. Martin, N.H. Taylor, Joseph A. Fitzmyer, John D. Nordling, Carolyn Osiek, Cain Hope Felder, and S.C. Winter.

Authority: Individualizing Social Struggle

According to Gillian Feeley-Harnick, Paul's intention in Philemon is to establish his authority and compel Philemon to honor his request.[335] Thus, the letter to Philemon addresses how one converts power into authority.[336] The core issue is no longer the conflict between Philemon and Onesimus, but rather who can command whom. By structuring her argument around the issue of authority in the letter, Feeley-Harnick views Onesimus as the gift, the instrument of God's broader design,[337] which is to resolve the authority issue between Paul and Philemon. In other words, Onesimus is merely a pawn, caught in the middle of the debate over who the ultimate authority is. To support her claim, Feeley-Harnick suggests that Paul was not ignoring Deuteronomy 23:16, even though Roman law requires that all fugitives be returned to their masters.[338] Furthermore, verses 18-19 illustrate a covert strategy by Paul to gain an advantage over Philemon, particularly since there may not have been any debts to repay, as Onesimus may have fled due to

---

[335] Gillian Feeley-Harnik, *"Is Historical Anthropology Possible? The Case of the Runaway Slave"* in, Gene M. Tucker & Douglas A. Knight Eds. **Humanizing America's Iconic Book**, Society of Biblical Literature Centennial Addresses, 1980, p. 117

[336] Ibid. p. 120

[337] Ibid. p. 120

[338] Ibid. p. 120

maltreatment.[339] Thus, while a struggle is mentioned here, it is not between conflicting socio-ideological interests and practices within the system, but rather between individuals.

This same tendency to individualize the social struggle taking place in the socio-historic environment is evident in the work of Norman K. Petersen, John M. Barclay, and Chris Frilingos. Regardless of the nature of the battle they identified, the argument shifts to the issue of individual authority.

Though Norman K. Petersen acknowledges that Onesimus's flight challenged slavery as an institution,[340] he views the letter as primarily concerning Paul's authority. Petersen highlights the nature of the social relations between Philemon and Onesimus within the social structure of their society and church.[341] In the broader world, Philemon is a master and Onesimus a slave; however, in the church, Philemon has no master role, and neither is superior or inferior; they are equals[342]. Upon Onesimus's return, Philemon faces three options: to remain Onesimus's master and justly impose punishment, to lend Onesimus to another master, perhaps Paul, or to grant Onesimus his freedom. All these[343] options are valid within the social structure of the imperial Graeco-Roman world.

In the church, however, Philemon has only one choice: to receive Onesimus as a brother, either out of obedience to Paul or out of goodwill.[344] In the church, Philemon can no longer lead a double life as both master and brother, as being a master conflicts with or is incompatible with being a brother. Petersen states, "it is logically and socially impossible to relate to the same person as both one's inferior

---

[339] Ibid. p. 121
[340] Norman K Petersen, **Rediscovering Paul – Philemon and the Sociology of Paul's Narrative World** (Fortress Press: Philadelphia, 1985), p. 94
[341] Ibid. p. 97
[342] Ibid. p. 97
[343] Ibid. p. 98
[344] Ibid. p. 98

and as one's equal." Thus, Onesimus being a brother to Philemon means that he cannot also be a slave to Philemon in any context. In other words, "being in Christ is a state of social being that governs the relationships between believers even outside the spatial and temporal boundaries of the church."[345] Given the relationship between Philemon and Onesimus, the course of action open to Philemon is to "liberate" Onesimus. In short, the issue here reduces to the identities of Philemon and Onesimus as equals before God.

However, whatever option Philemon chooses carries social implications. If he does not accept Onesimus as a brother, will he be excluding himself from his own household? Will he undermine the value of equality on which the emerging church stands, thereby beginning to unravel the community's social fabric? Here, Philemon's dilemma lies in thinking "not in terms of his role as master but of relinquishing it,"[346]57 shifting from thoughts of punishment to those of freedom.

However, Petersen does not view the letter developing in this way. Rather, he sees the letter centered on the theme of indebtedness— Onesimus to Philemon (in the worldly sense) and Philemon to Paul (within the church). Thus, the letter hinges on Paul's authority. Logically, if Paul possesses the authority to command Philemon's obedience, he also has the authority to discipline—now the issue concerns who holds the executive power and authority to enforce obedience.

In summary, for Petersen, Onesimus's desire to return raises the issue of identity equality, while Paul's intervention focuses on the issue of authority.[347] Thus, the letter demonstrates a shift from equality of identity to authority. The dilemma is that in a slave society like Imperial Graeco-Rome, master and slave are not brothers, and there is no equality of identity; authority signifies the complete control of the

[345] Ibid. p. 289
[346] Ibid. p. 290
[347] Ibid. p. 301

master over the slave as his property. Consequently, with all attention directed toward authority, Onesimus is effectively excluded from the letter, and the economic and social relations related to the household and house church are obscured.

Barclay similarly views the issue as centered on who determines Onesimus's future and when that future should come to pass. He identifies the central tension in Philemon as the fact that Philemon and Onesimus are co-equals within the house church, yet socially unequal within the household.[348] This tension prompts the question of whether Onesimus's conversion to Christianity should lead to his liberation from slavery, either now or at a later point in time.

On one hand, if Philemon grants Onesimus his freedom, it undermines the socioeconomic structure of imperial Graeco-Roman society. Therefore, freedom would be perceived as a reward for running away, which could encourage other slaves to convert to Christianity to secure their freedom. However, this leaves unresolved the question of who bears the cost of manumission and restricts, if not ruins, the ability of wealthier masters to maintain both their household and house church.[349]

On the other hand, if Philemon accepts Onesimus as both co-equal and socially equal, it carries implications for both the house church and the household. In the context of the house church, it raises questions such as: Who is the host, the slave or the master? Who is the leader? Is the offering taken as a contribution towards manumission? Are the household rules active in fellowship? What does brotherhood mean? Is brotherhood about equality in personal, spiritual, or material relationships?[350] In the household context, issues of disobedience, insubordination, and disrespect cast very long shadows. Who punishes

---

[348] John M. Barclay, *"Paul, Philemon and the Dilemma of Christian Slave-ownership"* in **New Testament Studies** Vol. 37 No. 2 April 1991, p. 183
[349] Ibid. p. 177
[350] Ibid. p. 182

whom, and for what? Who gives orders to whom, and who is expected to obey?

Essentially, Barclay observes no relief from the central tension: Can Philemon be both master and "brother" while Onesimus is both slave and "brother"? Can Philemon and Onesimus be co-equals yet still socially unequal? In other words, who holds the power to determine Onesimus's destiny, and when will that decision take effect? The crux of this position is that Onesimus becomes the object, not the subject, of his destiny. Onesimus's destiny is determined for him, not by him.

Unlike Petersen and Barclay, Chris Frilingos argues that Paul has the authority to determine Onesimus' fate while limiting the issue of authority to Philemon's household. The conflict takes place within the household. If Philemon agrees to Paul's request, then Paul implicitly wields administrative influence in Philemon's home. Once[351] more, Onesimus is a pawn, this time symbolizing Paul's domestic power within Philemon's household.[352]

To support his argument, Frilingos asserts that the imperial Graeco-Roman household was a site of social, economic, and political interaction, not merely a residence.[353] Moreover, Paul employs family language in his letter to undermine Philemon's authority and assert his claims to Onesimus.[354] Onesimus is Paul's child. Therefore, Paul possesses paternal rights (vv. 10, 12). As Paul's child, Onesimus has become a diligent servant and Paul's messenger (vv. 11, 13, 17). According to Frilingos, this "ownership" of Onesimus implies that Paul is now superior to Philemon. Thus, for Frilingos, Paul can dictate Onesimus's fate. But isn't running away a form of determining one's fate? I argue that it is. And will Onesimus heed Paul's statement? I think not! Claiming that

---

[351] Chris Frilingos, *"For My Child Onesimus: Paul and Domestic Power in Philemon"* in **Journal of Biblical Literature**, Vol. 19 No. 1 Spring 2000, 104

[352] Ibid. p. 104

[353] Ibid. p. 95

[354] Ibid. p. 100-102

Paul has the authority to decide Onesimus's future overlooks the fact that running away is risky and bold. Nonetheless, it was in Imperial Graeco- Rome, representing a significant power exercise.

What Feely-Harnick, Petersen, Barclay, and Frilingos have done is to centre the social struggle depicted in the letter to Philemon in individuals – Philemon and Onesimus - rather than in the socio-economic structure. But should the issue be confined to determining who has authority? Even if confining the issue to individuals is allowed, should it not be about Onesimus's freedom? It was Onesimus after all who was oppressed. Focusing on individuals will ultimately favor the status quo, meaning the system and its practices remain entrenched. To read Philemon from the point of view of authority is to read the letter from the point of view of the status quo, and hence, there will be a failure to deal with the systemic and structural issues. The issue here is not right relationships (righteousness) but right relations (justice). What the liberals have failed to recognize is that power is primarily a product of relation to the means of production[355] and is derived, therefore, from ownership of the means of production.

Reconciliation: Unchanging Oppressive Structures and Systems

The readings of B.M. Rapske, Ralph P. Martin, N.H. Taylor, Joseph A. Fitzmyer, John D. Nordling, and Carolyn Osiek also restrict the social struggle in the letter to Philemon to that which existed between Philemon and Onesimus, but from the perspective of reconciliation. However, reconciliation is approached on a personal level, which results in the neglect of social implications.

Rapske interprets the letter of Philemon as advocating for the forgiveness of any material injury and refraining from exercising the

---

[355] Max Weber, **The Theory of Social and Economic Organisation** (London: Free Press, 1964), p. 152

right to punish Onesimus for the act of running away.[356] Similarly, Martin views the request in vv. 8-20, which concerns Philemon's acceptance of Onesimus with clemency.[357] This argument is supported by v. 15. The act of Onesimus fleeing is seen as providential; therefore, he should not face punishment. In this context, v. 21 is understood as a call for manumission, supported by v. 17, which conveys the message to 'give him full acceptance" as a fellow Christian.[358]

Although Taylor approaches the issue from the standpoint of re-socialization, the core matters of forgiveness and acceptance remain unchanged. For Taylor, when Onesimus fled, he became de-socialized from the house church.[359] Therefore, he seeks Paul's mediation for reinstatement "not only as a slave of the household but as a brother in the house church."[360]71 The essence of conversion here is re-socialization, where the fugitivus theory and the case for manumission are dismissed. Onesimus could not be regarded as a fugitivus. As a fugitivus, he would not willingly choose to return to the inhumane treatment that awaits him. Consequently, Taylor sees manumission as diminishing Philemon's obligation without enhancing Onesimus' well- being and security.[361]

Taylor concludes that "on balance, it seems more likely that Paul is petitioning for Onesimus' restoration to his previous position in Philemon's household, enriched by his new relationship of Christian brotherhood with Philemon."[362] In short, servitude in the household is

---

[356] B.M. Rapske, *"The Prisoner Paul in the Eyes of Onesimus"* in **New Testament Studies** Vol. 37 No. 2 April 1991, p. 192

[357] Ralph P. Martin, **Interpretation – A Bible Commentary for Teaching and Preaching – Ephesians, Colossians and Philemon** (Atlanta: John Knox Press, 1991), p. 134

[358] Ibid. p. 144

[359] N.H. Taylor, *"Onesimus – A Case Study of Slave Conversion in Early Christianity"* in **Religion and Theology** Vol. 3/3 1996, p. 279

[360] Ibid. p. 274

[361] Ibid. p. 271

[362] Ibid. p. 270

sweetened by brotherhood in the house church, indicating that nothing has changed – Philemon is still the master, and Onesimus is still a slave.

Fitzmyer's understanding of reconciliation is also rooted in the idea that nothing has changed in the social structure. Building his argument on verses 15-16, Fitzmyer identifies three options available to Philemon: he can take Onesimus back without punishment, take Onesimus back and restore him to his position within the family and servility, or emancipate Onesimus and return him to Paul as a mission partner. However, each of these choices implies that Onesimus remains a slave. Although Fitzmyer notes that the emphasis in the letter is on love (verses 7, 20), indicating that the relationship between Philemon and Onesimus is no longer one of master and slave but rather one of brotherhood (verse 16), this simply means that Onesimus is now regarded as a Christian.

The arguments presented by Rapske, Martin, Taylor, and Fitzmyer suggest that the social structure would remain unchallenged. After punishment was set aside, clemency was enacted, and re-socialization was thorough. The socio-economic structure would have stayed exactly as Onesimus left it. Liberals seem uninterested in socio-economic and political analysis of systems and structures, no matter how blatantly oppressive and unjust. Instead, their priority appears to be reconciliation between individuals rather than pursuing social justice.

Similarly, the arguments of Nordling and Osiek, while not addressing prior punishment, do little to alter the understanding of reconciliation. Nordling posits that the radical nature of Christian forgiveness is set against the harsh laws of the world.[363] He acknowledges that manumission does not effect meaningful change in the material, structural, and legal relationships between slave and master. Nonetheless, he argues that Paul's concern seems to be perceptional and relational

---

[363] John D. Nordling, *"Onesimus Fugitivus: A Defence of the Runaway Slave Hypothesis in Philemon"* in **Journal Study of the New Testament** Issue No. 41 February 1991, p. 118

rather than structural.[364] Nordling focuses his argument on verses 16 and 17, interpreting "in the flesh" as pertaining to the household and "in the Lord" as referring to the house[365] church. Although these are two distinct domains, Paul desires equal treatment for slaves in both spheres. Consequently, Onesimus could act independently, exercising his own will, refusing to follow commands, and determining the punishment for anyone in the household as needed. Thus, Onesimus is granted privilege and honor. Furthermore, verse 17 employs the language of hospitality, where the one received becomes a friend. Yet, Nordling observes that in that society, "friendship could only have existed between social equals, and hospitality was only offered between social equals."[366]

Then, Paul wants Philemon to treat Onesimus as a social equal. However, for Nordling, social equality involved refusing to insult or degrade, offering protection, and respecting the honour and dignity of the slave.[367] Nonetheless, social equality is only one side of the social justice system; social inequality is not a separate issue. Both social equality and social inequality affect the same person within the same social justice system.

In short, Nordling sees Paul as desiring a familial relationship between Philemon and Onesimus, a transformation in the nature and quality of their relationship, while leaving the socio-economic structures unchanged.

Osiek also addresses the relational issue, albeit on a personal rather than a structural level. He observes that while Paul desires Onesimus as a mission partner, he must secure Philemon's approval, which necessarily requires reconciliation between Philemon and Onesimus.[368] Thus, being

---

[364] Ibid. p. 102

[365] Ibid. p. 102

[366] Ibid. p. 102

[367] Ibid. p. 102

[368] Carolyn Osiek, **Philippians and Philemon** (Nashville: Abingdon Press, 2000), p. 127

a mission partner is contingent upon this reconciliation. Osiek views verse 16 as the verse that underpins the letter.[369] Here, "in the flesh" refers to what Philemon and Onesimus are as human beings within their historically conditioned status, while "in the Lord" transcends all social distinctions or the statuses of master and slave.[370] Consequently, social distinctions dissolve since conversion alters the relationship between Philemon and Onesimus. Because of this alteration in social distinctions, Philemon can accept Onesimus as a social equal (v. 17) and choose to forgive and reconcile rather than seek justice (v. 18).[371] Nevertheless, nothing is done to address the deeply entrenched social inequality.

So far, the liberal interpretations of Philemon focus on the struggle occurring in the letter within the personal relationship between Philemon and Onesimus, rather than on the system and its structures and practices. By doing this, these liberal interpretations imply that Onesimus's fate depends on Philemon's kindness.[372] What places Onesimus in the correct relationship within the household economy is Philemon's undeserved love for Onesimus, rather than a new order of social equality. However, conflicts in personal relationships arise from the system. Without addressing the issues in the system, the struggle in the personal relationship will persist. To approach the individual separately from the systemic is to treat the symptom, not the root cause.

Reconciliation: Avoiding Systemic Evils

However, while the arguments presented earlier suggest that reconciliation relies on Philemon's graciousness, Cain Hope Felder and S.C. Winter perceive reconciliation as the result of the inner transformation brought about by God during conversion. For Felder,

---

[369] Ibid. p. 139

[370] Ibid. p. 140

[371] Ibid. p. 140

[372] R.S. Sugirtharajah, **Postcolonial Criticism and Biblical Interpretation** (Oxford: Oxford University Press, 2002), p. 112

Paul's emphasis in the text and letter highlights the power of the Gospel to transform human relationships and foster reconciliation, irrespective of class or other distinctions.[373] Where the Gospel's power is at work, families are established (*brother* in vv. 1, 7, 16, 20; *sister* in v. 2 and *"my child... whose father I have become* v. 10"); partnerships form, which imply and involve acceptance, trust, respect, shared responsibilities, and equality in participation (v. 17); and relationships develop based on love rather than on any legal obligations (v. 16). In this context, the changes resulting from reconciliation occur within personal relationships, not within the system.

For Winter, the change in the relationship is brought about by the fundamental shift in his being that Onesimus has experienced through baptism (v. 16).[374] Baptism has rendered the "ownership" institutionalized in slavery (vv. 15-16) and any rights granted by slavery (vv. 17-20) invalid.[375] Together, vv. 15-16 and 17-20 demonstrate that Paul does not recognize the authority of a Christian master over a Christian slave. Among the baptized, "slavery is not only wrong but invalid."[376]

Moreover, Paul substitutes the relationship between "owner" and "owned," recognized in the imperial Graeco-Roman legal system, with a relationship of indebtedness formed through parenthood in baptism.[377] The purpose of the argument is that "a transformation in relations between individuals causes a change in social status."[378] However, the argument is limited to social equality, regarding what occurs in personal

---

[373] Cain Hope Felder, *"The Letter to Philemon"* in **The New Interpreter's Bible** (Nashville: Abingdon Press, 2000), p. 885
[374] S.C. Winter, *"Philemon"* in Elizabeth Schussler Fiorenza, **Searching the Scriptures – A Feminist Commentary** (London: SCM Press Ltd. 1995), p. 307
[375] Ibid. p. 307
[376] Ibid. p. 307
[377] Ibid. p. 307
[378] Ibid. p. 308

relationships, and does not address social inequality, or what ought to be occurring in the system.

Compared to Felder and Winter, Craig S. De Vos argues that a change in perception is necessary, rather than a change in personal relationships or within the system. De Vos maintains the thesis that, due to the stigma associated with slavery in a male-dominated, servile culture of the imperial Graeco-Roman society, neither reconciliation nor manumission likely influenced the relationship between Philemon and Onesimus.[379] Even when manumission was granted or earned, it did not significantly change a person's fundamental character or behavior. Moreover, the patron-client relationship, which reflects an inequality of social power, continued to thrive. Ultimately, the structural change of manumission did not impact personal relationships.[380]

Thus, what Paul suggests reflects a fundamental shift in relationships, where Onesimus is seen as a brother or even an honored guest, rather than as a slave. This shift effectively challenges the male-dominated, servile culture and group-defined identity values of imperial Graeco-Roman society.[381] In other words, the essence of Paul's recommendation is to change perceptions or challenge stereotypes.[382] If you can change how a person is perceived, you can influence how that person interacts with others. Therefore, for De Vos, changing perceptions means changing relationships. Again, there is no direct attack on the system; rather, what happens in personal relationships is at the heart of the struggle.

In summary, Felder, Winter, and De Vos direct the argument inward, turning it into an abstraction that neglects the socio-economic

---

[379] Craig S. De Vos, *"Once a Slave Always a Slave? Slavery, Manumission and Relational Patterns in Paul's Letter to Philemon"* in **Journal for the Study of the New Testament** Issue 82/2001, p. 101
[380] Ibid. p. 92
[381] Ibid, p. 102
[382] Ibid. p. 103

and political dimensions of the letter. Concentrating on abstract concepts permits an oppressive social system and rationalizes oppression.

Those identified with liberal hermeneutics here have failed to connect reconciliation with liberation. There is no reconciliation without liberation. Reconciliation occurs at both personal and communal levels. On an individual level, reconciliation allows the "master" to also be a "brother," but it does not permit this on the communal level. At the communal level, systems and structures, along with their practices, are at work. Therefore, liberation relates to freedom from that which is oppressive and repressive within the system. In other words, not only must the oppressed become free, but the social systems, structures, and practices that oppress must change as well.[383] Freedom without material or social power is empty. Bringing a new order into existence requires dismantling the system that oppresses. Ultimately, reconciliation happens when individuals can affirm who they are (self-definition) and what they aspire to be (self-determination).

All in all, the previous points understand the socio-ideological and theological agenda at work in Philemon as occurring within personal relationships rather than within the system. However, Richard Horsley offers a different perspective. He argues that the issue concerns not just social equality, but also social inequality. Horsley disputes the idea that the problem of social inequality was ever concealed; it was merely overlooked. Thus, Horsley inquires, "How is it that only with Onesimus's conversion did the issue of social inequality emerge for the first time?[384] Why didn't this concern arise when Philemon was converted?[385] After all, Philemon was converted before Onesimus! Was there no issue with a member of the siblinghood remaining a slave-master if the slave himself

---

[383] J. Deotis Roberts, **A Black Political Theology** (Louisville: Westminster John Knox Press, 1974, reprinted 2005), p. 140

[384] Richard Horsley, *"Paul and Slavery: A Critical Alternative to Recent Readings"* in **Semeia** 83/84 1998 Slavery in Text and Interpretation, p. 179

[385] Ibid.

did not belong?[386] Regardless of conversion, social inequality was always inherent in the system. The true struggle occurs within the system. Here, Horsley genuinely connects reconciliation with liberation. It is in this intersection of reconciliation and liberation that social struggle is situated or fought.

In short, the liberal view emphasizes executive power or the struggle for power. This indicates that the conflict occurs within the upper echelons or among the executives of the socio-economic and political structure of imperial Graeco-Roman society. However, I believe the site of struggle in the letter to Philemon lies within the socio-economic and political structure and its practices, rather than in who administers the system. In other words, while liberal hermeneutics emphasize charity, prioritize reconciliation over social injustice, and highlight individualism,[387] they also show little interest in social analysis and consequently grant no agency to the socio- ideological dimensions of biblical texts.

Liberationist Hermeneutics

The question now becomes: where is the site of struggle in the letter of Philemon for liberation hermeneutics? Specifically, how does the socio-ideological and theological agenda that shaped Philemon influence the interpretations of liberationists? Did they advocate for a new social order for everyone, not just for free individuals? Having free individuals without a new order merely implies that the system of enslavement remains deeply rooted. So then, where is the site of struggle for liberationists? I understand liberation as freedom from structural and systemic bondage, which operates on three levels: analysis of lived realities (socio-analytical), theological interpretation of lived realities

[386] Ibid.
[387] Taken from class notes on lecture delivered by R.S. Sugitharajah on 'Liberal and Liberation Hermeneutics', February 23, 2005

(hermeneutical), and commitment to and involvement in social realities (pastoral). Therefore, I utilize liberation hermeneutics to interpret social processes with the primary intention of achieving human freedom from all forms of structural and systemic oppression and injustice.[388]

In what follows, I will analyze Theo Preiss, Amos Jones Jr., Robert E. Dunham, Clarice J. Martin, and Sabine Biebersstein's "readings" of Philemon as representative of liberation hermeneutics, which I have grouped under the liberation perspective. This grouping reflects the interpreters' interest in the social systems, structures, and practices in Philemon.

Coequality and Social Inequality in the Household

While Preiss and Jones Jr. focus on removing social distinctions, they do not emphasize effecting change in the social system and structure; however, their position still allows them to hold the struggle between house church and household in tension. For Preiss, the emphasis is not on what Onesimus did but on what Onesimus became.[389] Where Preiss misses the mark, however, is by not elaborating on the meaning and implications of what Onesimus did and became. I would argue that the emphasis is indeed on what Onesimus did. By stepping outside the system, Onesimus resisted it, which in turn determined what he became—not only a convert to Christianity but also free. Nonetheless, in asserting that it is a free person Philemon is to receive back, Preiss has identified the struggle that would arise between house church and household.[390] In other words, the issue is about co-equality and social inequality.

Where Preiss views the elimination of social distinctions as critical,

---

[388] Juan Luis Segundo, **Liberation of Theology** (New York: Orbis Books, 1976), pp. 7-38

[389] Theo Preiss, *"Life in Christ and Social Ethics in the Epistle to Philemon"* in **Studies in Biblical Theology** No. 13, Life in Christ (London: SCM Press, 1952), p. 34

[390] Ibid. p. 34

Jones Jr. considers social status paramount. For Jones Jr., the matter of equality involves a fundamental shift in the tangible social status of the slave, rather than merely an equality before God or within the emerging church.[391] However, Jones Jr. approaches this issue through his interpretation of ecclesia (Romans 12:2; I Corinthians 7:29-31; 2 Corinthians 11:32-33; Philippians 2:12-13, 3:20; Acts 17:7), wherein membership ensures liberation from sin and servitude.[392] According to Jones Jr., in the church, slaves were no longer bound by any obligations to their masters. Thus, the ecclesia constitutes a community of equals, devoid of masters and slaves. Nevertheless, even with the removal of social distinctions, what changes should be implemented in the social system and structures that sustain these distinctions? What matters more: a change in social status or a transformation of the social system and structure?

Preiss and Jones Jr. neglect to address the categories of master and slave as social classes. Being a slave placed Onesimus in a social class, indicating he had a master, Philemon. The term "master" also denotes a social category. How can this issue be limited to eliminating social status and incongruity without acknowledging the struggle between social classes? Indeed, it is the class structure that has led to slavery, stemming from the necessity of dominant classes in society to establish and preserve social structures and institutions that secure their positions of privilege and power.[393] To dismantle the class structure is to break down the dominant power base and foster a more participatory role in decision-making processes and production relations among the dominant.

---

[391] Amos Jones Jr., *"Paul's Message of Freedom"* in Norman K. Gottwald & Richard A. Horsley eds. **The Bible and Liberation** (Maryknoll, N.Y.: Orbis Books, 1993), p. 504

[392] Ibid. pp. 512-514

[393] Tim Hector *"Hopes and Aspiration at and After Emancipation"* Fan The Flame **Outlet Newspaper** April 24, 1998

The issue of class structure is critical in Dunham's interpretation. Dunham argues that Philemon, as both master and brother in the world, must reconcile with a slave who has become a brother.[394] In this context, what steps must Philemon take to transition from mercy to justice? Dunham identifies two steps. Firstly, Philemon must recognize that, through conversion, the old social distinctions of identities and status have disappeared.[395] Dunham arrives at this conclusion based on his interpretation of Galatians 3:27-28, which suggests that social distinctions are no longer significant within the community of the baptized.[396] Secondly, Philemon "must relinquish rights *(person as property)* in favor of what is right" *(the right to self-determination and self- definition).*[397] Social distinctions and inequality are dismantled immediately, transforming the old oppressive order into a new liberation order.

Coequality and Social Inequality in the Housechurch

All the arguments so far focus on the structures and practices within the system. However, Clarice J. Martin and Sabine Biebersstein investigate what occurred outside the system. In this context, Martin views running away as an act of self- determination and self-definition, thus exploring the praxis of resistance and equality within the faith community that gathers in Philemon's house.

Martin contends that Paul and Onesimus occupy the same social position— imprisonment. However, Paul holds a privileged status, as evidenced by his advocacy for Onesimus. In contrast, Onesimus views his humanity and religiosity as distinct from Paul's. Consequently, Onesimus considered even a perilous freedom to be preferable to

---

[394] Robert E. Dunham, *"Between Text and Sermon: Philemon 1-25"* in **Interpretation** Vol. 52 No. 2 April 1998, p. 191

[395] Ibid. p. 193

[396] Ibid. p. 193

[397] Ibid. p. 193

Christianized slavery and chose to escape.[398] While social location may not stem from class structure, praxis can vary. Additionally, social location does not necessarily arise from praxis.

Biebersstein poses the question: How can slavery be reconciled with the liberating message of the Gospel?[399] Before arriving at an answer, she situates the letter of Philemon within its socio-political context. For Biebersstein, the believers who gathered in Philemon's house were part of the minority Jewish community living under the dominant system of the Roman Empire. The Roman Empire divided society into the free and the unfree. In writing to this community, Paul employs familial language to address the recipients of the letter (vv. 1-2), describe his relationship with Onesimus (vv. 10-13), and convey the desired relationship between Philemon and Onesimus (v. 16).[400] By using such language, Paul implicitly creates a new social reality: a model of egalitarian relationships independent of rank, status, and gender (cf. Galatians 3:27-28).[401]

Furthermore, Paul uses economic terminology to describe the relationship between himself and Philemon by establishing a material basis (vv. 17-22).[402] Philemon came to faith in Christ through Paul's influence or witness and thus "owes himself" to Paul. There is a creditor-debtor dynamic between Paul and Philemon. From this business partnership, or the brotherhood among all three, Paul "directs" Philemon to do "more than I ask."[403] Brotherhood is only meaningful

[398] Clarice J. Martin, *"Womanist Interpretation of the New Testament: The quest for Holistic and Inclusive Translation and Interpretation"* in **Black Theology – A Documentary History**, eds. James A. Cone & Gayraud Gilmore (Maryknoll, N.Y: Orbis Books, 1993), pp. 226-236

[399] Sabine Biebersstein, *"Disrupting the Normal Reality of Slavery: A Feminist Reading of the Letter to Philemon"* in **Journal For The Study of the New Testament** No. 79, September 2000, p. 106

[400] Ibid. p. 113
[401] Ibid. p. 112
[402] Ibid. p. 114
[403] Ibid. p. 114

when material livelihood is secure or social equality is present.[404] Co-equality fosters brotherhood.

In summary, what Biebersstein has accomplished is to view the community of believers that gathered in Philemon's house, the household economy, as a microcosm of the Roman state and the house church as a community of freedom. In the Roman state, slavery was accepted as a part of society's order. As a result, society is divided between the ruler and the ruled. Here, the runaway is pursued and punished. However, in the house church, a way must be established, or permitted, in cases of the subversive actions of a runaway, for the Gospel praxis of resistance and equality. This holds the answer to the question Biebersstein posed earlier (how is slavery to be reconciled with the liberating message of the Gospel?): through the praxis of resistance and subversion by the oppressed within prevailing systems and structures that degrade and dishonor human beings.

From the interpretation of those identified under the liberation perspective, it is evident that a focus on institutional practices and the ideology that supports these practices characterizes liberation hermeneutics. This focus is reflected in the concern for victims of such practices, the transformation of unjust and oppressive institutional frameworks, socio-structural analyses, as well as the identification of oppression and oppressors, exploitation and exploiters in biblical texts, and the class and ideological positions and commitments of interpreters. In short, liberation hermeneutics is about "creating a new person and a qualitatively different society,"[405] as it challenges systemic and structural inequalities while emphasizing that equality and justice are attainable in this life.[406]

---

[404] Ibid. p. 114

[405] R.S. Sugitharajah, **Postcolonial Criticism and Biblical Interpretation** (New York: Oxford University Press, 2002), p. 65

[406] Taken from class notes on lecture delivered by R.S. Sugitharajah on 'Liberal and Liberation Hermeneutics', February 23, 2005

This characterization of liberation hermeneutics emphasizes that the interpretations of Philemon were carried out from a specific perspective. However, Jones Jr. is an African American, and both Clarice J. Martin and Sabine Bieberstein are feminist theologians, suggesting that their interpretations of Philemon arose from their unique viewpoints and specific experiences of oppression and domination. Consequently, the plight of Onesimus, the conflicts and injustices within the system, and the urgent need to transform that social order received considerable attention. Assumptions and hermeneutical skepticism influenced their interpretations of Philemon, creating a link between social location and interpretation.

As a result, Martin and Biebersstein's resistant "readings" stemmed from their experiences of marginality and oppression, along with their vision and hope for an alternative social order based on their identification of the oppressive ruling class interests and power embedded in the structure of the social system.

Postcolonial Type

Postcolonial is a contentious term and theory borrowed from literary studies and utilized in various ways.[407] The primary advocate of postcolonial usage within the realm of biblical studies is R.S. Sugirtharajah.[408] As a critical discourse, Sugirtharajah applies postcolonial theory to uncover suppressed voices, interrogate and expose the political and ideological agendas of interpreters, and reveal imperial assumptions

---

[407] See Bill Ashcroft, Gareth Griffiths, Helen Tiffin, **The Postcolonial Studies Reader** (New York: Routledge, 1995)

[408] See R.S. Sugirtharajah, **The Bible and The Third World: Precolonial, Colonial and Postcolonial Encounters** (Cambridge: Cambridge University Press, 2001); **Postcolonial Criticism and Biblical Interpretation** (Oxford: Oxford University Press, 2002); **Postcolonial Reconfigurations: An Alternative Way of Reading the Bible and Doing Theology** (London: SCM Press, 2003)

and intentions within biblical texts and their interpretations. Therefore, the postcolonial perspective centers on the biblical text, its interpretation, and the interpreter. In the context of this study, I apply postcolonial criticism to biblical studies to illustrate the suppression of Onesimus's voice, reexamine Philemon from the viewpoint of Onesimus, the dominated 'other,' and expose the consequences of imperial ideology and oppressive intentions present in the letter.

I will examine the interpretations of Philemon by Valentina Alexander, a female Caribbean theologian in the Diaspora; Renita J. Weems, a feminist African American theologian; and Burchell Taylor, a male Caribbean theologian.

Rereading Philemon from the Perspective of the Oppressed

Alexander places herself in the position of Onesimus and writes a letter to Philemon. She addresses Philemon not as a master but as a brother who no longer exists under oppressive material conditions, stating, "not because you are my master, but because you are my brother." Furthermore, she writes to explain, rather than beg for forgiveness, regarding her subversive act of running away, and to express her disagreement with Paul's plea for reconciliation between herself and Philemon: "I must write to you now to contest Paul's request, not that you should welcome me as a brother, but that you should still expect me to be your slave."[409] Alexander's focus is on the causes of domination and exploitation, as well as hermeneutical suspicion: why do master and slave relationships still exist? Why are the oppressed subjected to oppression? Thus, her focus is on the systems, structures, and ideologies that allow slavery to persist.

Consequently, for Alexander, the issue of brotherhood is closely tied to matters of partnership and participation. There can be no true brotherhood without involvement and collaboration. That's what the

---

[409] Ibid. p. 61

'hood'—the home of brothers—is all about. Thus, the fundamental division within the social structure is not between master and slave, but between master and brother. The antithesis or opposite of master is not slave, but brother. For Alexander, reconciliation is neither the actual issue nor the solution. Reconciliation does not eliminate the dominating and oppressive material conditions of slavery. In this context, Alexander presents three reasons for Onesimus's decision to run away.

First, Alexander suggests that she was weary of oppression. "When I ran away from you all those weeks ago, I felt fatigued, embittered, and resentful."[410] Weariness can be a revolutionary impetus. Rosa Parks, a civil rights activist in the United States, also grew weary of the injustices of racism, which led her to refuse to move to the back of the bus.

Secondly, Alexander asserts that human beings are not property but are endowed with the inalienable right to self-determination and self-definition. He stated, "No matter how much kindness you showed me, something in my heart continually reaffirmed that it was not right for me to belong to you and that I do not belong to myself."[411] There is no such thing as a free slave.

Third, Alexander argues that reconciliation and bondage are unsustainable.

Thus, Alexander posits,

> "...in his great love, Christ has removed my chains and set me free...I have something greater than ever belonging to myself now that he has made me his child and I belong to him...what an affront that would be to the Almighty God that should set me free and you should chose to enslave me again...Christ has come to set us free from our chains...we cannot let ourselves be

---

[410] Ibid. p. 61
[411] Ibid. p. 62

chained again, neither our spirits, nor our bodies, nor our minds....".[412]

In other words, while conversion does not separate the converted from their bodies, the freedom experienced in Christ is not one-dimensional. It is holistic, encompassing the social, economic, political, and spiritual aspects of life.

Exposing Oppressive Systems and Practices

Weems rereads Philemon within her interpretive community as an African American woman. In doing so, she raises three points. First, she identifies the central tension or site of struggle in the text/letter: a religious leader, Paul, is sending a slave back to a slaveholding Christian friend.[413] Here, Weems juxtaposes the class interests of Philemon and the destiny of Onesimus, highlighting Paul's complicity in safeguarding "the reputation of the budding church movement from being seen as a threat to the social and economic fabric of the Roman Empire."[414] In this way, Weems identifies the socio-ideological and theological interests at play in Philemon and suggests that social inequality leads to social conflict.

Second, Weems does not see Onesimus as a runaway, a fugitive from justice. On the contrary, Weems contends that Onesimus has escaped "because he did not want to remain a slave, even the slave of a Christian.[415] As a result of fleeing his harsh and oppressive situation, Onesimus, "despite his conversion or perhaps because of it, is not returning to his slave master willingly."[416] Escape represents the voice of the oppressed—an act of self-determination and self-definition.

---

[412] Ibid. p. 62
[413] Weems, **Reading Her Way Through the Struggle**, p. 43
[414] Ibid. p. 43
[415] Ibid. p. 43
[416] Ibid. p. 43

Third, Weems regards Paul's social location as privileged. For Weems, Paul's designation as a "Hebrew among Hebrews" suggests that his education and identity as a Benjaminite are not simply products of his birthright. As a Roman citizen, Paul enjoyed social and political advantages (Acts 23:22-29).[417] Therefore, Weems argues that Onesimus, who did not share these privileges, recognized his humanity and religiosity as separate from Paul's and would not willingly return to an oppressive environment.

Silence Speaks

Taylor also views Onesimus as someone who takes his liberation into his own hands. Although Onesimus lacks a voice in the text, Taylor believes that verses 10-13, 16, and 21 present a different perspective.[418] By running away, Onesimus engages in the most substantial form of protest or action he could undertake within the existing social context. In other words, Onesimus's escape speaks louder than words. Taylor suggests that Onesimus.

> "was simply not accepting slavery as something to which he must be subjected. He did not think that he was fated to be a slave by virtue of his class or any other feature of his humanity. This act of running away was protest action. It was an act of defiance and rebellion of the human spirit against oppression and indignity".[419]

As such, Taylor declared, "oppression in any form cannot be benevolent and cannot be reformed to make it truly acceptable to

---

[417] Ibid. p. 43
[418] Burchell Taylor, *"Onesimus: The Voiceless, Powerless Initiator of the Liberating Process"* in Howard Gregory, ed. **Caribbean Theology – Preparing for the Challenge Ahead** (Barbados: Cedar Press, 1995), p. 18
[419] Ibid. p. 20

the human spirit."[420] In this light, Taylor interprets v.16 as Onesimus' condition for return.[421] Here lies the voice of silence. As Taylor states, "Onesimus is the voiceless, powerless initiator of a liberating process."[422]

However, where Taylor sees protest, I see subversion. While protest can and does mushroom into large-scale civil action, it typically arises from individual or group grievances and seeks to address these wrongs. Not so with Onesimus's act of running away. Running away is akin to maroonage, as practiced by many slaves in the Caribbean during slavery. Specifically regarding Jamaica, maroonage consists of three phases.[423] First, there were individual acts of resistance, such as the Tacky revolt.[424] Furthermore, premeditated acts of revolt were not aimed at dismantling the system, but rather undertaken to gain personal or group freedom from institutional bondage while leaving the system intact.[425] Lastly, there were frontal attacks on the institution and system of oppression, striving for freedom for all, a new social justice system, and recognition of every individual as a moral, cultural, and social equal.[426] Onesimus's act of running away, though an individual act (one of many instances that was canonized), had broader social implications for social justice and equality, not just for the religio- household economy of the Philemon estate but for the Roman poleitia as a whole.

One implication is whether running away represents an oppositional stance or an act of resistance. According to Barton, there is a difference between opposition and resistance. Opposition contests the structures of

---

[420] Ibid. p. 20

[421] Ibid. p.

[422] Ibid. p.

[423] Don Robotham, *"The Development of Black Ethnicity in Jamaica"* in Rupert Lewis & Patrick Bryan **Garvey: His Work and Impact** (New Jersey: Africa World Press, Inc., 1994 2nd edition), p. 32

[424] Ibid. p. 32

[425] Ibid. p. 34 for example, The Maroon-British Treaty of 1739

[426] Ibid. p. 35 for example, the Sam Sharpe led rebellion in St. James in 1832

power from within the system,[427] while resistance takes a stand against the system from outside it.[428] Onesimus's absence from the household economy signified standing outside the system. A praxis of resistance is most effective for bringing about systemic change. Standing outside the system provides little to no opportunity for neutralization and control through absorption into power structures.

In Postcolonial hermeneutics, Philemon is reread through the unique perspectives of the interpreter—namely, an African American woman, a Black woman in the Diaspora, and an Afro-Caribbean male—allowing Onesimus, who is silenced in the letter of Philemon, to speak. This approach to rereading reconstructs biblical texts and grants agency to both the context of the interpreter and the material conditions from which these texts originated. Rereading or reconstructing is essential, particularly for the marginalized or subaltern, as biblical texts arise from various colonial contexts—Egyptian, Persian, Assyrian, Hellenistic, Roman—and were composed within royal courts.[429]

Rereading biblical texts this way uncovers that accounts of divine-human encounters, values, and struggles in these texts reflect the perspective of those in power. As Weems notes, "the voices embedded in the text of the Bible are primarily male, elitist, patriarchal, and legitimated.[430] Weems further warns against aligning oneself with the voice present in the text; by doing so, one may unwittingly align with the socio-ideological position and class interests of that voice.[431] Consequently, Sugirtharajah argues that before texts can be interpreted for their liberating potential or existential relevance, their ruling class

[427] Barton, **Afro-Creole**, p. 50
[428] Ibid. p. 50
[429] R.S. Sugirtharajah, **The Bible and the Third World – Precolonial, Colonial and Postcolonial Encounters** (Cambridge, U. k: Cambridge University Press, 2001), p. 251
[430] Weems, **Reading Her Way Through the Struggle**, p. 45
[431] Ibid. p. 42

interests, ideologies, stigmatization, and depictions in content, plot, and characterization require investigation.[432]

Exegetics and Eisegetics

What needs clarification now is where liberal, liberation, and postcolonial perspectives locate the site of struggle, as well as the socio-ideological and theological agendas at play in Philemon. The liberal perspective positions the site of struggle as occurring between individuals over who has executive power, rather than within the socio-economic and political system. Even in instances where socio-ideological interest and social practices are identified, particularly in the cases of Petersen and Barclay, the discussion often shifts back to the issue of authority.

The liberation perspective positions the site of struggle more within the context's systems, structures, and practices rather than in the biblical text itself. Here, the text is viewed as a production—a message to be received, understood, and applied—or as a medium to be analyzed. In other words, emphasis is placed on its contextual relevance. However, there is a danger in this approach. A contextual perspective implies that the text is solely ideological in its application.[433] On the contrary, since some texts were composed in royal courts, they possess socio-ideological roots, even if tied to oppressive practices.

From a postcolonial perspective, a socio-ideological and theological agenda always exists within biblical texts and their interpretations. Viewing the Bible as a product establishes the site of struggle within the text's economic, social, ideological, and cultural dimensions. However, postcolonialism seeks to explore how the socio- ideological and theological agenda of biblical texts is re-inscribed in stigmatization

---

[432] Sugirtharajah, **The Bible and the Third World**, p. 251

[433] Itumeleng J. Mosala, *"Biblical Hermeneutics and Black Theology in South Africa, The Use of the Bible"* in Gottwald & Horsley, **The Bible and Liberation**, p. 56

and portrayals in narratives and characterization.[434] It is essential to track what is stated in the biblical text and what is conveyed about the biblical text itself.

To track what is said in and about the biblical text, the interpreter must follow the lines of inquiry adopted by Alexander, Weems, and Taylor, who explored *whose perspective* the text was written from. What aspects of the text are oppressive? Where does oppression manifest within the text? If one approaches the text with an interpretive stance focused on the specificities and nuances of one's context, it is crucial to exercise great care to avoid aligning with the dominant voices and ruling- class ideas embedded in the text, given that biblical texts have their ideological roots in oppressive practices and the interests of the ruling class.

Conclusion

The previous analysis has uncovered various hermeneutical insights from both the slavery era and the modern period.

From the era of slavery:

- When a person's social position within the structure is privileged, they are less likely to question the causes of structural oppression.
- When agency is assigned to the material conditions that produced biblical texts, it raises critical awareness.
- If the reading strategy is not shaped by the unique aspects of one's context, there is neither questioning nor challenging of the status quo.
- When approaching biblical texts with a strong commitment to social justice and practice, both the reading strategy and the

---

[434] Sugirtharajah, **The Bible and the Third World** p. 252

material conditions that produced these texts hold authority and agency.

- When the materiality of biblical texts does not shape interpretation, a disconnect arises between faith and practice.

From the contemporary era:

- More than social location is needed to create a praxis of resistance.
- It is through a practice of resistance and subversion by the oppressed that dominating systems and structures are dismantled or altered.
- Presupposition and hermeneutical suspicion create a connection between social location and interpretation.
- Rereading biblical texts through the lens of one's context leads to a reconstruction of those texts.

Overall, the previous examination of how historical phenomena have been interpreted shows that a reading strategy based on the specificities and nuances of one's context, grounded in a genuine commitment to social justice and granting agency to both the materiality of biblical texts and the interpreter's context, leads to resistance. If a biblical hermeneutic is not developed that empowers the materiality of biblical texts and the context of interpreters, and if biblical texts are interpreted through the specificities and nuances of one's context while maintaining a stance of genuine social engagement, the unintended issue of contextualization in Caribbean biblical hermeneutical practice will likely continue.

What I propose, which meets the requirements of reading biblical texts through the particularities and peculiarities of the Caribbean context and grants agency to both materiality and praxis, is a biblical resistant hermeneutic situated within a Caribbean context. These resistant hermeneutic aims to eliminate the unintentional error of contextualization in Caribbean biblical hermeneutical practice and empower Caribbean hermeneuts to interpret the Bible through the lens of their own experiences with domination, exploitation, survival, and the struggle for sovereignty.

PART THREE

Proposal for and Implications of a Resistant Biblical Hermeneutic within the Caribbean

CHAPTER 5

TOWARDS A RESISTANT BIBLICAL HERMENEUTIC WITHIN A CARIBBEAN CONTEXT

Introduction

Struggles for survival and sovereignty have characterized, and continue to describe the existence of Caribbean peoples, even after many Caribbean islands gained political independence. Since the early days of colonialism in the fifteenth century, Europeans decimated the indigenous population. Africans, taken against their will, and later Asians were brought from their homelands to populate the islands for labor exploitation. Those who were brought over were compelled to resist, rebel, and subvert. Consequently, the masters of these individuals had to exert violent control and civilize their subjects to fulfill their exploitative aims. With long-lasting effects, this oppressive and 'civilizing' endeavor by the 'masters' led to structures of spirituality and theologies grounded in an alien culture and experience that was transported but not transposed, both suffering from a profound sense of unreality and disconnection.[435] It is this unreality and disconnection from these structures of spirituality and theologies that I encountered

---

[435] Hamid, **Troubling of The Waters**, pp. 6–8

in the weekly worship experience at my village chapel, and which continue to demand resistance and transformation.

In exploiting, dominating, and 'civilizing' circumstances, resistance becomes the way of life for those who struggle for self-definition and self-determination. Admittedly, not everyone who is culturally and spiritually enslaved by imposed foreign structures and systems desires to resist and undermine these foreign patterns. Many formerly colonized peoples lived in conditions dominated and exploited by foreign powers and cultural imperialism. In such situations of domination and exploitation, a resistant hermeneutic, with the Bible as a cultural weapon, offers Caribbean peoples a means to speak back in their own voice and confront any new order of colonialism. In this chapter, I will perform three tasks. First, I will formulate a biblical resistant hermeneutic titled *"Towards a Resistant Biblical Hermeneutic within a Caribbean Context."* My use of "towards" in the title for the resistant biblical hermeneutic signifies that it is neither the final nor the definitive reading strategy in biblical hermeneutics within a Caribbean context. Instead, the concept of "towards" highlights the dynamic and ongoing development of biblical interpretation in the Caribbean. Second, I will present a resistant reading of Philemon; and third, I will explore possible inferences from the resistant biblical reading strategy.

Component Parts of a Resistant Biblical Hermeneutic

There are five dimensions to this resistant biblical hermeneutic: cultural literacy consciousness, the praxis of resistance, culture as a "text," text as a cultural construction, and context. Altogether, these five dimensions highlight the socially constructed nature of biblical texts and their interpretations. These biblical resistant hermeneutic aims to raise an alternative consciousness and demonstrate how oppressive systems and practices can be challenged and exposed, so that such systems and practices can be reconfigured for socio-economic transformation or liberation.

The discussion of these five dimensions will flow toward the arrows. Each part is not separate and distinct from the others; they overlap and interact, only being separated for discussion purposes.

Diagram 5:1
A biblical resistant hermeneutic reading strategy

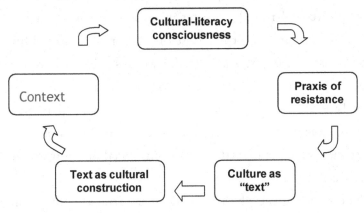

Cultural-literacy consciousness

Cultural literacy consciousness is not merely knowledge of the vernacular, dance, music, and rhythms of a people—meaning the forms or media of expression of a culture—but rather the cultural meanings and experiences associated with these forms and media. In other words, it encompasses how they influence the cost of living; educate, instruct, and raise awareness; and inspire challenges to or resistance against unjust systems. Concerns about forms and media are secondary issues. The main concern is what should be celebrated, along with how and why these celebrations are experienced.[436] Thus, this issue is not about indigenization or cultural renewal but about cultural meaning or the

---

[436] Idris Hamid, ed., **Troubling of The Waters** (San Fernando: Rahaman Printery Ltd., 1973), p. 161

experience of culture itself, as opposed to just a cultural experience (which is often tied to tourism).

Cultural literacy consciousness essentially refers to understanding ourselves as Caribbean people—who we are and who we can become, as well as why we are under- resourced and underdeveloped. It encompasses "how to be," geography, history, and the construction of a new way of being. It involves assessing and understanding our place and socio-geographic space in the world.[437] Garfield Sobers, the world's greatest all-round cricketer, played cricket in racist Rhodesia in 1970, exhibiting little or no consciousness or awareness of his place, unlike Vivian Richards, arguably the world's greatest batsman, who refused to play in apartheid South Africa in the 1980s for millions of dollars. In evaluating the actions of both cricketers, Hilary Beckles, a Caribbean social historian, suggests that Sobers "was not attuned to the historical and ideological nature of his social location within West Indies cricket."[438]

Understanding the physical world in its true size and proportion allows people to recognize their place (country). On world maps, many Caribbean countries appear as mere dots, and many others remain unidentified. Failing to perceive ourselves as having a place in the world can lead to a diminished sense of self and a lack of understanding of our history, causing us to be unaware of who we are today. Therefore, cultural literacy consciousness represents a movement toward our roots – a desire to establish identity, an awareness of how the region was populated, and an understanding of the historical, political, and economic processes at work in the region.[439]

---

[437] David I. Mitchell, ed., *With Eyes Wide Open – A Collection of Papers by Caribbean Scholars on Caribbean Christian Concern* (Barbados: CADEC, 1973), p. 107
[438] Hilary Beckles *"The Political Ideology of West Indies Cricket Culture"* in Hilary Beckles and Brian Stoddart eds., *Liberation Cricket, West Indies Cricket Culture* (Manchester & New York: Manchester University Press, 1995), p. 156
[439] Ibid. p. 107

What I'm acknowledging here is that the socio-geographic landscape of Caribbean readers of biblical texts is inherently plural and represents a highly contested and complex area of social existence. Cultural literacy encompasses the awareness of historical differences, diverse cultural sensibilities, various ethnicities, and the different religions of Caribbean peoples. Despite differences in ethnicity, class, gender, and religion, there are divided interests.

For instance, within the socio-geographic space of any interpretive faith community in the Caribbean, there will be members in marginalized subject positions[440] alongside those in dominant subject positions.[441] In other words, this community could include decision-makers, the unemployed, abused women, underpaid factory workers, non-nationals, struggling banana farmers, and individuals of African, Chinese, or Indian descent, among others, all at one time. Those in marginalized subject positions, experiencing systemic injustices, may view the system as oppressive, structured, and controlled to maintain power and privilege. Among those in dominant subject positions, there are two groups: those benefiting from the system and those who[442] are disadvantaged. Naturally, those who benefit will want the system to endure to preserve their power and privilege, while those adversely affected by the system will challenge and critique its practices, advocating for a more equitable social order.

The problem is that both the benefactors and the disadvantaged are part of the same village community, play on the same local sports team, shop at the same community supermarket, share membership in the same faith community, and interpret the same religious texts. What is needed here is not just cultural literacy that understands that one plus one does not necessarily equal eleven, or even that ten minus one equal

---

[440] I take 'subject positions' to mean identities. See Mary Ann Tolbert, *"Reading For Liberation"* in Fernando & Tolbert, **Reading From This Place,** p. 266.

[441] Ibid. p. 266

[442] Ibid. p. 266

nine. Instead, it is the awareness gained from recognizing the dominant and exploitative influences and agendas in the socio-geographic space.

Furthermore, if we only understand our class position, marginalized identity, and status, we know very little. The nature of people's indignities becomes clear when we comprehend the cultural significance of their class position, marginalized identity, and status—that is, why individuals struggle to find employment, face exclusion, have trouble paying bills, and endure discrimination. Indignities stem from people's class position, marginalized identity, and status. The indignities experienced connect a person's condition and consciousness, which can lead to resistance.

For example, when Douglass's slave master prevented his mistress from teaching him to read, claiming it would make him "unfit to be a slave," Douglass gained the understanding that "the pathway from slavery to freedom" lay in[443] literacy. Similarly, Roper argues that while Pentecostalism and Evangelicalism are fundamentally the people's church, they serve the poor without truly advocating for their interests, as they do not address the core issues of alienation and powerlessness.[444] Another instance involves a well-known rural Hindu priest from Guyana who, during a cricket match between the West Indies and India in 1953, "unleashed a stream of popular Hindu curse words, punctuated the air with his fists, unwrapped his sacred turban, turned to the crowd, and waved it triumphantly" because Ramchand, an Indian bowler, dismissed Pairaudeau, a white Guyanese batsman from Georgetown representing the West Indies.[445] Through this action, he connected with Indians despite his Guyanese nationality. His understanding and public display of emotion went beyond a mere acknowledgment of African and

[443] Frederick Douglass, *Narrative of the Life of Frederick Douglass* (Boston: Bedford/St. Martin's, 1993), pp. 40-41
[444] Roper, *The Impact of Evangelicalism and Fundamentalism*, p. 43
[445] C. Shiwcharan, *"The Tiger of Port Mourant – R.B. Kanhai"* in F. Birbalsingh & C. Shiwcharan, eds. *Indo-West Indian Cricketers* (London: Hansib Publishing Ltd., 1988), p. 54

Indian heritage; rather, it reflected a cultural literacy that recognizes the roots of oppression and exploitation.

To ground the elements of cultural literacy consciousness mentioned above— specifically, experienced indignities, the raising of awareness, and resistance—I would like to share excerpts from the stories of Malcolm "Jai" Kernahan and Terrence Thornhill, both from Trinidad, who became involved in resistance movements during the political upsurge of the 1970s, as shared with Brian Meeks,[446] a Jamaican political scientist.

Extract 1

Experienced indignities

Brian Meeks:	Tell me a little bit about yourself. Where are you from? How would you describe yourself?
Malcolm "Jai" Kernahan	Well, my father was an oil field worker, production department. We used to live in company quarters...near to Fyzabad. In 1953 when I was about four or five years old, he got blind and the company throw we out the house. Well, from that we become dirt poor, you know, because he had spent some money to buy some land and then he come and got blind. While working, some steel thing damage the eye and he lost his sight. He couldn't work again; they didn't need his service, so they told him to leave the house in a month's time. Well, we just become poor after that, you know. He went to one and two Obeah man to try and get back his sight – you the masses.

---

[446] Brian Meeks, *Narratives of Resistance – Jamaica, Trinidad, The Caribbean* (Jamaica: University of the West Indies Press, 2000), pp. 62-7

BM:	How many of you were in the family?
MJK:	three boys. Yeah, well, then we started to live by family. We had to go by uncle and live a little time. But one of the agreements we had come to with the oil company is that when we reach of age, the children would get work in the oil field. So we all knew that when we were of age we would get work in the oil field. But my father was a real militant oil field worker. I remember when I was a little fella they used to tell me how they used to beat people who used to break strike – scabs, no? – So I never got work in the oil field.

Malcolm formed his identity from the indignities and discrimination his father suffered at the hands of the social system. He linked his family's poverty to the social system.

Extract 2

Consolidating consciousness

BM:	So what did they tell you?
MJK:	Well, they just push me around, you know? "come back so and so,…come back so and so…". I get to hate the oil company and the white people and t'ing in them times, you know, so it was easy for me to fall into the Black Power Movement when that time came around. In 1967…they had a consciousness movement was building a lot of progressive literature started to find its way in Trinidad. Eldridge Cleaver's *Soul on Ice,* Walter Rodney's *Groundings With My Brothers,* and I started to read books. As a matter of fact, I have been in the struggle since '67.
BM:	What happened in '67?

182

MJK: Well, I always used to look at the Oil Field Workers' Trade Union as kind of militant organization. I admired George Weeks. Well, they had a fella by the name of Clive...who went to Cuba and he came back and said, "the only solution was armed revolution". I found that concept was nice and romantic and I get to like it, you know?...an then '69 came around and St. James had an organisation named WOLF – Western United Liberation Front – that was some soldiers...during this time too a dance troupe...came from Uganda and they had their hair in Afro with a part, and from that everyone used to wear dashikis and part of their hair in a certain style. And a kind of consciousness started to come along, a kind a blackness; and then we came and got involved with NJAC, but I was never a member of NJAC.

BM: Why?

MJK: I thought they were middle class. Talking about the dashikis and sandal...culturally, I couldn't deal with them.....As far as the "black man" was concerned, NJAC was middle class. Them fellas wasn't ready. They were only talking...But we still supported the movement. We marched with them, you know? And then from 1969-1970 we started to get *Peking Review* on the block and Errol Balfour he come around and started to talk about Marxism, and suddenly we started to see the struggle in terms of class.....

Malcolm's level of awareness was raised when he was unable to find employment and through his commitment and involvement in social justice movements and causes.

Extract 3

<u>*Resistance*</u>

BM: I want to come back to what was going on in your mind. That transition is a serious one, to decide to take up arms and fight the government. How easy was that decision?

MJK: ….My life was hard, real tough. So I say that I would rather die than live under the system. I don't want to live under the system anymore. Because you getting turn back everywhere you go to look for jobs; your name not recognised; you is nobody; you ain't living nowhere; you poor. If death come, no big thing…. To be honest, based on the vibes we had taken at that time, we couldn't do anything else. I believe that if I hadn't picked up a gun and gone to armed struggle I would be a mad or a vagrant. I couldn't fit into nothing in the society…. I think that the 1970 Revolution saved me.

For Malcolm, armed struggle against an unjust social system was 'salvation.' In traditional Christian understanding, salvation refers to the forgiveness of a wrong committed against another. For Malcolm, 'salvation' is not about forgiving those who have sinned. Instead, it involves personal commitment and active participation in the social struggle for justice to deliver those who have been wronged.

Extract 4

Social location

Brian Meeks:	Tell me a little bit about yourself?
Terrence Thornhill:	I was born July 27, 1949 in Glencoe. It was a residential area in a middle class setting... My father was one of the first black men to get degrees at university in England along with Eric Williams. His was in English at Cambridge. Both parents were teachers. My father was a head teacher and my mother was a common-entrance teacher. It was a middle class family. As far as I can remember, we always had a car; the house had hot and cold water. I went to Tranquillity Primary School and later to Queen's Royal College.

Extract 5

Consolidating consciousness

BM:	How did you become involved with the 'movement'?
TT:	I did track and field in school and went to the US in 1969 on a track scholarship to study at the Catholic University in Washington, DC. While there, seeing how black people were treated, I went through some changes in my life...then I started to see the sufferings of black people and identified with them. We started to talk about the Lord, Jesus Christ, how he was real and what they did to him; he went about trying to help and the suffering he experienced. And I was able to link His suffering to that of black people and see where the system always oppresses those who are good. That was November 23, 1970 and that day

it came to me very strongly that my life wouldn't be just to continue in school like this, but to search for that truth which Jesus brought to mankind and help somebody in the way of life....

Unlike Malcolm, Terrence views his identity as shaped by a privileged social position. However, despite his middle-class advantages, he was neither blind nor insensitive to the indignities faced by the oppressed.

Extract 6

Resistance

By May 1971, my teachers were asking me if I was still in their class....When I returned to Trinidad in June 1971, it was under a state of emergence. Guy Harewood was my good friend from primary school days... in those days, we had Mao's *Little Red Book*. One of his sayings was that "the political man is the real man". So as far as Guy and a few others were concerned, NJAC was only talking, theorising, but not willing to put their life on the line for the cause in the way that we thought it should be, in terms of guerrilla warfare. So Guy and them were branching off from NJAC, and just a little group talking among themselves. So I came back and met that. I started to go around with them. I had access to cars and so I used to go and purchase weapons with them, because the cars I had would be 'cool'. So I got involved, though I used to tell them, this set of revolutionary thing is not me, because I am for Jesus, which is peace. But then I listened to them, noted their sincerity and I was on a search for truth also. And there were slogans on the walls, like "armed revolution is the only solution" and "the voice of the people is the voice of God", and it was slowly coming to me that armed revolution is the way. I went back to the Bible because my whole experience was Bible oriented and every time I opened it I would read where Moses saw the Egyptians advantaging the Hebrews and he took a sword and killed an Egyptian. So my interpretation was that maybe we should take up the gun, because the people are being advantaged...

Although Terrence had conflicting identities and benefited from middle-class privileges, he still engaged in the fight for social justice because it was not about the privileges he possessed. Instead, it was about how the system disenfranchises people. We see in these narratives that for both Malcolm and Terrence, it wasn't merely their class positions and marginalized identities that drove them to join resistance movements. Rather, it was the cultural significance of the indignity of being pushed around to find employment—being unemployed, penniless, and socially dead—and their awareness of linking these aspects of their social existence to elements of the biblical agenda and practice that served as the impetus and epistemological lens for their involvement in resistance movements.

In sum, cultural literacy consciousness deals with causal particularities rather than universalities. It is not about the giveness of one's social location but what causes the social circumstances of that social location. In other words, it seeks responses to such questions as: What are the axes of power and privilege? How does causality run? How does my location shape me, and how can I shape my location? Cultural literacy consciousness takes marginality as a site of radical possibility, a space of resistance and refusal[447] as it begins by examining social reality from an external perspective. Thus, cultural literacy consciousness avoids being manipulated by the socio- ideological agendas of others and is safeguarded from unreality and disconnection.

The cultural significance of the sociality of existence within our socio- geographic space must influence Caribbean biblical hermeneutical practice, even if it is not necessarily the initial step in biblical interpretation. It is this cultural significance that offers the epistemological lens — our method of understanding biblical texts — which is crucial for interpreting these texts from the particularity and uniqueness of one's social location. Those from whom I gathered empirical evidence could not analyze Philemon without being aware of their history of slavery. Moreover, it provides the foundation and motivation, fostering an alternative consciousness for active commitment and participation in social struggle, inevitably leading to challenging and resisting oppressive systems and practices.

Praxis of resistance

The praxis of resistance involves acting as subjects for freedom, social equality, and just social relations, rather than being acted upon as objects in oppressive and unjust ways. In other words, a praxis of resistance is a strategy for social transformation in which biblical texts are read within the context of struggle and with a commitment to social justice. By praxis of resistance, I mean a subjective commitment, taking sides in the "action" and supporting those who fight against oppression for social justice.

The praxis of resistance does not refer to the Anansi-style praxis of resistance found in Caribbean folklore, which is akin to hideology:

---

[447] bell hooks *"marginality as a site of resistance"* in Russell Ferguson, Martha Givens et al **Out There: Marginalisation and Contemporary Culture** (New York: The MIT Press, 1990), pp. 341-43

"preserving an inner freedom beneath the mask of compliance."[448] In Caribbean folklore, Anansi represents a mode of resistance and embodies the personality of the oppressed. Anansi survives by his wits and cunning, defeats animals and humans in contests of intelligence, and generally triumphs; he always earns the praise of those without power, even in defeat, along with the approbation of the powerful.[449]

Rawick argues that Anansi's exploits empower the oppressed—an empowerment that those in control of the decision-making process would neither grant nor facilitate.[450] In this context, Genovese views Anansi as both a victim and a symbol of spiritual resistance, who acknowledges the limits of what is politically possible.[451] Through Anansi, the oppressed can assert their humanity and overcome their mental slavery, which reflects their objective circumstances.[452] Thus, for Rawick, Anansi, as an oppressed figure, engages in an individualistic struggle—working in concrete ways "on behalf of himself"—not to revolutionize oppressive systems, but rather "to change his circumstances and thereby gain enough footing to rebel."[453]

However, Barton argues that although Anansi outsmarted Massa and was never caught, even after all his exploits and victories, the system and structure that upheld Massa's power and privilege remained firmly in place.[454] While the system was weakened and structures laid bare, Anansi ultimately served to reinforce the existing order. His actions,

---

[448] Richard D.E. Barton, **Afro-Creole, Power, Opposition and Play in the Caribbean** (Ithaca & London: Cornell University Press, 1997), p. 49

[449] Martha Beckwith, **Jamaica Anansi Stories** (New York: American Folk-lore Society, 1924), pp. xi-xii

[450] George P. Rawick, **From Sundown to Sunup, The Making of the Black Community** (Westport, Connecticut: Greenwood Publishing Company, 1972), p. 100

[451] Eugene D. Genovese, **Roll Jordan Roll, The World the Slaves Made** (New York: Vintage Books, 1976), p. 254

[452] Rawick, **From Sundown to Sunup**, p. 100

[453] Ibid. p. 100

[454] 20 Barton, **Afro-Creole**, p. 62

being individualistic rather than collective, meant that Anansi was merely a rebel, not a revolutionary.[455]

In essence, Anansi opposed the system but did not resist it outright. He remained within the system while employing strategic moves. Anansi never stepped outside the system to attempt to transform it. What the Anansi-style praxis of resistance illustrates is that, despite opposition, the foundational structures of the system, though challenged, remain unchanged. In other words, the praxis of resistance fundamentally differs from psychosocial resistance because the goal of resistance is to alter the system and the norms of these structures.

The praxis of resistance does not imply analyzing the human situation from which existential questions of faith arise, nor does it consider how symbols of the Christian message—such as the Cross, Holy Spirit, Resurrection, and Sacrament—are utilized to address these concerns. Examining the human situation by posing existential questions of faith and employing symbols from the Christian message is essentially contextualizing that message. This contextualization can become a private endeavor, conducted safely from the confines of the study, office, manse, or rectory, or during weekly Bible study in a church building—often ignoring socio-economic and political issues, leading to discussions confined to ideas, private existential matters, or theodicy. Through contextualization, we interpret the world. The praxis of resistance I refer to represents a concrete commitment to strive for social transformation, aiming to reshape unjust social systems and practices while expressing and interpreting faith in God through this tangible effort.

Furthermore, I do not mean "to be where the action is." On the contrary, the practice of resistance is a practical response to the "action" and to the conditions of life. "To be where the action is" may not necessarily stem from an understanding of the cultural meaning of social

---

[455] Ibid. p. 62

existence, derived from any clear ideological stance or commitment, nor from an analysis that oppression is caused by the social system. One participates in the "action" to liberate the oppressed and challenge the oppressive social order. "To be part of the action" must emerge from social strategy, not personal agendas.

Furthermore, my interviewees, or for that matter the weekly Sunday worshippers, the Caribbean pulpit, and the group that assembles weekly for Bible Study, could not have come to interpreting Philemon from a position of concrete commitment and involvement in social struggle for justice and spiritualised the understanding of freedom, slavery and reconciliation, shaving them of their materiality. Seldom do we gather around the Bible in the Caribbean out of praxis of resistance. When we do gather, we do so to mine biblical texts for their spiritual meaning and personal spiritual development, not intending to re-engage with the sociality of existence, to identify and resist oppressive systems and practices, and to denounce such practices as opposite to God's justice.

Culture as "Text"

Culture as "text" acknowledges that readers of biblical texts do not simply materialize from nowhere. Even if they did, they would "land" and "settle," if alive, in some socio-geographic space that has, or soon will develop its own history. Likewise, it recognizes that words function to create a "world" or version of reality. In biblical texts, both the text and the text-maker are not only communicating but also performing an action, generating a "world" that exists in rhetorical presentation.[456]

One observation of this study is that Caribbean biblical hermeneutical practice aims to understand the socio-historical contexts in which God is revealed. Furthermore, the study is developing a reading strategy

---

[456] Walter Brueggemann, *"That The World May be Redescribed"*, **Interpretation**, Vol. 56 No.
4 October 2002, p. 361

that connects the "readings" of social reality from both the authors of biblical texts and Caribbean readers. I argue that the influences and experiences of one's socio-geographic space serve as a legitimate "text", representing a version of social reality.

As a result, the "canon" of the socio-historical praxis of the people of God is not limited to the sixty-six books of the Bible. Although the biblical canon is closed, revelation continues in God's unfolding story within the socio-historical praxis of humanity. This unfolding narrative suggests that the reality illustrated by biblical writers is not the sole legitimate representation of social reality. The biblical perspective is merely *one window* through which to view the world, *one mirror* reflecting life and ourselves, and *one lens* that helps us see what might otherwise go unnoticed. In other words, culture as "text" perceives the Bible as not being *from* God but *about* God. It approaches the Bible not from a top-down viewpoint—God to humanity—but from the bottom up, focusing on human efforts to comprehend what they can about God.

What, then, are the influences and experiences, the socio-historical realities, that have shaped and continue to shape the Caribbean reader's understanding of biblical texts? What is the source of the influences and experiences that shape Caribbean peoples' perspectives on the world and biblical texts? What aspects of Caribbean social history provide insights for biblical interpretation? What influences and experiences reflect and impact the social lives of Caribbean people? How do Caribbean individuals come to understand themselves? What influences and experiences of Caribbean peoples make the practice of resistance effective?

This study argues that these influences and experiences are rooted in the socio-cultural history of Caribbean peoples. Thus, as noted earlier, Mulrain uses jumbie stories and laughter as an interpretive lens for examining biblical texts, allowing the texts to retain their mythology while subverting despair and inspiring confidence to face the future. Gossai employs the game of cricket to address the issue of identity in the Old Testament book of Ruth. Jagessar explores Caribbean literature to uncover how writers utilize biblical theological traditions and constructs to reinterpret their meanings considering the influences and experiences of Caribbean peoples. Middleton engages with Caribbean music to modernize and expand stories in biblical texts, incorporating Caribbean socio-historical realities. Spencer Miller analyzes popular Caribbean aphorisms to reveal power relations in biblical texts.

Let me also share an experience of a house group of about 15 to 20 people led by Father Leslie Lett, who frequently gathered for prayer and Bible study in an Anglican parish on the Caribbean island of St. Vincent.[457] This experience illustrates how culture is a "text" and how theology unfolds. The selected text for study was 2 Corinthians 4:7-16a. Earlier in the day, a peaceful demonstration had been disrupted by state violence, with tear gas being indiscriminately deployed throughout the city. Fr. Lett resisted the group's push for him to publicly denounce state terror during Sunday Mass until after the following conversation:

Ellisson:	"But Father, the Mass is the right place to speak out; people done start to lose jobs and who going to feed their children…we have to share our food with them so they can fight for justice, for in the Mass Jesus teach us how to share bread and the cup that all may have to eat and drink and nobody get weak and perish".
Thomas:	"And, too, Jesus teach us in the Mass how to struggle for justice and against oppression, for in Mass he teach us how to have our bodies broken and our blood shed, like what happen this afternoon; the Mass is about Jesus struggling with us".

---

[457] Fr. Leslie Lett, **Third World Theology, The Struggle for the Kingdom**, Jubilee Research Centre, 1986, pp. 7-8

Then we agreed that the tear gas was the incense and that Mass was celebrated in the city's streets that afternoon! The streets were the Sanctuary because wherever the people share, wherever their blood is shed and their bodies broken in the struggle for justice for the weak in an oppressed community, there is the "real presence" of Jesus; there is the Sanctuary, the privileged locale of access to God.

The discussion then centred on the church's Sanctuary:

Jane: "This means that we have to change up how we think about the church Mass – it's too holy-holy and don't help people to see what we are talking about here tonight".

Jane: "This means that we have to change up how we think about the church Mass – it's too holy-holy and don't help people to see what we are talking about here tonight".

Veronica: "I think that in the church Mass Jesus tries to make us learn how to discern him; the trouble is people only learn how to discern him in Bread and Wine, and they don't learn how to discern him in poor people, in beat-up people, in the people who are down-pressed. That is why St. Paul said if people don't discern the Lord's presence in the ordinary people in the community they eat and drink damnation, not salvation, in the Mass".

Winston: "In other words, we need both Sanctuaries and they can't be separated because in a way, they are one and the same".

Veronica: "Salvation and worship is about struggling for justice, like Jesus; no wonder he said not all who say 'Lord, Lord, will enter the Kingdom'. And the word that

comes out of the Lord's mouth that we must live
by is the word of poor people, small people – if we
listen to them we hear Jesus' word".[458]

In this experience, it was the "tear gas as incense," "streets as
sanctuary," and discerning Jesus in Bread and Wine, "in battered
people, poor people, and oppressed people," the people's experiences
and struggles, that became the primary "text" (a window, a mirror,
a lens) for interpreting 2 Corinthians 4:7-16a. What I am submitting
here is that socio-cultural analysis conditions, shapes, informs, and
influences biblical appropriation. Caribbean jumbie stories, laughter,
cricket, Caribbean literature, music, aphorisms, and the struggles of
Caribbean peoples for justice, self-definition, and self-determination
serve as legitimate windows, mirrors, and lenses—or "texts"—through
which to engage in biblical interpretation. Nevertheless, one must
remember the cultural significance of those socio-cultural influences
and experiences, the ideological stance and commitment of the reader,
and the socio-ideological agenda and theology present in biblical texts.
The cultural meaning of social existence, ideological commitment, and
the reader's stance, along with the socio-ideological and theological
agenda of biblical texts, come together to create a reading strategy that
leads to resistance against oppressive systems and practices. As Winston
expresses in the house-group conversation mentioned above, "we need
both Sanctuaries, and they can't be separated."

In summary, culture as "text" involves more than just various
readers employing different reading strategies. Rather, readers interpret
texts in diverse ways, influenced by the multiple social groupings they
both represent and belong to.[459] These interpretations are constructed
by positioned and interested readers, who read from different and

---

[458] Fr. Lett, **Third World Theology**, pp. 6-
[459] Segovia & Tolbert, **Reading From This Place**, pp., 28-31

complex social perspectives.[460] In this study, culture as "text" focuses on interpreting biblical texts through the lens of one's sociocultural context.

Moreover, the incident cited above emphasizes the elements of the biblical resistant hermeneutic I am advocating and highlights my critique of Caribbean biblical hermeneutical practice. It embodies a cultural literacy consciousness that perceives tear gas as incense, the streets as sanctuary, and the "real presence" of Jesus as experienced where blood is shed. Bodies are broken in the struggle for justice and against oppression. This perspective provides the epistemological lens through which to interpret 2 Corinthians 4:7-16a from the specifics of the context. Similarly, this understanding empowers both the materiality of the biblical texts and the context of interpreters, ensuring that the biblical text is approached from a position of praxis of resistance with a clear ideological stance and commitment. Additionally, it bridges the gap between faith and praxis, as the street is neither the opposite of sanctuary, nor is the sanctuary the opposite of the street. From this new understanding of body and blood, the Mass is no longer celebrated as unrelated to the sociality of existence.

In other words, the cultural significance of social existence offers a means of understanding biblical texts. It thus inspires a tangible commitment to and engagement in the fight for justice and against oppression. Furthermore, it enables resistance to oppressive systems and structures, granting agency to the materiality of biblical texts and the context of interpreters.

Text as Cultural Construction

The notion of text as cultural construction acknowledges that biblical texts were not composed in isolation, nor does a reader approach these texts in a void. The Bible originated within a specific socio-cultural

---

[460] Ibid

context and was crafted from a distinct perspective. Consequently, biblical texts represent "readings" of the social realities experienced by their authors. This indicates that the Bible is a "produced" text, a construction, and a reflection of a socio-historical practice. In this framework, the biblical text is decentered, as the emphasis shifts from the text itself to the creation of "worlds." As Catherine Hall articulates, it is "a focus on history as constructed, not given; on the imagined community as created, rather than simply existing; on identities brought into being through particular discursive work."[461]

The trouble is that those "worlds" are constructed by the ruling classes, who also authored biblical texts.[462] Therefore, the concern of biblical interpreters is whether and in what way a religious perspective finds expression in biblical texts or reflects the socio-economic relationships and conditions of a specific society. This concern impacts the notion of the "word of God." For what is referred to as the "word of God" may represent the conversion of ruling class interests that transcend social divisions. So, whose truth is conveyed in the Bible? The ruling class's or God's? Is the representation of God in the Bible, then, trustworthy? What, one might question, constitutes biblical truth?

Since biblical texts have their ideological roots in oppressive practices, written as they were in royal courts and thus dominated by ruling-class ideas, interests, and voices, the challenge of biblical hermeneutics is to identify those embedded ideas, interests, and voices within the biblical text. Weems explains that hermeneutics consists of two parts in the biblical interpretive process.[463] The first part is the reading process.[464] This involves an interaction between the text and the reader, striving to uncover the meaning of the biblical text. The text's socio-historical

---

[461] Catherine Hall, *Civilising Subjects* (Cambridge: Polity Press, 2002), p. 9

[462] Robert B. Coote & Mary P. Coote, *Power, Politics and the Making of the Bible, An Introduction* (Minneapolis: Fortress Press, 1990), pp. 4-11

[463] Weems, **Reading Her Way Through**, p. 36

[464] Ibid. p. 36

context and rhetorical features are analyzed alongside the reader's presuppositions, social location, and hermeneutical skepticism.

The second half of the biblical interpretive process focuses on the actual biblical text. Weems argues that it is essential to recognize the narrative voice of the text to prevent aligning oneself with the elitist, patriarchal interests and ideas that are embedded within it.[465]

Although Weems may have suggested that biblical interpretation consists of two interconnected halves, each half is not independent. Biblical hermeneutics is an ongoing process where one factor influences the next, and interpretation and meaning continuously evolve.

Overall, the movement of a biblical resistant hermeneutic presented in this chapter shifts **from** struggling against oppression to achieving liberation and social equality, as it envisions a new organizational structure free from exploitation and expropriation. While we have gained freedom as a people in the Caribbean, a cohesive community has yet to be[466] established. Thus, the issue of emancipation from socio- economic and political bondage is not merely theoretical; it is a tangible ontological dilemma of **"how to be,"** of existing in our socio-geographic space known as the Caribbean. Given the Caribbean's history of colonialism and neo-colonialism, "how to be" arises from experiences of pain, suffering, and underdevelopment.

Furthermore, my resistant reading strategy does not favor any specific Bible reading approach—behind the text, within the text, or in front of the text.[467] On the contrary, it utilizes all three strategies to place the text in real-life contexts. In front of the text, reading strategies involve an awareness of cultural literacy and a practice of resistance

[465] Ibid. p. 45

[466] Leonard Tim Hector, *"Ralph Gonsalves and the New Idea of a Caribbean Civilisation"* in **Outlet Newspaper**, March 9, 2001

[467] Gerald West, **The Academy of the Poor – Towards A Dialogical Reading of the Bible** (Sheffield: Sheffield Academic Press, 1999), pp. 124-142

as the text is engaged from the reader's ideological perspective and concrete commitments. It also seeks answers to these questions: Who is the reader? How does the reader live? And where does the reader live? On the text, reading strategies emphasize the literary world of the text in a dialogue with the reader's world. Behind the text, reading strategies examine the context from which the text originates or view the text as a cultural construction and culture as "text." The resistant biblical reading strategy fosters a new way of knowing, seeing, and being.

By employing all three Bible reading strategies, the biblical resistant hermeneutic connects the socio-ideological conditions of the text's production with the cultural meaning of social existence and the socio-ideological position and commitment of the reader. It also raises the following *interpretive questions*:

- **What is the 'place' of the reader?**

  What are the class, ideological position, and commitment of the reader? What is the reader's way of knowing the text? Why are things (political, economic, historical) the way they are?

- **What is the 'place' of the text?**

  What are the socio-historical, political, and economic circumstances that produced the text?

- **What is the text doing?**

  What class, ideological, gender, or power interests does the text serve or challenge? What form does opposition or conflict take between the groups involved in the biblical text? How does the text resolve any opposition or dispute that may be taking place in the text? What religious perspective or understanding of God is expressed in the text? Whose voice dominates or is silenced? Does the text take sides?

- **What does the reader do in response to the biblical text?**
  Should the reader oppose staying within the social system and using strategic manoeuvres to challenge it? Or should the reader resist standing outside the social system, denouncing it, and announcing an alternative social order? Or should the reader spiritualise the understanding of the biblical text by disregarding the socio-economic and political dimensions?

Below, I outline the resistant biblical hermeneutics by showing how it relates to the analytical reading strategies used in this study.

Table 5: 1

A biblical resistant hermeneutic reading scheme

Analytical reading strategies	Aspects of resistant biblical hermeneutic	Consequence
Infront of the text	- Praxis of resistance - Cultural-literacy consciousness - What is the 'place' of the reader?	- What should the reader do in response to the biblical text? :oppose, resist (separate, denounce, announce), spiritualise understanding of text
On the text	- Literary world of the text - What is the text doing?	
Behind the text	- Text as cultural construction - Culture as 'text' - What is the 'place' of the text?	- New ways of seeing, knowing and being.

Resistant Reading of Philemon

To integrate the discussion in this study, I engage in a resistant reading of Philemon that gives agency to both the materiality of the letter and the context of a Caribbean interpreter. I aim to address the gap I have identified in Caribbean biblical hermeneutical practice. Even if I exegete the letter first and establish the cultural meaning second, the materiality of both the text and context is still given agency. This process is not about the sequence of interpretation but about the agency assigned to the material conditions of both the biblical text and the interpreter's context.

I address all four interpretive questions within the biblical resistant hermeneutic.

What Is The 'Place' of the Reader?

First, I will read Philemon from the perspective of hospitality workers primarily in the Caribbean hotel industry. Thus, I will answer the question: *what is the 'place' of the reader?* In the Caribbean hotel industry, duties are generally performed on a shift basis. Pay tends to hover above the minimum wage level, and to ensure they have enough money to meet family and personal expenses and commitments, employees often work more than one shift, put in extended hours, or take on multiple jobs. This social reality of long hours with little pay or exploitation informs the epistemological perspective when reading Philemon. The question to consider is: what is the cultural significance of long hours of hard work with minimal compensation?

To begin with, it is exploitative. There is an inequality between wages and labor that favors the employer. Additionally, with low pay, hospitality workers and their families suffer diminished quality of life, as income influences the quality of education children receive, the housing families can afford, and the goods and services they can purchase. Moreover, both the exploitation and the decreased quality of life lead to the indignity of not being able to provide for families that experience a better quality of life.

Experiences of indignity result directly from the nature of relations to the means of production. In the Caribbean, with its history of a plantation economy and its current dependence on tourism, banking, government, and offshore banking as the basis of the economy today, the mode of production is capitalist. In this capitalist system, the forces of production include land, the seas, and skills (human resources). Within the socio-economic structure, hospitality workers do not participate in decision-making processes and are not part-owners of anything in any establishment within the industry. They are simply members of the working class. In other words, defining and determining the quality of life stems from production relations.

Essentially, what we have in this socio-economic structure is an establishment exercising its economic decisions (such as how many to employ, how much to pay, and how long and often they should work) within the context of a country's economy (including social security benefits, employment benefits, and tax structure), which is heavily influenced by the ideology of the ruling class and is subservient to foreign interests. Any contest or conflict among hospitality workers that leads to strike action is not limited to personal dynamics (between employer and employee) but also involves structural factors (including employer/employee relations and the broader socio-economic system). In other words, by striking, hospitality workers are not merely resisting the establishment's economics but are instead challenging the socio-economic framework of their industry.

Essentially, striking is praxis. In this sense, one acts as a subject for social transformation rather than being treated as an object, which would worsen one's exploitative working conditions.

Moreover, striking has various social implications, as it impacts not only a specific establishment but also the socio-economic framework of an industry and the foreign influences and interests connected to that sector. Striking represents an exercise of social power and the subtle politics of the exploited class. Through striking, individuals resist power by evading its grasp and limiting its material and symbolic claims.[468] More specifically, striking serves as the "elsewhere"[469] for the exploited class, a place from which to challenge and express aversion to domination. Additionally, striking embodies the "body politics" of the exploited class, signifying the act of physically removing oneself from exploitative working conditions, thereby gaining a significant amount of bargaining power. Essentially, "although the body is never free from the encroaching grasp of official power, it remains a site where power can be contested on nearly equal footing."[470] In the end, to strike is to reclaim one's dignity, protect one's (physical) body against the exploitative and abusive claims of an industry, and destabilize that industry without resorting to violent and direct confrontation.[471]

Through cultural literacy consciousness, I am creating an alternative understanding of what it means to work hard and long for little pay while being marginalized by the social system. From this perspective, one sees the roots of social injustice as the socio-economic structures, systems, and practices, not just a single establishment.

Equally important, I am examining the social aspects of existence in relation to matters of faith. "Body politics"—the abusive, extractive, and exploitative claims of the ruling class—are as socio-economic and political as they are theological. Such claims undermine God's purpose for creation, which is the well-being of humanity, or erode the Divine image in which humans are created. Challenging the vested interests

---

[468] Obika Gray *"Discovering the Social Power of the Poor"* in **Social and Economic Studies** 43:3 (1994), p. 184

[469] Barton, *Afro-Creole*, p. 50

[470] Obika Gray, **Discovering the Social Power**, p. 186

[471] Ibid.

and injustices of the ruling class fosters God's kingdom of righteousness and justice in the present.

What Is The 'Place' of the Text?

Second, regarding *'place'* in the letter to Philemon, I have already outlined this in detail in chapter three (pp. 117-147). To summarize, we discussed then that the economics of Philemon's household are integrated into the household economy structure of imperial Graeco-Rome. The socio-economic structure of imperial Graeco- Roman society comprises two classes: the ruling class and the dominated class. What complicates the issue in Philemon is that the household simultaneously serves as the house church, which highlights the tension between social inequality (in the household economy) and social equality (in the house church). As such, the household economy structure of imperial Graeco-Rome creates the socio-cultural environment from which the Philemon text emerged, with social inequality and social equality representing the socio-economic relations and circumstances through which religious faith finds expression in the text.

What Is The Text Doing?

Third, the letter centers on how to interpret Onesimus' (a slave in the household, a brother in the house church) act of running away and what Paul means by urging Philemon (the master of the household, a brother in the house church) to accept Onesimus "no longer as a slave but as a brother" (v. 16). In other words, the letter now seeks to answer the question: *what is the text doing?* As it stands, the letter calls for interpretation from Philemon's perspective, focusing on his graciousness in forgiving Onesimus for having the audacity to run away, or from Paul's viewpoint as mediator, highlighting his skills in negotiating reconciliation between the two opposing parties. Both perspectives emerge from a position of privilege. Without an epistemology that seriously considers Onesimus' marginalized position — which is given minimal mention in the letter and thus seems insignificant — interpretation will not arise from this standpoint. Yet, the letter is intertwined with both the vertical and horizontal material relationships between Philemon and Onesimus.

In the vertical position, that is, Philemon and Onesimus' relationship in the house church, the conflicting and exploitative relationship between the ruler and the ruled stands starkly exposed, with all its dominating practices, class injustices, and vested interests laid bare. On the horizontal plane, that is, Philemon and Onesimus' relationship in the household, the incompatible difference between master and brother within the household of faith cries out for redemption, revealing the urgent need to embody righteousness and justice in the household economy.

Consequently, from the perspective of hospitality workers, Onesimus's act of fleeing is viewed as anti-hegemonic, an "elsewhere" from which to express disapproval of the socio-economic structure he does not wish to be part of. Conversely, that "elsewhere" also reveals the nature of the alternative community he desires to inhabit: one where he has the right to self-definition and self-determination. Through his "body-politics," Onesimus may not have achieved social equality in the Roman Empire. However, in that imperial context, social equality is not defined by its feasibility; instead, it is about exposing an unjust social system and practices to slightly open the door to social justice.

What Does The Reader Do In Response to the Biblical Text?

Finally, after explaining the cultural implications of long hours of hard work for little pay and making an analogous and dialogical connection with Philemon, hospitality workers can re-engage with the social aspects of their existence— specifically, how readers respond to the biblical text. Instead of viewing the Bible merely as an account of the socio-historical practices of a specific time and group striving to be God's people, it becomes a tool in the fight against exploitation, advocating for dignity, improved quality of life, and authentic existence.

The hospitality workers do not resist the socio-economic system by going to work each day without advocating for better working conditions and fair wages. They resist in three ways. First, by refusing to work under exploitative conditions that are unbeneficial, non-participatory, and where they have no stake, the hospitality workers separate themselves from the socio-economic system; second, they denounce the socio-economic system as unjust after recognizing the cultural implication of hard work for little pay and linking that exploitation to biblical texts; or they might abandon the struggle for social justice out of fear of victimization or repression, or perhaps in favor of only praying about it; third, they announce an alternative vision of workers' participation in decision-making processes and having a stake in the benefits that come from continuing the fight to establish a just social order. While go-slow tactics (opposition) may also be considered a form of resistance, if the goal is to transform or create a new order of justice, then one must resist, not merely oppose. However, if there is victimization and repression, it indicates the formation of interest groups – on one side, the establishment and industry aiming to protect vested interests and privilege, and on the other, the hospitality workers striving to build a just social order – and the struggle continues.

Even so, readers face three options as they consciously choose to resist or change dominant and oppressive social structures. First, survival, or finding a way to accept injustices while maintaining one's sense of self; second, rebellion—continued subversive activities aimed at transforming the oppressive social system; and third, revolution, which involves the outright overthrow of the ruling oppressive system.[472]

---

[472] Stephen Duncombe, **Cultural Resistance Reader** (London, New York: Verso, 2002), pp. 7-8

Brothers or "Slaves" of Caribbean "Masters"

Two of the inferences to draw from the above are, one, that fundamental principles of justice, dignity, self-definition and self-determination do not change with time and circumstances (pp. 151-198) and two, since the Caribbean is a "created" community (p. 31) the perpetual struggle of Caribbean people has always been to emancipate themselves from the imposed trapping of foreign values, customs and control. Now, what we have seen in imperial Graeco-Roman society and Pauline theo- politics and slavery are the following – one, production relations determine and define subject positions and the quality of life in the socio-economic structure and system; two, economic interests decide how persons are treated; three, mechanisms of "freedom" set up by the dominant class in society only serve to reinforce bondage, oppression and exploitation; and four, creating systems and structures of social justice between master and slave is a sign of the presence of the reign of God. Over time, these principles of rights, justice and freedom remained unchanged, despite changes in regimes of culture in society.

Matters of social equality, social justice, freedom, domination, and servile fidelity, raised in the duality of brothers along with master and slave relationships in Philemon, are significant in the Caribbean context. While it is true that, aside from the islands of Montserrat and the British Virgin Islands (still British dependencies), along with the Dutch dependencies of St. Martin (St. Maarten), St. Eustatius, Curacao, Aruba, and Bonaire; the French territories of Guadeloupe and Martinique; and the American territories of Puerto Rico and the United States Virgin Islands, which include St. Thomas/St. John and St. Croix, most other Caribbean islands have unfurled their flags of political independence from their former European colonizers individually. Each has its own Governor, Prime Minister, Parliament and Senate, Mr. Speaker or Madam Speaker, national anthem, national flag, national dress, electoral democracy, and standing army as evidence of their "independence."

Yet, who owns and controls the financial sector and telecommunications networks? And is it not true that the largest portion of the budget goes toward repayment of the national debt? It is true! Despite the political and economic advancements made through the sacrifices and courage of our heroes, both dead and alive, it is still evident that our real "masters" sit in offices and boardrooms in continental Europe and North America. Are we brothers with our former "masters"? Or are we still "slaves"? In fact, up to and through the 1980s and early 1990s, North America was referred to as "Big Brother,"[473] and may still be today. If it was not in name, then it was in practice. The duality of "brothers" yet master and slave is as relevant to first-century imperial Graeco-Roman society as it is to the present-day Caribbean.

In the Caribbean, neither slaves nor their descendants played a role in the abolition process.[474] Abolition was enacted by the establishment through parliamentary means.[475] Consequently, only the system of labor exploitation changed. Property relations remained unaltered. This situation persists today. Until property relations are modified so that descendants of slaves are not simply propertyless wage earners, disconnected from property ownership, but are instead capable of generating wealth, the social revolution of abolition remains incomplete.

Conclusion

In summary, the Bible has primarily served as a tool of criticism in biblical hermeneutical practices within a Caribbean context. As rightly pointed out by Spencer Miller, this usage is evident in the fact

---

[473] Bible study on 2 Kings 18: 17-37 by William Watty, *"Big Brother and Weaker States"* in Allan Kirton and William Watty eds, **Consultation for Ministry in a New Decade** (Barbados: CADEC, 1985), pp. 9-18
[474] Richard Hart, **Slaves Who Abolished Slavery** (Barbados, Jamaica, Trinidad & Tobago: University Press of the West Indies, 1985, 2002), p. 336
[475] Ibid. p. 336

that biblical study occurs within the framework of denominational agendas and is predominantly a matter of faith, rarely motivated by a quest for justice or liberation.[476] The necessary remedy for this situation is a resistant reading strategy established by this study, in which readers are culturally aware and engaged. The socio-structural issues in both the context and biblical text are identified and addressed. Here, the hermeneutical movement does not primarily occur from biblical text to context. Instead, it aims to uncover the cultural significance of the reader in context, emphasizing the need for the reader to approach the biblical text with commitment, from within their social reality, and with the patience required to discern the socio-ideological and theological agenda embedded in the biblical text. In doing so, the "reading" of the Bible is not conducted to acquire knowledge, for spiritual development, or to critique behaviors, but rather to equip the reader with the insights needed to interpret and defend life.

Fundamentally, the biblical resistant hermeneutic "first discovers the questions to which the biblical texts provide answers and identifies the problems that the biblical texts address."[477] Reading biblical texts in this manner grants agency to both the material conditions that produced these texts and the contexts in which they are interpreted. The Bible may serve as the answer or solution, but what are the questions or problems? Without this alignment in the socio-structural analysis of biblical texts and the context of the interpreter, the potential to expose, challenge, and resist oppressive social structures and practices is significantly reduced, if not entirely absent.

---

[476] Althea Spencer Miller "Lucy Bailey Meets the Feminists" in Kathleen O'Brien, Musa W. Dube, et al eds. **Feminist New Testament Studies – Global and Future Perspectives** (New York: Palgrave MacMillan, 2005), p. 221
[477] Mosala, **Biblical Hermeneutics**, p. 192

CHAPTER 6

IMPLICATIONS OF DEVELOPING A RESISTANT BIBLICAL HERMENEUTIC WITHIN THE CARIBBEAN INTRODUCTION

Regardless of the exegetical starting point in biblical hermeneutics—whether it's the context of the biblical text or the context of the interpreter—knowledge of place is essential. I have argued that understanding the socio-ideological, economic, political, and theological circumstances that produced the biblical text is crucial, as is grasping the socio-cultural, ideological, and economic meanings of the realities that the interpreter navigates when interpreting biblical texts. Engaging with biblical texts within specific social contexts enhances our recognition of their meanings.[478] The biblical text cannot interpret itself. From this perspective, I have found that resistance to oppressive social systems and structures emerges when this material and cultural understanding is given agency, especially when it aligns with a concrete commitment to and active participation in the struggle for social justice. What implications does this have for the specific context of the Caribbean in reading biblical texts as products? More specifically, what are the meaning-effects of a Caribbean biblical resistant hermeneutic?

---

[478] Vaage ed., **Subversive Scripture**, p. 12

I suggest that a Caribbean biblical resistant hermeneutic has six implications: how one defines the Bible, how one "reads" the Bible, the sites for doing theology, understanding the ground and structure of Caribbean religions, the way the spirituality of Caribbean peoples is structured against resistance, such as worship and salvation, and the relationship between culture and theology.

Defining The Bible

In bringing together the world from which the biblical texts are produced with the world from which the reader 'reads,' the nature of biblical literature becomes a critical issue. In addition to the examples cited above (see Introduction pp. 6-8 on JEPD and the Gospels), I will refer to other instances that illustrate the material conditions from which biblical texts emerged, reinforcing the point that biblical texts are already an interpretation, an 'action,' and a record of involvement in God's call, whether toward obedience or disobedience.[479]

For instance, one does not need to look far or long in the Bible to see that biblical texts themselves are interpretations. At the beginning, in chapters one and two, there are two accounts of the same creation story (Genesis 1-2:4a and 2:4b-24). Effectively, the Bible contains differences not only between books but also within individual books.[480] In Genesis 1-2:4a, vegetation and animals are created before Adam, followed by man, and then later, woman; however, in Genesis 2:4b-24, Adam is created before vegetation, animals follow Adam, and man and woman are created together on the sixth day. What we have here is not a factual

---

[479] ²Jose Miguez-Bonino *"Marxist Critical Tools: Are They Helpful in Breaking the Stranglehold of Idealist Hermeneutics"* in R.S. Sugirtharajah ed. **Voices From the Margins – Interpreting the Bible in the Third Word** (London: Orbis Books/ SPCK, 1995), p. 64

[480] David Robert Ord & Robert B. Coote, **Is the Bible True? Understanding the Bible Today**

account of the world's origin but rather an understanding of worlds, the meaning of life, and how life is perceived.

In Israel's theological traditions, Genesis 1-2:4a is assigned to the Priestly account, with its emphasis on order, blessing and Sabbath and is dated to the time of exile in Babylon, 586-538 B.C.E.[481] Exile was a time of crisis in the life of Israel as they were without temple, monarch and land. When symbolic systems are lost, up- rootedness, despair, and hopelessness are experienced. Theologically, the loss of the temple meant that God chose to abandon Israel or that God was powerless. The loss of the monarchy meant that Yahweh had broken promises of land and becoming a great nation or was not strong enough to keep promises, and the loss of the land indicated that Yahweh abandoned his promise or could not make it happen. As such, Genesis 1-2:4a is understood as the Priestly account, a re-imagination of what humanity is in the light of exile[482] as God's cosmic intent remains one of empowerment and well-being for all (Genesis 1:28). In contrast, Genesis 2:4b-24 is attributed to the Jahwist or J account, which legitimizes King David's rule. Regarding the creation narrative, it is important to note the presence of the Serpent and how the man and woman were cursed and expelled from the garden, condemned to hard labor after acquiring the power "to know."[483] The essence of the story emphasizes that everyone must partake in the labor of constructing the Davidic Empire.

Similarly, Hugo Assmann cited the case of various New Testament writers' ideological appropriation of Jesus' own earthly program.[484] Assmann has noted the tendency of New Testament writers to connect Jesus' earthly program with Isaiah 61:1-7. However, Isaiah 61:1-7

[481] Terrence Fretheim, **Creation, Fall and Flood** (Minneapolis: Augsburg, 1969), p. 23

[482] Hans Walter Wolf and Walter Brueggemann, **The Vitality of Old Testament Traditions** (Atlanta: John Knox Press, 1982), pp. 101-113

[483] Ord & Coote, **Is the Bible True?** pp. 72-73

[484] Hugo Assmann, **Theology for A Normal Church** (New York: Orbis Books, 1976), p. 68

addresses the class interests of the exiled Judean ruling class in Babylon. In this passage, the exiled Judean ruling class transcribes the ideology of the Exodus, which speaks of the liberation of captives and the oppressed, to fit their own narrative of return.[485] Thus, the text focuses on the luxury and privilege expected in Zion,[486] rather than liberation, which contrasts sharply with Jesus' own earthly program.

Therefore, biblical texts consist of a complex mix of different positions and groups, reflecting various and often contradictory traditions throughout history and arising from diverse situations.[487] These differing positions, groups, and traditions allow for the existence of "not a biblical message but 'biblical messages,' not a biblical God but 'biblical Gods.'[488] It is important for readers to avoid too quickly embracing, owning, and claiming the 'message' and the 'God' of the Bible without understanding biblical texts, their socio-ideological agendas, and the context. Doing otherwise could enable the oppressed to collude with their oppressors in their oppression.

Biblical texts are not without problems. The writers of the Bible cannot be excused for their contributions to the oppression of women, the abuse of children (Genesis 22), the degradation of the environment, and the glorification of war (Revelation), simply because such issues are attributed to interpretations over the years rather than the biblical texts themselves.[489] Due to the way biblical texts are written, they sometimes fail us through patriarchal bias (Genesis 22) or the glorification of violence (2 Samuel 12:11). As Fretheim notes, "to save the Bible from complicity in patriarchy and violence, and thereby maintain its authority in the face of such challenges, we engaged in exegetical egg-dances and

---

[485] Ibid.
[486] Ibid.
[487] Mosala, *Biblical Hermeneutics*, p. 29
[488] Mosala, *Biblical Hermeneutics*, p. 28
[489] Lecture delivered by Dr. Terrence Fretheim on *"Is the Portrayal of God Reliable?"* at the Vancouver School of Theology, Summer School Public Lecture Series, July 6, 1995.

the scissors and paste approach by using texts that positively influence the interpretation of troubling passages." However,[490] attempting to save the Bible from complicity dismisses the sinfulness and limitations of its writers, implying that human failings and frailties do not manifest in biblical texts. They do. It is essential to problematize the commonly held view of inspiration, recognizing that the human mind – sinful and finite – will not perceive everything about God rightly. Human beings will not always understand each other perfectly. In other words, the issue does not always rest with the interpreter and never with the biblical text.

In Caribbean biblical hermeneutical practice, there is a willingness to avoid viewing biblical texts as already possessing a definitive interpretation or being inherently ideological. For instance, Jennings defines the Bible as the "record of and witness to the primordial revelation of God, particularly in the context of Yahweh, the God of Israel, and in Jesus of Nazareth."[491] The Bible's singular universal message is applied to Caribbean existential realities. When this happens, the Bible is interpreted through an ideological lens. Nevertheless, the Bible is inherently ideological; it was written from a specific perspective and understanding, shaped by contextual circumstances. It is impossible to adapt the universal to fit the individual. As a result, we often strive to make the biblical text conform to our own understanding, asserting truths in advance. True contextualization occurs only when the interpreter grasps the universal or sees it through the lens of the universal.

I suggest that the specific aspects of the Caribbean experience can be viewed through the lens of the word of God (the particular). However, the word of God (the universal) cannot be understood solely by considering the specific aspects of the Caribbean experience. The

---

[490] Ibid.
[491] Jennings, *The Word in Context*, p. 3

word of God is not restricted to the Bible. It can also be found in the uniqueness of Caribbean experiences, which can also be seen as "text."

Therefore, the Bible, regarded as the word of God, serves as an abstract starting point for Caribbean biblical hermeneutics. However, even if one approaches the hermeneutical task through the lens of Caribbean experiences as an epistemological guide to reading biblical texts, one must still engage with these texts and identify the socio-ideological agendas that are present.

All this highlights a distinction between the Bible and the word of God. The Bible reveals the socio-historical context of God's intention and will for humanity as understood by a specific people in a particular time and place. The word of God emerges from engaging with the particularities and peculiarities of the socio-historical realities of a particular context while discerning the theo-politics of biblical texts. The Bible is not the word of God (dictation); instead, the word of God is found within the Bible (revelation).

"Reading" The Bible

In a biblical resistant hermeneutic, culture is considered "text," meaning that understanding biblical texts begins with the lived experiences of readers and their cultural-literacy awareness of those experiences, rather than starting with the biblical text or viewing pastors or church leaders as the sole sources of knowledge and meaning. As mentioned earlier, the drug and mug approach represents the current reading practice of Caribbean biblical hermeneutics, seemingly aiming to gather knowledge for spiritual formation and faith development. Therefore, the drug and mug reading strategy does not grant any agency to the material conditions of either the biblical text or the context of the interpreters. Additionally, there is no intention to separate oneself or the church from oppressive social systems and practices, condemning those systems and practices, and advocating for God's justice.

For the biblical resistant hermeneutic, "reading" is not about co-creating data or amassing knowledge. Instead, it involves constructing an alternative consciousness that fosters the development of a just world and society. To achieve this, both teachers and group members must have a clear understanding of the cultural significance of lived experiences as a prerequisite for challenging the dominant power dynamics in any given situation. Thus, it's not merely about gathering "facts" but about embracing an "activist" agenda.

This "activist" agenda requires democratizing the interpretive process, where interpreting biblical texts is carried out by communities of interest and in the community's favor. I envision, on one hand, the pastor or church leader (in a privileged social position) and, on the other hand, the community of interest (including marginalized individuals, farmers, domestic workers, fishermen, construction workers, civil servants, abused women, etc.) that come together to study the Bible on a weekday in the village chapel. If this experience is to embody an "activist" agenda, those gathered cannot relinquish the interpretation of biblical texts to the recognized "expert," the pastor or church leader, and thus become passive consumers of their wisdom and discernment; instead, they must become active participants in the encounter. Being active participants entails co-constructing knowledge as a collaborative effort.

However, I am further considering that if the agenda is to become genuinely "activist," farmers, domestic workers, fishermen, and others need to study the Bible as distinct groups rather than in a mixed assembly, as is currently the case, which is unproductive and socially redundant. Interpreting biblical texts through the particularities and peculiarities of their lived realities as specific social groups[492] will lead to analyzing the causes of those realities, making judgments, organizing for different

---

[492] Vaage, **Subversive Scriptures**, p. 14

and just outcomes, and addressing the universal rather than allowing the universal to dictate it.

It is not that the pastor or leader lacks a role to play; he or she does. However, they must become what Antonio Gramsci refers to as an "organic" intellectual.[493] According to Gramsci, the "organic" intellectual is responsible for organizing and constructing a social class's[494] contradictory consciousness, meaning that the pastor's or church leader's organizing role is also ideological. Their teaching of the Bible aims to transcend and educate as a practice of freedom.[495] For this to occur, the teaching approach needs to be constructivist,[496] which involves problem-solving, meaning- making, and dialogically-based methods. In a constructivist teaching approach, education involves constructing meaning from situations that seek to understand and transform social reality. The pastor's or teacher's role is that of a reflective practitioner.[497] With congregants, there is both reflection-in-action and reflection-on- action, so that for both parties, knowing is 'in action' or 'praxis knowing.' Furthermore, the constructivist approach implies that the pastor or church leader not only empathizes with the group but also stands in solidarity with them in their daily struggle to live, survive, and make ends meet, growing alongside them in understanding

---

[493] Antonio Gramsci, **Selection From Prison Notes** (London: Lawrence and Wishart, 1971), p. 6

[494] Gramsci, Selection From Prison Notes, p. 10: "the mode of being of the new/organic intellectual can no longer consist in eloquence, which is an exterior and momentary mover of feelings and passions, but in active participation in practical life, as constructor, organiser, 'permanent persuader' and not just a simple orator; from technique-as-work one proceeds to technique-as-science and to the humanistic conception of history, without which one remains 'specialised' and does not become 'directive' (specialised and political); see also Anne Shawstack Sassoon, Gramsci's Politics (London: Groom Helm London, 1980), p. 139

[495] bell hooks, **Teaching To Transgress, Education as the Practice of Freedom** (New York, London: Routledge, 1994), p. 3.

[496] M. Williams & R.L. Buder, **Psychology For Language Teachers: A Social Constructivist Approach** (Cambridge: Cambridge University Press, 1997), p. 51

[497] Ibid. pp. 53-6

the lived realities they urgently need to transform into a framework of social justice.

Admittedly, challenging or changing what gives meaning to one's life, or questioning the structures in which faith was formed, can lead to a crisis of faith. While this can be liberating, it is also quite difficult. Despite this reality—perhaps even because of it—if Caribbean biblical hermeneutics is to truly liberate by resisting social systems and practices that oppress, then even the Bible, which is the foundation of its faith experiences, must be interpreted differently.

Doing Theology from Non-Traditional Sites

With biblical resistant hermeneutics' dual focus on the materiality of biblical texts and the context of interpreters, discourse responding to the activity of God, or theology, stems from the socio-historical practices of biblical texts' composers and interpreters. Traditionally, theological perspectives in the Caribbean emerge from three starting points: God-Jesus-Holy Spirit, human beings, and the world, culture, or experience. The emphasis is on belief, positioning the theological perspective's starting point in God-Jesus-Holy Spirit, which renders it somewhat speculative. In contrast, biblical resistant hermeneutics inverts the starting points of theological perspectives: world, culture, or experience, human beings, and God-Jesus- Holy Spirit, raising the question, "What are the non-traditional sites for doing theology in the Caribbean?" Therefore, the biblical resistant hermeneutic does not aim to conduct theology using Western academic frameworks but prioritizes material conditions as authentic sites for theology.

Budget and census are two neglected areas that do not receive the attention they deserve as genuine sites for doing theology. Yet, it is in budgets that ruling class ideology or ideas take on material force, where public policies for human development are articulated, and where the church's commitment to the socio-economic needs of its members is inscribed. Its ministry to the whole person has its social reference. The interest lies not only in discussing the issues from political and economic perspectives but also in examining what the church should do and say in defense of life and embodying God's love and justice among human beings.

Budgets

Budgets are quantitative tools. While they may not be the most effective means of drawing qualitative conclusions, budgets offer insights into qualitative realities such as housing, health care, education, social services, and the commitment to agricultural development. Essentially, budgets connect economic development and justice to the religious values of fairness (appropriate relationships between employer and employee, ruler and ruled), righteousness (moral relationships between employer and employee, ruler and ruled), and the common good, all of which contribute to the bottom line. There is no conflict between the practice of faith and economic justice. Budgets serve as moral documents.[498]

Below, I will present three questions that will highlight the theological issues advocating for social change and serving as a foundation for social transformation. To this end, I have provided three pie charts illustrating the budgets for 2001 and 2006 for the Caribbean island of Antigua for analysis.

The questions are:

- In terms of the budget's expenditures, which sector of the economy receives the largest portion and why? What are the social implications?

---

[498] Jim Wallis, **God's Politics** (Oxford: Lion, 2005), p., 241

- On the income side of the budget, which sector of the economy contributes the largest portion, and why? What are the social implications?
- Generally, what are the negative and/or positive impacts of the social justice concerns addressed by the budget? What economic justice issues (such as spending cuts or increases in health, education, social services, or taxes) are raised in the budget?

Clearly, the question of "who" on the expenditure side of the budget highlights that the largest portion of the budget is not found within the national economy. If it were, we would be asking about "which" sector within the national economy. The reality is that an external entity receives the largest share, which is unrelated to either generosity or surplus; there is no surplus available to be generous with. This situation illustrates our dependence on foreign influences and forces, suggesting that we do not control our responses to the events impacting us. Essentially, we relinquish what we need. The two budgets below illustrate this point.

Budget 2006

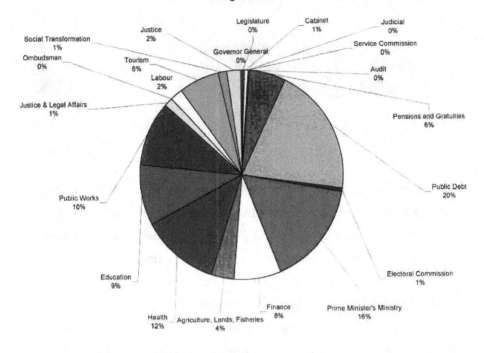

Budget 2001

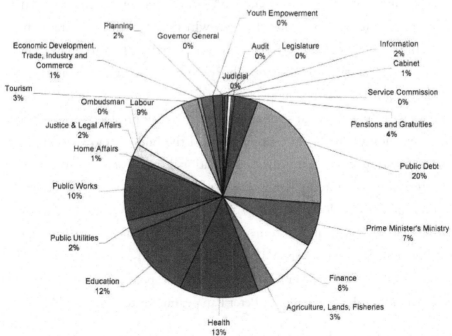

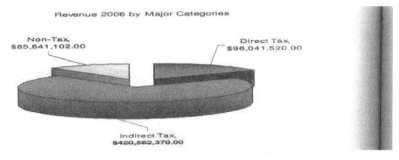

Table 6:3

In both budgets, public debt receives the largest share at 20%; remarkably, this percentage remains unchanged five years later, despite being under two different political administrations. Not much has shifted. Rather than a change in social, political, and economic orientation and policies, we merely experienced a change in political leadership. We have been borrowing to survive. In other words, we have been digging one hole to escape another. Paying such a high price to foreign entities for our survival diminishes, if not completely eradicates, investments in human and economic development—such as health, education, agriculture, and fisheries—which inevitably deteriorates the quality of life for citizens. Essentially, we are paying for our oppression.

Similarly, the question of who or which sector contributes the largest portion of the budget on the income side highlights that it may still be a national grouping, rather than a productive sector of the economy, providing a larger share of the budget. However, these contributions may not be invested in national causes or projects, as they often end up in foreign hands. For instance, over three-quarters of the revenue for the 2006 budget of Antigua comes from indirect taxes, with consumption and customs service taxes accounting for more than fifty percent of the revenue. If we randomly select a basket of essential goods – such as Quaker Oats, Orchard pineapple juice, Jewell rice, Carnation milk, Purity flour, Peter Pan peanut butter, Maxwell House coffee, and McCormick seasoning[499]–we observe that none of the labels indicate that they are "made in Antigua." We lack our own products or styles. Even with the concessions made to consumers by the current government, the cost of living remains externally controlled, deepening our dependence. Furthermore, the high cost of living negatively impacts the quality of life.

The issue I am raising here is that the quality of life and the cost of living are both systemic and structural challenges, as well as theological ones. A wholesome quality of life and the root causes of a high cost of living are not opposed to theology. Through a biblically resistant hermeneutic, cultural literacy will recognize budgets as moral documents that have social implications for the quality of life of citizens and ultimately for hope. It also advances the critique, exposure, and denouncement by biblical interpreters of elements that do not contribute to the community's overall well-being and organization for social justice and change.

Census

If budgets help us reach qualitative conclusions, then the census will provide quantitative findings. A nation's census offers raw data about the living conditions of its people. This enables us to approach theology from the perspective of the human condition and the lived experiences of the population.

What needs to happen here is the development of a social profile for a social class, group, or area regarding housing, health, crime, unemployment, education, marital status, etc., using census data to identify areas of need, trends, and possible causes of social problems. From this information, strategies can be created to address difficulties,

---

[499] See 2006 Budget Statement entitled "**Gearing Up For Growth**" delivered Wednesday November 30, 2005 by Dr. The Hon. L. Errol Cort, MP, Minister of Finance and The Economy, pp., 72-76

solve problems, and thereby foster alleviation, relief, and social well-being. Building a social profile is not the same as stereotyping any class, group, or area; the profile is based on facts, not assumptions. For example, let's create a social profile of housing provisions in St. John's City, Antigua, based on the 2001 census.

Diagram 6:1
Housing provisions in St. John's City, Antigua

	Total	Male	Female	Total	Percentage
Population	24,452	11,400	13,051		
Majority age group 35 -39	2,268	1022	1245		
Majority area – Gray's Green		193	181		
Number of persons per household	6,577			5	
Type of ownership - squatters	6,577			14	
Construction material	6,577			3,582 wood; 1,358 concrete	
Source of water supply	6,577			1,680 public stand-pile; 284 private	
Number of rooms per household	6,577			2,325 with 3 rooms	
Rented quarters	6,577			2,944	
Owned property	6,577			3,324	

What we are observing here, in terms of housing quality, are socially depressed communities in the vicinity of St. John's city. This has social implications for health, crime, children's education, poverty, and overall quality of life. In these circumstances, the path to well-being is not upward social mobility, as desirable or commendable as that may appear, but rather the construction of a just social order. Communities of faith in these areas should not simply gather to worship God, centered on celebrating the Sacrament of the Lord's Supper and biblical proclamation, as this does not lead to advocating for a new social order. This pattern persists. Such a lack of social activism highlights the disconnection between the structures of spirituality, the social nature of existence, and the redundancy of the biblical reading approach. A biblically resistant hermeneutic grounded in people's lived realities has an "activist" agenda as its aim and would, therefore, help bridge the gap between the structures of spirituality and the social nature of existence, as well as address the redundancy of the biblical reading approach, resisting the causes of poor quality of life.

Understanding the Ground and Structure of Caribbean Religions

Given the material interest of a biblical resistant hermeneutic, the foundation of Caribbean peoples' experience of God did not emerge from Caribbean socio-historical realities. Allow me to clarify this point.

When Africans and, later, indentured laborers from India were forcibly brought to the Caribbean against their will, they carried their religions with them. In Africa, predominantly West Africans had a way of being—a belief system centered on a Supreme Being, gods, humans, and the world.[500] The following diagram illustrates that structure of being:

---

[500] G. Parrinder, *Religion in Africa* (New York: Praeger, 1969), p., 27

Diagram 6:2
Structure of belief of West Africans

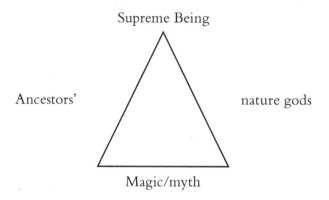

Supreme Being

Ancestors'   nature gods

Magic/myth

In the Caribbean, however, that belief structure was dismantled. Several strategies were employed to disrupt African spiritual and cultural organization. For instance, separating individuals from the same tribe and region aimed to prevent solidarity and organized resistance against oppression. African nature gods, which belong to specific locales and tribes, did not survive long in the Caribbean.[501] Consequently, the inability to unite as a tribal community and worship made it impossible to reignite and reweave their belief structure or way of life. However,[502] this does not imply that indigenous African religious ideas did not persist. Despite significant changes, what endured and emerged retained recognizable 'African' features – Obeah, Myalism, Rastafarianism, Revivalism, Shouters, Jordanites, and Pocomania.

---

[501] Elizabeth Thomas-Hope *"The Pattern of Caribbean Religions"*, pp. 9-5, Geoffrey Parrinder *"The African Spiritual Universe"*, pp. 16-24 in Brian Gates ed. *Afro-Caribbean Religions* (London: Ward Lock Educational, 1980); see also George Mulrain *"African Cosmology and Caribbean Christianity"* in Burton Sankeralli ed. *At the Crossroads – African Caribbean Religion and Christianity* (Trinidad and Tobago: Caribbean Conference of Churches, 1995), pp. 50-51

[502] Don Robotham *"The Development of a Black Ethnicity in Jamaica"* in Rupert Lewis & Patrick Bryan eds. **Garvey: His Work and Impact** (Trenton, New Jersey: Africa World Press, Inc. 1994), pp. 26-28

Consequently, a significant loss was ontology, their way of being. In the Caribbean, spiritual relationships and the order of life and world view were disrupted to such an extent that, in the diagram below, the base became the apex (*see diagram below 6:6*). The way of being was magical; the epistemological lens through which to see and interpret the world became one of magic. Magical practices were centered on rituals to secure the assistance of malevolent powers in addressing life's challenges and the struggle against oppression. The most expressive form of magic was Obeah. For the Africans, spiritual agents were responsible for personal and societal acts of dehumanization, not the system under which they lived. Thus, the enemy was within, not outside.

Diagram 6:3
Africans ontology in the Caribbean

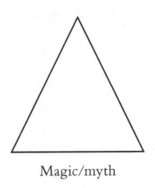

Magic/myth

For example, Mrs. Flannigan shares a story she once heard from one of her servants. A slave's wife had mysteriously lost one of her gowns. Soon after the loss, the wife began to experience strange sensations. She decided to consult an Obeah man to find out the possible cause of her distress. Upon seeing her, the Obeah man declared that the wife had "enemies," and it was their intrigues that brought on her illness. However, if she returned another day and brought "all the money she could gather," he would cast the evil spirits out of her. The servant who was listening asked if the wife gained anything from the experience, to which the storyteller replied, "She says she does, but I don't know; I don't see her looking any better; had to pay a lot of money though; Obeah doesn't like it if you don't give much."[503]

Another way to "discover" who committed evil was to place a door key between the pages of a Bible, specifically on the eighteenth and nineteenth verses of the fiftieth Psalm. After securing the key in the closed Bible, both the accuser and the accused would place a finger on the handle or the exposed part of the key and recite the incantation, "By St. Peter, by St. Paul, you tief me fowl" (or whatever was stolen), to which the accused would respond, "By St. Peter, by St. Paul, me no tief you fowl." If the accused were guilty, the key would turn in the Bible.[504]

For slaves and ex-slaves, their "enemies" or the sources of their suffering— whether from the loss of personal belongings, the pain and fatigue from physical labor, or deprivation—were not seen as the oppressive social system; instead, the Bible was viewed as a conjuring book.

In addition to Obeah, the neo-African religions of Myalism, Pocomania, Voodoo, and Shango emerged from this alienated and divided existence. They symbolize the Africanization of Christianity. However, my intention here is not to prioritize the socio-historical experiences of Africans as an ethnic group. Doing so would overlook the faith expressions of the indentured laborers from Asia, who were allowed to practice their Hindu and Muslim faith by the ruling elite, despite experiencing the same social realities of disconnection and alienation. Therefore, my goal is not to engage in ethno-cultural hegemony. Still, it is a fact that no other ethnic group suffered to the same extent from manipulation, discrimination, and calculated denigration as Africans.

The plantocracy and missionaries exploited these circumstances of

---

[503] Mrs. Flannigan, *Antigua and the Antiguans, Volume II* (London: Saunders & Otley, 1844), p. 53

[504] Ibid. p. 55-6

alienation and division. It was primarily at night in their quarters and deep in the bushes, away from the oversight of the masters and their cohorts, that Africans experienced their way of being or rehumanized themselves through music, dancing, and rituals.

In the light of day, the missionaries, with their religious mix of biblical religion, Catholicism, which emphasised punishment, and Protestantism, which concentrated on justification by faith through grace, wielded religious power and authority with little regard for the belief structures of Africans or Indentured Indians. The undisguised ideology of the European churches was to bring the "one gospel" into different cultures, thereby promoting a monoculture or denying the right to be different.[505]

The biblical religion espoused by the European churches represented nothing less than the imposition of a universal narrative: the biblical story of one particular people, Israel, and of one faith expression, Judeo–Christianity, centered on Jesus Christ as the world's savior. For the European churches, biblical religion began with Jesus Christ as the eternal Son of God and extended to the Incarnation, earthly life, death, resurrection, and exaltation of Jesus Christ (Christology from above); or started with the history of Jesus Christ as the eternal Son of God and then moved to the Incarnation (Christology from below). Here, I have highlighted the belief structures of white European Christianity and those of the enslaved and formerly enslaved Africans. In white European Christianity, the belief structure progresses from the Supreme Being (God) to Jesus Christ, then to context. Conversely, for the enslaved and formerly enslaved Africans, the movement flows from the Supreme Being (God) to humanity, then to society. While white European Christianity struggles to establish or gain belief, enslaved Africans are focused on surviving day to day and striving for authenticity. The

---

[505] Harold Sitahal *"Dealing with Plurality in the Caribbean...The C.C.C and Pluralism"* in Sankeralli *At the Crossroads*, p. 225

former (white European Christianity) imposes the universal upon the particular; the latter (Caribbean religions) interprets the universal.

So, rather than Myalism, Pocomania, Shango, Voodoo, Islam, Hinduism, and Rastafarianism being the faith expressions of Caribbean people—all of which are rooted in Caribbean culture—Christianity takes that role. Officially, Christianity is not indigenous to the Caribbean way of life, as it is based on the beliefs and practices of Catholicism, Methodism, Moravianism, Anglicanism, Seventh-Day Adventism, and many other fundamentalist expressions of faith.

Structuring of Spirituality Against Resistance

One consequence of this alienated existence and the imposed nature of faith expressions in the Caribbean is that spirituality is shaped in opposition to oppressive social systems and practices. The structure of worship and the understanding of salvation support this point.

Over the past fifteen years as a minister in the Methodist Church, I have had numerous opportunities to lead worship. And that is part of the problem. Worship feels like a command performance by the preacher, resembling a sit-and-stand exercise routine. The preacher directs, and the congregation follows. The whole experience, as it is now, is individualistic yet communal, an isolated event though primarily social, largely uncreative yet intellectual, very intellectual, and non-participatory despite being responsive. Congregation members are mostly passive consumers instead of active participants in developing an awareness of our social existence. This lack of social awareness is, to a significant degree, the issue.

Paradoxically, at play, in cricket (see below pp. 275-277), Caribbean people know the system as the enemy. But, at worship rituals, they see themselves as the enemy, in dire need of forgiveness from guilt and sin. It is still the same today. Today's worship is still structured to comfort the afflicted, not to afflict the comfortable.

Interested folk Culture Worship

What structures the worship experience to connect with the sociality of existence and thereby serve as resistance is what I will refer to as *interested folk culture worship*. However, I know that worship is transcultural,[506] meaning it surpasses the specific ways of being of people and places. In any culture, one must recognize that one is praying, baptizing, and celebrating Divine memory. Nonetheless, worship is also contextual, counter-cultural, and cross-cultural.[507] Contextually, worship re- expresses the ways of being of a local or specific culture. In its counter-cultural dimension, worship aims to resist and transform foreign or non-specific influences and practices, exposing dehumanizing and oppressive values that may condition the ways of being of peoples and places, challenging worshippers to live differently. In its cross-cultural manifestation, worship acknowledges that there is something in all ways of being, in all communities, that is worthy of worship. This means that for worship to be genuinely counter-cultural or a radical space of resistance, it must be contextual. Interested folk culture worship is both counter-cultural and contextual.

Worship centered on folk culture addresses specific social issues, incorporating guitars, drums, calypso, and reggae music into the liturgy. Instead of congregants attending weekly services led by the Holy Spirit's guidance through a preacher or liturgist, the worship experience over the course of a month, quarter, or a designated week concentrates on themes like unemployment, domestic abuse, HIV/AIDS, obesity, and drug addiction. Relevant prayers, hymns, songs, Bible readings with proclaims, and sermons are tailored to these issues. A worship team, drawn from the congregation and comprising youths,

---

[506] James Scherer & Stephen Bevans, **New Directions in Mission and Evangelism** (Maryknoll: Orbis Books, 1999), pp. 180-84; see also, Knolly Clarke *"Liturgy and Culture in the Caribbean"* in Idris Hamid, **Troubling of The Waters**, pp. 141-63
[507] Ibid.

women, men, farmers, fishermen, and so forth, prepares all elements of the service. During the worship experience, individuals from the community or congregation who are impacted by these issues are invited to "testify," exhort, pray, and receive prayer from others. This approach makes worship authentic and opens up radical possibilities as it raises awareness and encourages the community to actively engage in social transformation. In essence, a specific community of shared interests comes together for the benefit of the entire community in worship.

In essence, folk culture worship significantly influences relationships and ministry within the local congregation. Traditionally, membership in the local congregation is based on geography, comprising a community of believers gathered from the residents of a specific area. In other words, the church is shaped by where people live, even though there is a prevailing understanding that the church is based on spiritual experiences or 'beliefs.' Nevertheless, geography plays a crucial role in shaping interests. Social realities exist wherever people reside, and geography remains the defining factor in relationships and ministry within the local congregation. Therefore, one 'believes' to belong.

I propose that a community of interests should form the basis of membership rather than geography, so that local congregations are built around how people live instead of where they live. This way, worship arises from the lived realities or social interests of the local community, meaning that spiritual structures are no longer isolated phenomena, detached from the social aspects of existence. Now, one belongs to 'believe.' Additionally, the proclamation from the Bible and the weekly Bible study sessions inevitably focus on the social realities that directly affect the daily lives of congregants.

Salvation has typically not been viewed as having any material implications. In the Caribbean, understanding salvation has been limited to liberation from sin and guilt. By highlighting this limitation,

I do not intend to diminish the benefits of grace – the assurance that the resources of divine mercy and forgiveness are always available, gifts ready to be given to all who ask for them. Instead, I recognize that salvation is liberation from unjust social structures, alienation and despair, as well as the human indignity and oppression that destroy people's lives.

What our former colonial masters did to advance their exploitative agenda, and what many churches in the Caribbean continue to do, leading to their irrelevance, is fail to engage with people in the concrete realities of their lives. They separate faith from people's cultural, political, and economic circumstances. When individuals are connected within the social fabric of their existence, some understanding of the alienation experienced and the forms of oppression and discrimination felt emerges; consequently, salvation must aim towards being liberated to live in community with both God and neighbor, or towards establishing justice and righteousness in the entire community.

Essentially, understanding salvation as redemption—liberation from the grip of sin and death—and emancipation—freedom from structural and systemic oppression that prevents people from fully realizing their humanity—directs salvation toward resistance. For a biblical resistant hermeneutic, salvation represents a pursuit of social justice.

Cultural Expressions as Hermeneutical Practices of Resistance

Furthermore, with a biblically resistant hermeneutic that views Caribbean peoples' ways of being as the authentic basis of their experience of God, utilizing those specific ways of being as a lens should inform the peoples' discourse about their experiences of God. In Caribbean social history, the relationship between the histories of two of the Caribbean's most cherished and unifying cultural expressions, cricket and carnival, and the development of theological perspectives supports this point.

To examine the relationship, I will analyze the socio-cultural significance of cricket, both on and off the field, within the context of the social forces at work during the colonial period (1492-1838), the post-emancipation era (1838-1960), and the post-independence phase (1960s onward). Additionally, I will consider the contextual and historical development of theological perspectives related to the social forces influencing play off the field, the style of play on the field, and how cricket informs hermeneutical practices within the Caribbean context. I use cricket as the cultural symbol of British imperialism in the Caribbean and as a driving force behind the Caribbean people's quest for self-identity and self-determination.

Colonial Era

Social Forces and Style of Play

Cricket's origin in the Caribbean was coincidental.[508] The credit for its introduction goes to the English military, not the English planters. Although its introduction was incidental and thus not part of the planters' civilizing project, its potential as a tool of domination was quickly recognized and exploited by them. What the planters contributed was a culture of terror[509]—an intimidated minority facing an overwhelmingly large majority that they did not regard as human beings but rather as frightened property.

The English military played cricket as a means of relaxation. Observing the military at play, the frightened and enslaved Africans eagerly embraced the game, mastering its fundamentals and grasping

---

[508] Tim Hector *"Will We Continue to be Annihilated and Humiliated"* Fan The Flame **Outlet Newspaper** December 1, 2000

[509] Tim Hector *"The OECS in Time, Space and Sports"* Fan The Flame **Outlet Newspaper** April 21, 2000

its principles and assumptions. They believed it represented a potential opportunity for self-expression and humanization that the ruling elite deliberately denied them. What was enjoyable for the English military was laden with socio-cultural and political significance for the enslaved Africans.[510] Therefore, who plays and who does not, along with which club or country they represent, who captains, fields where, and bats at what position, all reflect social roles and carry social meaning. Thus, social roles, relations, and tensions are played out on the cricket field. In essence, cricket mirrors the society in which it is played.

During the colonial period, the white European plantocracy was in full command of the political, economic, and cultural reins of power, which was exercised to maintain social distance between the white minority and the black majority. In cricket, the social distance was demonstrated in the prejudicial and discriminatory selection policy.[511] The enslaved and formerly enslaved were routinely excluded from both playing in and leading club or national teams. This was not based on either merit or ability but on race and colour. In all spheres of West Indian life, whites were held as superior and blacks as inferior. So, if one had inferior skills but was white, one played and represented the club and nation, but if one had superior ability to all comers but was black, one was marginalized. Marginalisation for the blacks, however, was a site of resistance. Hilary Beckles, one the Caribbean's foremost historians, was obliged to conclude that the politics and history of the times "were driven by the same ambition: how to keep the black man in his place and maintain white institutional hegemony".[512]

Cricket, therefore, was a highly contested cultural and politicized

---

[510] C.LR. James, *Beyond A Boundary*, p., 66

[511] Maurice St. Pierre, *West Indian Cricket Part 1, A socio-histoircal Appraisal* in Hilary McD. Beckles, **Liberation Cricket, West Indies Cricket Culture** (New York: Manchester University Press, 1995), pp. 120-123

[512] Hilary McD. Beckles, *"The Political Ideology of West Indies Cricket Culture"* in Beckles & Stoddart *Liberation Cricket*, p. 150

activity.[513] For the enslaved and formerly enslaved, cricket was a paradox: a game West Indians love to hate as it is a game of the colonizer that serves as a reminder of their imposed social, political, racial, cultural, and personal inferiority.[514] English players adopted a no-risk approach on the field, improvising nothing and taking fewer chances. Furthermore, one must adhere to the rules and assumptions (the umpire's decision is final, and spectators do not cross the boundary) and the morality of the game. Since cricket was an import, the style of play would reflect the English tradition. In English culture, cricket was played and watched with restrained enthusiasm, showing limited faith in the game, with little to no emotion expressed in victory or defeat, accompanied by polite applause and standing ovations to recognize outstanding achievements or milestones.[515]

Unlike the English style of play, the enslaved and formerly enslaved Africans engaged in the game with clear passion and aggression. They would cross boundaries without hesitation to celebrate successes or express disapproval of the umpire's decisions and the strategies of the players. The game fostered a sense of shared participation between players and spectators. With little hope for upward social mobility and a focus on white standards, the aim was to perform and outshine the white players. Cricket served as an outlet for their frustrations; thus, batsmen struck the ball fiercely, bowlers bowled with speed, and spectators crossed boundaries.

Cricket, as a culture, served both as a mirror and an arena. As a mirror, it reflected the colonial racial domination of Whites over Blacks. As an arena, the game acted as an outlet for anger and frustration against

---

[513] Neil Lazarus, *"Cricket and National Culture in the Writings of C.LR. James"* in Beckles & Stoddart **Liberation Cricket**, p. 390

[514] Burton, *"Ideology and Popular Culture"*, p. 104; see also Patterson, *"The Ritual of Cricket"*, p. 142 in Beckles & Stoddart **Liberation Cricket**,

[515] James, **Beyond A Boundary**, pp. 212-222; see also Tim Hector *"Crisis in Society and Cricket – Women to the Rescue"* Fan The Flame **Outlet Newspaper** June 25, 1999, p. 3

the oppressive social system and allowed individuals to express their opposition. In short, we see white European domination supported by an ideology of race and class, which is evident in a contested cultural performance.

Theological Perspectives

During the colonial era, colonizers made every effort to ensure that slaves and their descendants remained disunited and disorganized, preventing them from reshaping their former African customs and practices. Both self-determination and self-identification were consciously and systematically denied and eradicated during the establishment and maintenance of slave plantation societies. Nevertheless, the colonizers could not extinguish the consciousness of the African way of life, which was evident in Africans' understanding of life, death, and supernatural forces. To survive, slaves and their descendants had to adopt the religious beliefs and practices of Christianity, the faith of the colonizers, seeming to assimilate into European values and customs for personal advancement within the social system while still pursuing their quest for self-identity.

What emerged from this approach to survival and the quest to reclaim a lost identity was the syncretic religions of Myalism, Pocomania, Shouters, and Shakers, characterized by their emphasis on magic, spirit possession, and biblical episodes such as the Exodus and the experience of the early church at Pentecost (Acts 2). These syncretic religions, despite their tendency to engage in ecstatic worship—which provided a temporary escape from the harsh realities of suffering and injustice—represented a way to humanize themselves, find meaning, and resist hegemony.

In sum, the way of being in this colonial period shows the strife between the policy of white European Christianity to impose and deculturize and the quest of the enslaved for authenticity, self-discovery, self-hood, and self-realization, as the ground for their experience of God was unrelated to their socio-cultural circumstances.

Post-"emancipation Era

Social Forces and Style of Play

In the wake of widespread social unrest and demands for better working conditions, increased salaries, and political self-determination, culminating in adult suffrage and the formation of the West Indian Federation, the years from 1960 to 1966 were characterized by a rising nationalist consciousness and a sense of solidarity among West Indians. In cricket, the significant triumph of these struggles was the appointment of Frank Worrell, a black working-class Barbadian, as the first non-white captain of the West Indies cricket team, alongside a selection policy ostensibly based on merit and ability. However, these notable changes in leadership and self- determination in cricket were not mirrored in the political and economic realms. The black working-class masses "exercised abstract political power in an economic vacuum, leading to a lack of confidence in social life and a reluctance to accept the status quo."[516]

As Worrell worked to instill confidence in the players, he introduced a new style of play and fostered a fresh team ethic. Each player had previously focused on individual success, leading to a roster of outstanding individual talents. Now, under Worrell's leadership, a collective of exceptional cricketers collaborated to achieve shared goals.[517] While the gameplay still showcased flair, style, and calypso-inspired batting—with both textbook and unconventional shots—it was all executed with the necessary self-discipline.

As a result, during the quest for political self-determination and

---

[516] Tim Hector *"Will We Continue to be Annihilated and humiliated"* Fan The Flame, **Outlet Newspaper** December 1, 2000
[517] Ibid.

the direct challenge to race and class, as seen in Trinidad, Barbados, and Jamaica achieving political "independence" during this period, the Worrell years as captain from 1960 to 1966 were particularly expressive of social aspirations.

However, what Worrell built so diligently was destroyed between **1968 and 1977**. By May 1962, the West Indian Federation had collapsed, leading many West Indian islands to seek and gain insular "independence." Insular "independence" is like chasing the wind, for it was nothing more and nothing less than "foreign economic control ruling, with a black political directorate reigning."[518] Additionally, these years saw the rise of the Black Power movement, which emphasized black self-identity and social justice. Furthermore, post-political "independence" issues of unemployment and underdevelopment began to take a serious toll.

Based on the theory that style in cricket must be viewed in relation to the social environment,[519] it is not surprising that individualism, exceptional personal styles of play, insularity, and poor leadership became prominent once again in cricket performances. This era produced individual geniuses, such as the incomparable Garfield Sobers, an Afro-West Indian, and the great Rohan Kanhai, an Indo-West Indian. Sobers represented and upheld the West Indian style of play, characterized by flair, charisma, and both disciplined and unruly aggression. In contrast, Kanhai embodied both the West Indian style of play and the search for identity. Thus, while in the Worrell years one team represented many different islands or masses, in the Sobers and Kanhai years, individuals represented the masses, the various islands. Both Sobers and Kanhai were "representatives" and "historic players."

---

[518] Ibid. p. 4
[519] James, **Beyond A Boundary**, p. 219

Theological Perspectives

White European Christianity held the dominant position in these socio-political and economic circumstances. It made little effort to "come to terms with the meaning of faith and the challenges to faith in its context."[520] This was done with the explicit support of the ruling elite and complicity in their socio-economic and political agenda focused on control and profit maximization. Ignoring the fact that Africans and Indians did not represent a single collective but distinct peoples from varied cultural backgrounds, each with its own traditions and customs, the foreign missionaries forged ahead with the proclamation of their "one universal gospel" rooted in the biblical narrative of "one race," Israel, and of "one faith expression," Judeo-Christian. No effort was made to utilize the cultural traditions and customs, in whatever form they survived the Middle Passage or adapted in the West Indies, as a lens through which to understand the biblical story. The aim was to create a Christian colonial identity; to Christianize was to civilize, and to civilize was to Christianize. Within this civilizing-Christianizing project, the masses complied as they sought to outmanoeuvre their oppressors—white Europeans—at their own game, thereby striving to emulate European lifestyles and values.

In 1960-1977, we have been working out of the theory, in both cricket and theology, that theology, not theological perspectives, can represent a collective of people with their own histories and cultural identities. In cricket, a team can be made up of players from different nationalities and/or ethnicities. One team can represent these differences in the common goal of winning. Yet, what was made possible in cricket ought to have proved impossible to do in theology. It proved possible, however, because theology is understood as that word spoken about God

---

[520] Kirton, *"Current Trends in Caribbean Theology"*, p. 99

in a particular context, which is timeless, universal, and unchanging[521] and can be interpreted across various contexts. Still, as Watty points out, "if theology is timeless, universal, and unchanging, then there is no need to transport it from one country to another, as people in all nations would have already had access to the one known truth about the One Eternal, unchanging, and universal God."[522] When theology is transported, it tends to distort and inhibit contextual understanding.

Post-"independence" Era

Social Forces and Style of Play

In the late 1970s and 1980s, conditions worse than insular "independence" emerged in political and economic matters. The state and style of play shifted in the 1980s, 1990s, and 2000s. With the onset of structural adjustment, globalization, and the deepening roots of American cultural imperialism in Caribbean societies, it became clear that they had never achieved the political and economic "independence" for which they had fought and won.

Moreover, with mass migration to greener pastures in ways that are both genuine and ingenious—baffling even the most astute immigration authorities—and not for the first time in Caribbean history, 'home' was experienced as a different reality wherever possible within the Caribbean itself, but mainly in North America, Britain, and Canada. Those who migrated to North America and changed their allegiance to the American flag were designated 'Resident Alien'; those who moved to Britain and Canada had their ethnicity listed before their country of adoption. Notably, those born overseas found themselves in a position where they belonged neither to the Caribbean nor their country of birth.

---

[521] William Watty *"Decolonisation of Theology"* in Idris Hamid ed. **Troubling of the Waters**, p. 53
[522] Ibid. p. 52

'Home,' too, was a different reality for many cricketers. With the internationalization, professionalization, commercialization, and marketing of cricket, lucrative contracts with overseas teams, particularly in England and Australia, business enterprises, and the West Indies cricket board became the day's order. Cricket was now a commodity and no longer expressive of any West Indies cricket team culture, now of British citizenship, who has lived, and still lives, in England for many years.

At home, just like abroad, the issue of identity was alive and real. Caribbean societies are doubly diasporic.[523] When the indigenous inhabitants, the Amerindians, were exterminated by marauding Europeans, Africans and Asians were brought to the Caribbean for plantation labor. Since the end of World War II to the present day, many Caribbean people have migrated to Britain, North America, and elsewhere. In each migration, identities had to be constructed. Consequently, a debate has emerged about whether there is a Caribbean identity or if Caribbean and identity are connected.[524]

What was significant, however, for the 1977-1980s was that West Indian societies were structurally adjusted at precisely the time when the West Indies cricket team was dominating world cricket. While the West Indies cricket team was dominant, West Indian societies struggled to survive each day. The challenges to overcome were no longer represented on the field of play but in the rising tide of global economic globalization with its networks of corporations and markets. Cricket was now no longer tied to struggle and politics but to economics.

As a result, while in the 1970s and 1980s the style of play was still

---

[523] Patrick Taylor ed. **Nation Dance: Religion, Identity and Cultural Difference in the Caribbean** (Bloomington/Indiana: Indiana University Press, 2001), p. 10
[524] See Barry Chevannes *"Jamaican Diasporic Identity − The Metaphor of yaad"* and Abrahim H. Khan *"Identity, Personhood and Religion in Caribbean Context"* in Patrick Taylor ed. **Nation Dance** (Bloomington/Indiana: Indiana University Press, 2001).

flamboyant and aggressive, marked by controlled panache and flair, and filled with improvisation that broke free from imposed 'limitations,' it became significantly different in the 1980s, 1990s, and 2000s. Now, in a globalized world with West Indian economies facing pressure, the style of play appears tentative, defensive, uncertain, and lacking in strokes, focusing on graft and simply occupying the crease without producing runs, becoming unentertaining, even with stars like Brian Lara and Carl Hooper on the field. As early as 1963, C.L.R. James noted that "in cricket, the West Indies have evolved a style of their own, even if in independence as a whole they have yet to do so." In summary, in these globalized times, the West Indies cricket team struggles between "the ways of their raising and the influences of an imported culture."[525]

Essentially, the failure of West Indian societies to develop a distinct style for independence has undermined and ultimately led to the collapse of our approach to cricket. The struggles on the field mirror the broader economic challenges faced by Caribbean nations in sectors like sugar, bauxite, oil, bananas, and offshore banking. In short, we no longer possess a product or[526] a unique style of our own. In West Indian societies, there is no distinct identity on or off the field. Ultimately, one aspect reflects the other, and vice versa.[527]

Theological Perspectives

Previously, it was noted that during the 1960-1966 period, missionaries were reluctant to engage with existential issues and the cultural specificities of Africans and Indians as sites for theological

---

[525] Tim Hector *"Lara in Cricket Time and Social Place"* Fan The Flame, **Outlet Newspaper** April 9, 1999

[526] Dorbrene E. O'Marde *"West Indies Cricket: Is the Music Loud Enough?"* speech delivered at the Carifesta V11 Symposium on "Continuing to Define Ourselves in a Changing World" August 23, 2000 held in St. Kitts/Nevis.

[527] Hector, *"Will We Continue"* Fan The Flame, **Outlet Newspaper**, December 1, 2000

reflection. In contrast, the post-independence years of 1968-1977 and the 1977-1980s witnessed the rise of religiopolitical movements such as Rastafarianism and the Revivalist cults, including Revival Zion, Streams of Power, and the[528] Jordanites. This era also saw the establishment of CADEC (Christian Action for Development in the Caribbean) and ARC (Action for the Renewal of the Churches) emerging from the Caribbean Conference of Churches. Rastafarianism represents a rejection of White Christianity and its ideology in favor of a religious view that roots its understanding of the Supreme Being in black identity, using indigenous symbols for worship. Revivalism seeks to connect with African roots and religious heritage. Through CADEC and ARC, the Caribbean Conference of Churches champions ecumenism, social development, and social justice. All three religio-political organizations are united in the struggle for self-discovery, empowerment, identity, and the recovery and reaffirmation of African culture and heritage.

However, radical attempts by Rastafari and the Caribbean Conference of Churches to reconnect with African roots and religious heritage, as well as to promote "social change in obedience to Jesus Christ and in solidarity with the poor,"[529] have lost both their impact and momentum simultaneously. The American invasion of Grenada in 1983, the subsequent demise of the Grenada Revolution, unprecedented American cultural penetration, and the rise of Pentecostal and Fundamentalist sects are contributing factors. For instance, Rastafarianism has become more about style and fashion than a lived reality, while the Caribbean

---

[528] Kortright Davis, *Emancipation Still Comin' – Explorations in Caribbean Emancipatory Theology* (Maryknoll, New York: Orbis Books, 1990), p. 52; see also Neil Parsanlal *"In Search of a Black Theology for the Caribbean: Rastafarianism and Revivalism"* in *Caribbean Journal of Religious Studies* Vol. 17 No. 1 April 1996, pp. 5-7

[529] **Called To Be, Report of Caribbean Consultation for Development, Trinidad, November 1971** (Barbados: CADEC, 1972), p. 23; see also pp. 24, 33-34

Conference of Churches now focuses on HIV/AIDS and the uprooted people of the Caribbean.

What is happening here is that the church and the neo-African religions are turning inward, thus distancing themselves from their socio-economic, political, and cultural context of origin. Turning inward is not the right direction. The day may be postponed but is inevitable when Caribbean people must reject the monotheism and monoculture of foreign and traditional churches or faith expressions and reconnect with the socio-religious cultural traditions, practices, and customs of their heritage. Such reconnections represent a shift toward Caribbean theological perspectives of peoplehood,[530] as ties are established and reestablished with all the cultures, religions, and traditions that define us as Caribbean people. For the sake of authentic existence, that day cannot come soon enough.

The foregoing analysis reveals that cricket integrates, humanizes, and equalizes.[531] In this regard, cricket is as cultural as it is theological, as culture is the wellspring of theology.

Cricket as Hermeneutical Practice of Resistance

Cricket is a game of order. The umpire is the authority, and his decisions are final. The field of play is a 'sacred' space. To cross that 'sacred' space, the boundary line, is to trespass. And trespassers are penalized.

Yet in the history of West Indian cricket, this order has been challenged, and that 'sacred' space traversed when the cricketing public deems the rule of that order unjust. Such a feat requires public acknowledgment, especially when opposing tactics are considered unfair. For the West Indian cricket community, the boundary is

---

[530] Burton Sankeralli, **At The Crossroads**, p. 224

[531] Tim Hector *"From Vivi to Sir Vivian"*, Fan The Flame **Outlet Newspaper**, May 26, 2000

artificial. Throughout West Indies' cricket history, it is not uncommon for the cricketing public to disrupt play on the field in protest of the rule of that order, reflecting the upheaval and disruption of the social order in society. At these times, cricket becomes a mirror, an arena, and a social drama.[532]

In 1953, at the Bourda cricket ground in Guyana, turmoil in society spilled over onto the field of play. The year 1953 marked the electoral victory of the People's Progressive Party in Guyana. Soon after, the British forced that party from office and suspended the constitution. It was a time of rising national consciousness. On the field, the West Indies cricket team was locked in a battle against all teams, including England. England held the advantage in the match, having already scored 435 runs in their first innings, while the West Indies had 139 for 7.[533] McWatt and Holt, two West Indian batsmen from Guyana, were staging a comeback when umpire Badge Menzies ruled McWatt run out, a decision deemed dubious by the cricketing public. Bottles were thrown onto the field, disrupting play for a time. Notably, the cricketing public's open disapproval was aimed at umpire Badge Menzies, not the English players.

In 1960, at the Queen's Park Oval in Trinidad, the societal struggle against American imperialism again played out on the cricket field. Trinidad and Tobago was engaged in a battle to reclaim the Chaguaramas military base from American control. It was also a time marked by the quest for political self-determination from Britain. On the cricket field, the West Indies cricket team was again in conflict against England, of all teams. Once more, England held the upper hand. The West Indies found themselves in dire straits at 98 for 8 when Ramadhin, alongside

[532] Orlando Patterson *"The Ritual of Cricket"* in Beckles and Stoddart eds., **Liberation Cricket, West Indies Cricket Culture,** p. 141
[533] Maurice St. Pierre *"West Indies Cricket – Part 11, An Aspect of Creolization"* in Beckles and Stoddart eds., **Liberation Cricket, West Indies Cricket Culture,** pp. 132-134

Singh, initiated a recovery, while England had scored 382. Trinidadian umpire Leekow controversially called Ramadhin, the West Indian batsman from Trinidad, run out under questionable circumstances, resulting in the West Indies all out for 112. The cricketing public erupted in riot. However, the protest was aimed at the perceived bias of umpire Leekow, not the English players.

In 1968, at the Sabina Park cricket ground in Jamaica, class conflicts and societal tensions once again spilled over onto the cricket field. During the 1960s, the social stratification that characterized Jamaican society was evident through the unequal distribution of income, color prejudice,[534] and the seating arrangements in the cricket stadium. The elite and middle class, typically of lighter skin tones, were seated in the covered and shaded stands, while the working class, often consisting of Black individuals, sat in semi-covered stands or stood in open areas. This social stratification was clearly on display at Sabina Park that day. On the cricket field, the Black West Indian team was losing to the white English team. England had made 376 runs, while the West Indies had only scored 143, prompting England to ask the West Indies to follow on. At 204 runs in the second innings, the Jamaican umpire Sang Hue made what appeared to be an unfair caught-out decision against Butcher, a West Indian batsman from Guyana. The cricketing public responded by throwing bottles from the semi-covered stands and open areas, and they invaded the field of play. The police were called in to restore order. The entrance and involvement of the police heightened the drama, as "the actors lived their roles." Similar[535] to the situations in Guyana and Trinidad, the anger of the cricketing public was directed at the Jamaican umpire, Sang Hue, rather than the players.

The point of the above three examples is to show that the umpire symbolised resistance against the system. One should note here that

---

[534] Patterson *"The Ritual of Cricket"* in Beckles and Stoddart eds., **Liberation Cricket, West Indies Cricket Culture,** p. 146
[535] Ibid

resistance was generated by and centred in the socio-existential realities of the cricketing public – rising nationalist consciousness in Guyana, the struggle against American Imperialism in Trinidad, class conflicts and tensions, and black consciousness in Jamaica. The umpire, perceived as the symbol of order and control, the chief upholder of the system, and the guardian of the assumptions, rather than the players, was seen as the cause of injustice and partiality. The umpire was the one to attack; his decisions were the ones to challenge and overturn despite the game's boundary and assumptions. Now, this manner of resistance is instructive for the Caribbean biblical hermeneutical practice. In the examples cited, culture is the "text". The Readers are the cricketing public who are literate and conscious of their socio-existential realities. Their "reading" of the "text" led them to resist the perceived unjust system. They were not just readers of the word but doers of the word. In short, where biblical hermeneutics is done using an "inside out" reading strategy, from the text to the context, especially without the socio- ideological agenda at work in the text identified, unjust and oppressive systems remain untouched, though perhaps exposed and criticised, however, where biblical hermeneutics is done using the "outside-in" approach, from context to text, where the socio-ideological agenda at work is divined, unjust and oppressive systems are exposed, challenged and resisted.

The "inside-out" reading strategy focuses on redemption, while the "outside- in" approach emphasizes resistance and eventual liberation. In unjust and oppressive systems, human beings are at stake—their humanity, their way of being, and their self-realization. Engaging with biblical texts without considering the reader's context and the social reality of the reader is to overlook the system as a source of oppression and suppression, leading readers to seek liberation only from the personal bondage of sin and death. Conversely, reading texts through the epistemological lens of contextual realities allows one to recognize the system as a root cause of oppression or suppression. Consequently, readers strive for liberation from the structural and systemic bondage that dehumanizes them and hinders their full human potential.

It is not unreasonable to assume that many of the cricketing public in attendance at the cricket match are Bible reading and weekly Sunday worshippers in their chapel of membership. Yet, while in the cultural context of cricket they are inclined to understand the cultural meaning of a bad decision at a cricket match by the "system" (the umpire) and respond by resisting, they do not resist the "system" (oppressive social structures and practices) because of interpreting biblical texts. Even when the "umpire" in the wider society is identified, they are hesitant to "cross boundaries". This hesitancy is due to the way in which they are taught to understand and interpret biblical texts, despite the cultural-literacy consciousness demonstrated at a cricket match. Without a socio-structural analysis of biblical texts – what were the political, ideological, theological, economic circumstances that produced this text? Does the text take sides? Whose voice dominates or is silenced in the text? What religious perspective of God is expressed in the text? What is the reader's way of knowing into the text? – there is no socio-structural understanding of contextual realities, which will lead to a strategy to re-engage the sociality of existence. Despite this, my argument is that the manner of resistance at the cricket match is instructive for biblical hermeneutics within the Caribbean context.

Additionally, the disruption of play and resistance to the system in Guyana in 1953, Trinidad in 1960, and Jamaica in 1968 demonstrate a connection between the social struggle for self-determination and self-identification, as well as 'play,' resistance, and subversion.[536]

The preceding discussion is shown in the table below:

---

[536] Richard D.E. Burton *"Creolization, Ideology and Popular Culture"* in Beckles and Stoddart eds., **Liberation Cricket, West Indies Cricket Culture**, pp. 92-93

Table 6:4

Cricket and theology in socio-historical praxis

Periods	Social Forces	Style of Play/way of being (Cricket)	In Theology	Style of Play/ way of being (Theology)
Colonial	System of oppression and negation White European domination Ideology of race Deracination, Alienation	English: dull and regimented Africans: risky, exuberant, expressive, aggressive *1953: disruption of play, Bourda, Guyana*	Theology of imposition, Deculturisation , Shango, Obeah, Voodoo, Pocomania, Jordanites, Shouters	Struggle between the policy of white European Christianity to impose and deculturalise and the quest of enslaved Africans for self- discovery, self- hood, self-realisation and authenticity
Post– "emanci – pation"	Rise in nationalist self-consciousness Sense of common history, culture and political identity Appointment of first Black cricket captain	Dash, panache, uninhibited, attacking with due respect for disciplined necessity, Team ethic *1960: disruption of play, Queen's Park Oval, Trinidad*	Theology of imitation	Non-creative, imitative, disconnect with existential realities, unreality and unrelatedness, distortion and prevention of contextual understanding of theology

Post-"indepen dence"	Collapse of Federation, Cultural evaluation, Post-"independence" political problems, Beginning of IMF structural adjustment programme	Individually brilliant players, loss of team ethic, cavalier, aggressive *1968: disruption of play, Sabina Park, Jamaica*	Theology of development, Decolonisation of theology, Black Power movement, Rastafarianism, Revivalism,	Rejection of white European Christianity but not by the masses, struggle for self-identity, social justice and development, Reassertion of African culture and heritage,
	Structural adjustment, Underdevelopme nt, Unemployment, Reign without rule	Attractive, daring and judicious, attacking to release 'limitations' imposed	Caribbean Conference of churches, Pentecostalism, Fundamentalis m	Commercialisati on of religion, Electronic church
	Foreign control made more foreign, Globalisation, 'home' as different reality, Dependent growth, Loss of particularities, Cultural penetration and imperialism	Tentative, defensive, strokeless, unentertainin g, occupation of the crease without production	**My suggestions:** **Need to reconnect with socio-religio-cultural heritage, practices, customs and traditions and resistance.** **Caribbean theological perspectives of peoplehood.**	

From the above table, the following conclusions can be drawn:

- The colonial, post-emancipation, and post-independence periods witnessed a thoroughgoing struggle against and resistance to foreign forms, systems, and ideology—a battle that the missionaries did not enjoin. The Africans, their descendants, and the Europeans found themselves in foreign lands. The Africans went from freedom to captivity, and the Europeans came to hold captives. In these circumstances, the missionary church was opposite to its raison d'etre.

- Nationalist consciousness and affirmation have been diminished in the neo-colonial global order.
- The more economic growth relied on foreign investment, the more denationalized the cultural systems became, and the more inward and pastoral the church appeared.
- Resistance is the authentic way of being for Caribbean peoples, as they are more likely to determine their future and define their identity for themselves when they resist alienation and domination.
- When we consume or are consumed by the products and ways of others, we neither become ourselves nor resist outside domination.

Carnival as Hermeneutical Practice of Resistance

In addition to cricket, carnival—another of the Caribbean's key cultural expressions—also highlights the connection between social struggle for self- determination, self-identification, 'play', resistance, and subversion. Carnival offers valuable insights into biblical hermeneutical practices within the Caribbean.

The French planters introduced carnival in the Caribbean at the end of the eighteenth century.[537] However, Black communities adopted and transformed the manner and content of the masquerade during the post-emancipation era to incorporate African traditions and customs,

---

[537] Thomas Bremer & Ulrich Fleischamann, eds., **Alternative Cultures in the Caribbean** (Frankfurt: Vervuert Verlag, 1993), p., 140

allowing it to continue evolving over the years.[538] In its original form, the carnival was a festival where French planters mimicked the *nègre jardin* or field laborer. The planters blackened their faces and wore the tattered clothing of enslaved African field workers.[539] However, this was not mere mimicry or 'play'; it served as another means of dehumanizing the enslaved Africans.

Nonetheless, when the emancipated Africans in their canboulay embraced the festival or midnight procession that included singing and dancing, armed with sticks and torches as they marched through the streets,[540] this was not merely an imitation of the French Planters but rather symbolic and revolutionary in content and intent. Torches symbolized the dawn of a new day of freedom. A process of transculturation occurred as the emancipated Africans transformed the *negre jardin*, a parody designed to dehumanize them, into a *canboulay*, which served as a mask of a mask or a liberating practice—a safe way to engage in dangerous activities. Here, the masquerade's political potential as "rituals of rebellion" was clear. However, the fact that it also provided a release from the stress and strain of oppressive and exploitative plantation life meant that it ultimately did little more than reinforce the status quo.[541] In such circumstances, the masquerade was reduced to a "role serious, not real serious" state.[542]

Such differences in content and intent indicate that carnival, both past and present, represents a contested cultural performance.[543] On one hand, there is a ritualized role reversal involving both oppressors and

---

[538] Errol Hill *"Traditional Figures in Carnival: Their Preservation, Development and Interpretation"* in **Caribbean Quarterly** Vol. 31 No. 2 June 1985, p. 20

[539] Ruth Wust, **The Trinidad Carnival From Canboulay to Pretty Mass**, unpublished M.A Thesis, Berlin (1987)

[540] Ibid.

[541] Abner Cohen, *"A Polytechnic London Carnival as a Contested Cultural Performance"* in **Ethnic and Racial Studies,** 5:1 January 1982, pp., 23-41

[542] Barton, **Afro-Creole**, p., 245

[543] Cohen, *A Polytechnic London Carnival*, p., 37

the oppressed; on the other, there is the "lampooning of liberty"[544] by the oppressed. In this context, the carnival masquerade seeks to balance consensus with conflict, control with spontaneity, and compliance with subversion.[545] When this balance tips in favor of consensus and control, carnival becomes stylized. A stylized masquerade signifies that power is contested ritually and thus becomes entrenched. However, when it shifts toward conflict, spontaneity, and subversion, carnival transforms into "ritualized[546] resistance"—a genuine symbol of freedom that disrupts the imposed patterns of society, fostering a new understanding of self and society, all the while maintaining a sense of gaiety.

These two traditions – *negre jardin* and *canboulay* – are in flux within contemporary Caribbean carnival culture. While the concept of creating images of images remains – artists and their masqueraders portraying social realities or continuing the human experience –the absence of facemasks and the loss of irony, along with their immediate critical, political, and revolutionary edge and intent, is evident. This absence and loss are largely due to middle-class participation, the institutionalization of carnival administration, and the branding of carnival with a focus on marketing and profit. Consequently, the emphasis has shifted from mimicry and irony to asserting selfhood. The days when mas' was a political and revolutionary act are gone. Now, the subverters have become subverted.[547] For V.S. Naipaul, "carnival is neither an illusion nor a direct reflection of social reality but a stylized rendering of society's concerns and values." The[548] emphasis is now on color, making carnival a riot of hues, more stylized than political or revolutionary. It

---

[544] Victor Turner, *"The Spirit of Celebration"* in Frank Manning, ed. **The Celebration of Society: Perspective on Contemporary Cultural Performance** (Bowling Green, Ohio,1983), pp. 187-191

[545] Capelleveen, **Peripheral Culture,** p. 140

[546] Ibid. p., 141

[547] Barton, **Afro-Creole,** p. 278

[548] V.S. Naipaul, **The Middle Passage** (London: Deutsch, 1962), p., 90

has become a performance that has lost connection to subversion and resistance.

Accordingly, the carnival masquerade reflects a broader Caribbean struggle or dilemma: economic benefits versus the quest to convey cultural history and reality.[549] In essence, the Caribbean dilemma is about "how to eat and remain human,"[550] as the economic often seems hostile to the artistic, and the cultural to the economic. This tension between the cultural and economic represents an arduous struggle, yet it is nonetheless a version of Caribbean reality. This is our epistemology, our way of knowing and interpreting."

I acknowledge that carnival has the potential for resistance. Carnival also illustrates the "outside in" approach to reading "text," as indicated above. In a carnival, masqueraders display costumes and masks. They dress as queens, kings, and band princesses, representing their understanding of socio-political and economic realities. Such an interpretation of social realities is, in effect, a direct challenge to structures, hierarchies, and values, albeit symbolic and filled with gaiety. This shows that oppressive systems need not be challenged violently all the time. 'Play' or masquerading serves as a revolutionary tool—a safe way to engage in dangerous actions. The prophets of Israel and Jesus employed prophecy and parables to convey harmful messages safely. It is to the detriment of the Caribbean peoples' liberation from oppressive and unjust systems in their societies that carnival has become more about gaiety than a revolutionary tool. Essentially, carnival is a revolutionary tool and should be utilized as such.

---

[549] Dorbrene E. O'Marde, *"Calypso in the 1990s"* in **Antigua Carnival Souvenir Magazine**, April1990, p., 40

[550] George Lamming, Opening address Rex Nettleford cultural conference, U.W.I Jamaica March 1996 in **Caribbean Quarterly** Vol. 43 Nos. 1&2 March-June 1997, p. 6

Conclusion

The previous discussion emphasized the critical importance of understanding one's context and knowledge of place, whether concerning biblical texts or societal conditions, in resisting oppressive social systems and practices. Randall Bailey warned, "Unless one is aware of one's cultural biases and interests in reading the text and appropriating the tradition, one may be seduced into adopting another's culture, which is detrimental to one's health and well-being." Finally, it is essential to evaluate those realities and organize for social transformation while ensuring that theology emerges from praxis and is grounded in the lived realities of the people. It is a biblically resistant hermeneutic that will dismantle the alluring aspects of a foreign culture, establish knowledge of place, and ultimately promote authenticity of existence.

CONCLUSION

In this study, I argue that biblical texts emerge from a lived context. In this context, political, theological, and socio-economic perspectives, practices, and systems are inscribed and re-inscribed in the interpretation of experiences. In other words, biblical texts do not represent mere dictation. Instead, they are composed from perspectives arising from specific experiences.

Based on this argument, I draw the following conclusions:

1. Interpreting biblical texts within the Caribbean context, beginning with the human condition or lived experiences, gives more agency to the interpreter's material circumstances than to the material circumstances from which the biblical texts emerged. This, in turn, lessens the effectiveness of biblical texts as tools of analysis for social change and justice **(Chapter 1)**.

2. Where biblical hermeneutics are conducted within institutionalized systems and conventions, biblical texts are constrained **(Chapter 1)**.

3. Interpreting biblical texts from a position of power and privilege removes their political, ideological, social, and economic aspects and implications **(Chapter 1)**, and consequently,

4. When biblical texts are stripped of their political, economic, ideological, and social interests and practices, the necessity

to take sides in the social struggle for change and justice is significantly diminished, if not eliminated **(Chapter 2)**.

5. When biblical texts are examined with a concrete commitment to and engagement in social struggles for change and justice, this leads to resistance against oppressive systems and practices **(Chapter 2)**.

6. When there is socialization of the means of power and governance in society, which involves participation and partnership within the social system, social relationships characterized by equality and justice are established **(Chapter 3)**.

7. Reconciling personal relationships within social systems marked by inequality and disparities in power and status does not free us from systemic or structural injustices and inequalities **(Chapter 4)**.

8. Revisiting biblical texts through the unique experiences of the interpreter reveals the ideology, biases, silences, vested interests, and dominant voices present within these texts **(Chapter 4)**.

9. A reading strategy that is (i) critically aware of the cultural significance of contextual realities, (ii) arises from a concrete commitment to and engagement in the struggle for social change and justice, (iii) aims to establish the 'place' of the biblical text (the social, ideological, economic, and theological aspects that produced the text), and (iv) 'place' of the reader (the class, ideological commitment and stance, as well as hermeneutical presuppositions) results in resistance rather than opposition to oppressive systems and practices **(Chapter 5)**.

From the argument and findings above, I acknowledge that biblical texts are authored by individuals involved in *politics*. With this recognition, it becomes crucial for interpreting biblical texts as powerful agents of social change and justice to examine both the *political nature* of these texts and the *politicization* of the hermeneutical process.

Below, I will clarify how I am using the terms politics, political, and politicization in this context.

By *politics*, I refer to "administering the power and governance of the state"[551] or managing public policy within the entire spectrum of human relations in society. The focus here is on administration, which allows this study to engage with the debate on the relationship between Church and State. Although such a debate is not the main focus of this study, the issues of faith and politics are intricately woven into the argument that the Bible is a constructed text. Therefore, it is crucial to recognize that what matters is for both faith and the administration of public policy to be held in tension, rather than being polarized. The State is neither independent of God's rule nor exempt from morality. The Church should not shy away from facing ridicule and victimization when trying to influence public policy and protect its image. Faith should not merely hover over the complexity of human relations in society or public policy. Concrete commitment and involvement must be fully embraced in the practice of faith.

Furthermore, it cannot be overlooked that the Church exists within a socio- political-economic context. The Church engages with society and is an integral part of it (John 17:15-18). People must be related to and responded to within the full scope of the concrete realities of their lives. Therefore, the social, cultural, and economic conditions of people's lives cannot be separated from matters of faith. The interaction between faith, practice, and politics must foster a social process that strives for human emancipation and development.

If politics is understood to encompass the total complexity of the social, cultural, political, and economic facets of human relations in society, then Philemon is a political biblical text. Whether we interpret the letter to Philemon as primarily addressing the exercise of authority

---

[551] Leonardo Boff, O.F.M., **Faith On the Edge, Religion and Marginalized Existence** (San Francisco: Harper & Row Publishers, 1989), p. 39

by Paul over Philemon or by Philemon over Onesimus, or as focusing on reconciliation rather than social justice, or vice versa, or viewing running away as a means of subverting the social system and its practices is irrelevant. All these perspectives concern people involved in administering public policy or responding to the effects of such policies. In the letter to Philemon, the key players include the master, who is also the manager of a household economy and thus a member of the ruling elite that administers public policy. The slave is an exploited member of the dominated class, countering oppressive public policy. Therefore, all aspects of the social structure and system in Philemon possess political dimensions.

By "political," I mean "a specific view of social reality" or one's "understanding of social organization."[552] In other words, regarding the governance, power, and socio- economic structure of society, one is concerned with such questions as: how is power attained, and how is society governed? Are these systems oppressive? Are they democratic? Do they favor the rich over the poor? Who holds power? Who controls the productive forces? Who owns what, how much, and why? Which ideas and beliefs prevail? How do social forces compete?

The point is that biblical texts engage with this political process and provide a specific perspective on the social realities of their context. Despite the ambiguities surrounding Paul's request to Philemon, it is undeniable that Paul is confronting a social reality—the institution of slavery and the subversive nature of escaping—that affects how society organizes itself.

By *politicization*, I refer to the process of educating or raising awareness among people and organizing them to have a voice and a role in the political process.[553] For individuals to critique, challenge, revolutionize, and engage in the decision-making process of society and become

---

[552] Ibid. p. 38
[553] Ibid. p. 40

stakeholders in the social organization of their socio- geographic space, there must be a politicization of the interpretive process. Failing to politicize the interpretation of Philemon would mean not focusing on or analyzing the governance, power relations, and household economy of imperial Graeco-Rome. This would effectively sterilize the letter by spiritualizing its social, ideological, and economic dimensions.

In effect, the resistant biblical hermeneutic within a Caribbean context involves politicizing the hermeneutical process. One consequence of using the analytical tools employed in this study is the political utilization of biblical texts. The resistant biblical hermeneutic in a Caribbean context applies historical-materialist and postcolonial criticism to biblical studies and contextual Bible study as analytical tools to (i) reveal the social, ideological, economic, political, and theological dimensions of biblical texts; (ii) uncover both dominant and suppressed voices and interests within biblical texts, and reinterpret texts through the socio-cultural experiences of the interpreter; (iii) ensure that the hermeneutical process does not sanitize biblical texts of their political agency while seeking to draw lessons from specific contextual issues. When biblical texts are not used politically, they lose social relevance and their effectiveness as instruments in the struggle for social change and justice.

A critique of two examples from biblical hermeneutics within a Caribbean context demonstrates that the impact of biblical texts is diminished when the interpretive process is not politicized. In this regard, I will analyze the exegesis of 1 Corinthians 14:34–36, concerning the issue of women becoming clergy, as discussed in the article *'The Word in Context: The Essential Criterion for Doing and Reflecting Authentic Caribbean Theology'* and *'Deuteronomic Themes in a Caribbean Context.'*

For Jennings, two critical factors in hermeneutics are how the Bible is understood and what he refers to as double contextualization.[554]

---

[554] Jennings, *The Word in Context*, pp. 3–4.

Jennings defines the Bible as the "record and witness to the primordial revelation of God, particularly in the uniqueness of Yahweh, God of Israel, and Jesus of Nazareth."[555] Double contextualization involves "interpreting and applying the Bible within its original context and interpreting and applying the Bible to our own context."[556] For Jennings, the essential issue here is to determine what the text meant to the original audience, considering the specific milieu of the time when it was written.[557] Building on this understanding of the Bible and double contextualization, Jennings presents three exegetical questions for interpretation: to whom was the Apostle speaking? What specific situation were the words addressing? What do the words or phrases signify? In summary, Jennings emphasizes that he aims to avoid confusion between the context and content of the text.[558]

Although Jennings attempts to place the text correctly, his focus on revelation suggests that the Bible is a socio-ideological product. The original message and audience Jennings seeks to recover may well belong to the legitimized ruling, elitist, and patriarchal class responsible for composing biblical texts. This recovered message may not necessarily reflect God's intentions if the socio-ideological agenda within the text remains unidentified. It is not simply a matter of determining "to whom" and "to what specific situation words were addressed." One must also recognize the ideology at play in that address which shaped and influenced the specific situation. If Jennings had pinpointed the socio-ideological agenda in the text, he would have observed that the question of women becoming clergy indicates a power dynamic within ecclesiastical structures and systems. In other words, it is the ruling ecclesiastical authorities who decide who serves as clergy in the church. Therefore, had he utilized this level of analysis, Jennings would

---

[555] Ibid. p. 3
[556] Ibid. p. 4
[557] Ibid. p. 4
[558] Ibid. p. 8

acknowledge that an ideology of male patriarchy and marginalization operates here, and as a result, the text either serves or challenges class or gender interests.

For Jennings to identify the socio-ideological interests at play in the text, he needed to trace it back to its socio-historic origins. This does not mean comparing "how similar or different the first-century ecclesiastical situation is to current realities,"[559] as Jennings does. Rather, it requires recognizing that the ecclesiastical situation, shaped by the metropolitan context of Corinth and the broader imperial Graeco-Roman society and state, forms the backdrop of the text. According to Richard Horsley, the metropolitan context of Corinth consisted of uprooted individuals who were not influenced by their traditional social connections and commitments, yet were still under the control of the imperial order and the power dynamics of the provincial elite, encompassing a network of patron-client relationships and family structures.[560] The imperial Graeco-Roman state and society was characterized by a patriarchal-hierarchical social structure where women were marginalized and excluded from leadership and participation in societal decision-making processes, leaving Christians subject to the patriarchal societal order. Within this social framework, the conflict between equality and hierarchy in imperial Graeco-Roman society is mirrored in the ecclesiastical situation.

Within the text or in the letter of 1 Corinthians itself, this conflict is evident. According to 1 Corinthians 11:2-16, women are permitted to speak or prophesy when the community of faith gathers. However, 1 Corinthians 14:34-36 revokes that right. Is there a contradiction here? Is 1 Corinthians 14:34-36 a later addition to the text? In other words, is it an attempt to align women with the ideology of a patriarchal- hierarchical

---

[559] Ibid. p. 4
[560] Richard A. Horsley *"Submerged Biblical Histories and Imperial Biblical Studies"* in R. S. Sugirtharajah ed. **The Postcolonial Bible** (Sheffield: Sheffield Academic Press, 1998), p. 169

society?[561] Was Paul addressing only married women?[562] Or did early church tendencies influence the social practices of the church in Paul's name? Was the church at Corinth an alternative community resisting the Roman imperial order?[563] For De La Torre, the possibility exists that the text was neither a commentary on the injustices around the role of women in the church and the ideology of a patriarchal- hierarchical society nor a set of instructions for the community of faith to follow. Instead, it intended to "illustrate the consequences of being a woman within a patriarchal society."[564] The consequences of submission, subordination, and exclusion of women by patriarchy represent the socio-ideological agenda at play in 1 Corinthians 14:34-36.

The challenge with Jennings' interpretive approach is that he becomes entrenched in an exegetical strategy that starts with the text as the word of God, rather than considering the marginalization of women in the church or society due to patriarchy. Initiating exegesis with the biblical text merely seeks to recover the broader universal message of the text and apply it to a specific context. The risk with this method is that if the interest or voice embedded in the biblical text is not recognized, one might inadvertently align with an interest or voice that contradicts one's own. The universal is not found in the particular, but the particular exists within the universal. If the interest or voice of the biblical text is overlooked, Jennings may still fall into the confusion between the context and content of the text that he aims to evade, and the double contextualization approach might indeed lead to double the trouble.

What is critical, therefore, is the social reality from which one begins

---

[561] Miguel A. De La Torre, **Reading The Bible From the Margins** (Maryknoll: Orbis Books, 2003), p. 170

[562] Elizabeth Shussler Fiorenza **In Memory of Her: A Feminist Theological Reconstruction of Christian Origins** (New York: Crossroad, 1983), pp. 230-33

[563] Horsley, **Submerged Biblical Histories**, pp. 170-71

[564] De La Torre, **Reading the Bible**, p. 170

the exegetical process, whether that of the reader or the biblical text. In other words, whether one starts "from the outside in" or "from the inside out" is the essential issue. On one hand, the "outside in" approach positions the reader in his or her place as he or she engages with the biblical text through his or her social reality, influenced by one's class, ideological stance, and commitment, meaning, with a consciousness of cultural literacy. This perspective shapes interpretation, as the "outside in" approach provides the reader with an 'elsewhere' from which to stand and read. On the other hand, the "inside out" approach encourages the reader to explore the socio-historical, economic, and political factors that shaped the text. This exploration aids the reader in identifying the socio-ideological and theological agenda present in the text, revealing what the text accomplishes and, consequently, what the reader must do.

Inevitably, Jennings' exegesis does not lead to resistance for four reasons. First, he approaches the biblical text without considering the epistemological lens of the cultural meaning of the marginalization of women in the Caribbean context. Second, Jennings fails to engage with the text from a praxis of resistance or with any acknowledgment of a concrete commitment or involvement against patriarchy; if he did, he did not recognize it as a critical part of the interpretive process. Third, although efforts were made to understand the context of the biblical text, this was not intended to give agency to the ideological, socio-economic, and theological interests and agendas that generated the text. Lastly, there is no clear ideological stance, commitment, or strategy arising from the exegesis of the text by which to re-engage with the sociality of existence, particularly regarding the marginalization of women in the Caribbean context.

Holder follows the hermeneutical path he identifies as cut by Hamid and Watty in the 1970s and taken as the model by other Caribbean hermeneutes throughout the 1980s and 1990s. He identifies a path to take "seriously the experiences of Caribbean peoples and relate these experiences to theological insights of the biblical tradition".[565] He divines the hermeneutical assumption behind this reading strategy thus: "the Bible as the word of the Lord can speak to and illuminate the experiences of Caribbean peoples".[566] To demonstrate this reading strategy, He uses what he calls Deuteronomic themes of "Land, Identity and Leadership" and relates these to Caribbean experiences. First, Holder discerns that there is a *nahalah* or inheritance challenge of Deuteronomy, which gives the right of land ownership.[567] Next, he makes the hermeneutical leap to the Caribbean experience wherein the plantation economy of colonial times bequeathed a system that deprived Caribbean peoples of land ownership. Holder charges that it is the responsibility of Caribbean governments to ensure that Caribbean peoples experience "their *berakah* or blessings through their relationship with their nahalah".[568]

Regarding identity, He sees cultural imperialism as a social reality preventing Caribbean people's self-identity from having "the space to grow and firmly establish itself".[569] This condition, He confesses, led him to Deuteronomy "to find some theological insights about identity that can address [the] Caribbean condition".[570] He points out that cultural imperialism threatens the identity of those to whom Deuteronomy is addressed. Holder does not say from whom the threat comes and why. Next, He posits that Deuteronomy deals with this cultural penetration by taking the addressees back into their past and infers that Caribbean people can only understand where they are when they understand from whence they came.[571]

In both examples, Holder's exegetical starting point is the Bible

---

[565] John Holder, *Is This The Word of The Lord*, p.p. 135-36
[566] Ibid. p. 136
[567] Ibid.
[568] Ibid.
[569] Ibid.
[570] Ibid.
[571] Ibid.

as the word of God, followed by attempts to contextualize the (original) message(s) derived. Essentially, the reading strategy focuses on contextualization, recovering the Bible's message for contemporary Caribbean social realities.

Holder does demonstrate cultural literacy consciousness. However, by starting the exegetical process from the "inside out"—focusing on the original meaning of the text or viewing the Bible as the word of God—he becomes hindered by concerns that prevent him from recognizing the socio-ideological issues within the text. This "inside out" approach restricts the reader's interests and experiences from influencing their interpretation. It is essential to acknowledge that the biblical text is already an interpretation, a version of reality that takes a stance, even when the starting point is the biblical text. Identifying the ideology behind these biblical versions is crucial. Additionally, Holder attempts to reconcile the universal with the particular.

Undoubtedly, land and identity are significant and pressing issues in the Caribbean. However, when interpreted outside of a distinct social reality, these issues may still be considered significant and pressing, yet not fully embraced by Caribbean people, as the specific causal factors remain unaddressed. In other words, through Holder's reading strategy, we may find answers from the Bible to questions not asked by Caribbean people. It is only when biblical interpretation is rooted in the realities of people's lives that it addresses the cause. In summary, when exegesis adopts an "inside out" approach—starting from the social reality of the text without recognizing its socio-ideological context—it transforms the Bible into a tool of criticism. Conversely, when it utilizes a reading strategy based on the "outside-in" approach, drawing from the social reality of the reader, the Bible serves as a tool of struggle.

In effect, Holder's exegesis of certain Deuteronomic themes does not lead to resistance due to four factors. First, Holder's understanding of Deuteronomy stems more from the contextual origins and purpose of the text rather than from the cultural significance of land and identity in his Caribbean context. Although he identifies colonial plantation economic practices related to land ownership and cultural imperialism as adversely affecting Caribbean peoples' self-identity, the focus is on the context and purpose of Deuteronomy, not the specific causes of the land and identity issues in the Caribbean. Analyzing the roots of the land and identity problem would imply that the contextual realities of Caribbean peoples provide the epistemological lens necessary for interpreting Deuteronomy. These contextual realities, arising from the analysis, would not only inform the reading of Deuteronomy but also guide action. Two, Holder does not mention any explicit commitment or engagement regarding cultural imperialism or land ownership issues that he struggled with; if he did, he did not incorporate it into his interpretive process. If that were the case, such a praxis of resistance would lead to a different approach to Deuteronomy and a different outcome from his exegetical efforts.

Third, the agency attributed to Deuteronomy relates to the "knowledge of the context, date, and purpose of Deuteronomy," rather[572] than the socio-ideological interests and agenda present within it. Identifying the socio-ideological interests and agenda of Deuteronomy, regardless of where this exegetical activity may fit into the process, would risk overlooking ideas and interests that could be detrimental to the issues of land and identity in the Caribbean. Caribbean hermeneutes cannot afford to approach biblical texts as if they were not composed from a specific perspective and out of contextual realities, which must be understood before applying biblical texts to contemporary situations.

Fourth, there is no strategy for re-engaging with the social nature of existence or, in Holder's case, for contending with cultural imperialism and the legacies of the colonial plantation economy.

---

[572] John Holder, *"Some Deuteronomic Themes in a Caribbean Context"* in **Caribbean Journal of Religious Studies** 14 (1993): p., 6

This study shows that resistance occurs when one has first analyzed the cultural meaning of social realities, second engaged in a praxis of resistance against what may be oppressive in those social realities, third given agency to the materiality of biblical texts and the context of the interpreter, wherein the socio-ideological agenda and social practices that produced the text are identified, and fourth implemented a strategy for re-engaging the social realities.

In sum, this study has not claimed that biblical texts are direct consequences of political, economic, and social circumstances. Rather, it has taken seriously the view that religious perspectives expressed in biblical texts convey the ideology, political and socio-economic relations, and circumstances of a particular society.

Suggestion for Further Research

The way forward involves utilizing aspects of the socio-cultural history of the Caribbean as an epistemological lens for biblical hermeneutics, employing the biblical- resistant hermeneutic developed by this study. For instance, Black Power, the Middle Passage, Anansi as a folk hero, and community can serve as an epistemological lens. Black Power is characterized as a defiance and protest movement against socio-economic conditions of oppression, domination, and discrimination.[573] It aims to promote economic and political independence and the development of a native philosophy and culture.[574] It is important to note that in the Caribbean context, the term Black Power is complicated by factors such as the variety of racial types and mixtures and the process of class formation. Nevertheless, the reality of the struggle against socio-economic conditions of oppression, domination, and discrimination that it represents and addresses will not hinder its application as an epistemological lens through which to interpret biblical texts.

---

[573] Hamid, **Troubling of the Waters**, pp. 106-117
[574] Ibid., p. 122

Disintegration is one of the significant issues in the Caribbean. Colonialism has burdened Caribbean societies with the legacy of fragmentation into social classes, island states, various languages, and different religious denominations and movements. In the biblical narrative, it is notable how Israel transitioned from an extended family to a tribal league, then to a monarchical state, followed by a priestly aristocracy, and ultimately to a church. Thus, community is a key theme in the Bible. Its story revolves around a specific community of people. Therefore, viewing community as a lens may provide valuable biblical hermeneutical insights into Caribbean integration.

The Middle Passage involved the crossing of the Atlantic by approximately 9 to 15 million Africans who were captured, chained, and forced to leave their homeland for the Caribbean and the Americas.[575] Olaudah Equiano, a former slave who purchased his freedom and became an abolitionist, described the transatlantic crossing as a "wretched situation... aggravated by the irritation of the chains, now unbearable, and the filth of the necessary tubs where the children fell and almost suffocated. The screams of the women and the groans of the dying rendered the entire scene of horror almost unimaginable."[576] In these anguished and hopeless circumstances, Equiano and his fellow Africans viewed death as a release. Therefore, biblical texts such as the Psalms and Job, along with biblical motifs like the crucifixion of Jesus, can be reinterpreted through the lens of pain, despair, injustice, and death.

The point I want to make here is not that the socio-cultural aspects of Caribbean history should lead us to conclusions about the biblical text and then seek religious justification for them. Rather, it is that these socio-cultural concerns should shape the biblical interpretive process. An integral part of this interpretive process is its interaction with the socio-ideological interests and social practices reflected in biblical texts. The

---

[575] Eric Williams, **Capitalism and Slavery** (London: Andre Deutsch, 1964), pp. 3-35

[576] Olaudah Equiano, **Equiano's Travels** (London: Heinemann, 1967), p 29

goal of re-engaging with the social aspects of existence, with the aim of fostering a just social order, must always guide these two dimensions. Neglecting this interpretive process means that biblical hermeneutics in a Caribbean context will continue to engage with biblical texts for personal spiritual growth rather than for societal transformation.

BIBLIOGRAPHY

Caribbean Social History

Baptist Missionary Society (BMS) Periodical Account V (1813).

Barrett, Leonard E. *Soul Force* (New York: Anchor Press, 1974).

Barton, Richard D.E. *Afro-CreoLe*, Pow% Opposition *and Plal* in *the Caribbean* (Ithaca and London: Cornell University Press, 1997).

Beckford, Robert, *Dread and Pentecostal A Political T}reologyfor the Black Church in Britain* (London: SPCK, 2000).

Beckles, *Hilary Black Rebellion in Barbados, The Struggle Against Slavery 1627-1838* (Bridgetown: Caribbean Research and Publications Inc., 1987).

Beckles, Hilary and Shepherd, Verene, *Caribbean Freedom: Society and Economy From Emancipation* to *the* Present (Bridgetown: Caribbean Research and Publication, Inc., 1989).

Beckles, Hilary and Stoddart, Brian *(eds)*, *Liberation Cricket, West Indies Cricket Culture* (Manchester and New York: Manchester University Press, 1995).

Beckwith, *Martha famaica Anansi Stories* (New York: American Folklore Society, 1924). Birbalsingh F. and Shiwcharan, C. (eds), *Indo-West Indian Cricketers* (London: Hansib Publishing Ltd., 1988).

Bisnauth, Dale, *History of Religions Im the Caribbean* (Jamaica: Kingston Publishers, 1989)

Brathwaite, Edward Kamau, Wars *of Respect, Nanny and Sam Sharpe*, Agency for Public Information, Kingston, Jamaica, 1977.

Bremer, Thomas and Fleischamann, Ulrich (eds), *Alternative Cultures in the Caribbean* (Frankfurt: Vervuert Verlag, 1993).

Caldecott, Alfred, *The Church* in *the West Indies: West Indian Studies No. 14* (London: Frank Cass & Co. Ltd,, first published 1898, Reprinted 1970).

Campbell, Horace *Rasta* and *Resistance From Marcus* Garvey to *Walter Rodney* (London: Hansib Publishing Limited, 1985).

Coleridge, William Charges Delivered to the Clergy ofthe Diocese of Barbados and the Leeward *Islands*, (London: J. G. & F. Rivington, 1835).

Davis, Charles T. and Henry, LouiS;Gates, *The Slave's Narrative* (Oxford: Oxford University Press, 1985).

Dookan, Isaac, A *Pre-Emancipation Histon ojthe* Caribbean (London: Collins, 1974).

Mrs Flannigan, *Antigua **and** the Antiguans*, Volume 11 (London: Saunders & Otley, 1844)

Gatesl Brian *(ed)IAfo-Caribbean ReLigion* (London: Ward Lock Education, 1980). G^{enov}esel Eugene D.p *Roll Jordan Roll - The WorLd the Slaves Made* (New York:Mntage Books, 1974).

Goveia, Elsa, SLavery in the British Leeward Islands at the end of the Eighteenth Century (New Haven, CT and London: Yale University Press, 1965).

G^{ri}^{m}shawJ Annal *The C. L R. James Reader (Ox£ard* UK and Cambridge, MA: Blackwell, 1992)

LaTrobe, Benjamin, A Succinct View of the Missions Established Among the Heat}lens by the Church of the Brethren or Unitas Fratum, in a Letter to a Friend (London: M. Lewis, 1771) Letter dated 26 November 1770.

Hall Catherine, *Civitising Subjects* (Cambridge: Polity Press, 2002).

Hall, R., 'Acts Passed in the Island of Barbados 1643-1672, No. 42" in Hilary Beckles *(ed.) Black Rebellion in Barbados - The Struggle*

Against Slavery 1627–1838 (Bridgetown: Caribbean Research and Publication, Inc. 1987).

Harrisp Raymund, *Scriptural* Researches on *the Licitness of the Slave Trade* (London: 1788)

Hart, Richard, *Slaves Who Abolished Slavery* (Barbados, Jamaica, Trinidad and Tobago: University Press of the West Indies, 1985, 2002).

Higman, B. W, *Writing West Indian* Histories (London: Macmillan, 1999).

Hill, Robert A. (ed.), *The Marcus* Garvey and *UNIA* Papers (Berkeley, CA: University of California Press, 1983-1985).

Hinton, J. H., *Memoir of WiLliam Knit)b*, *Missionary* jn *yamaica* (London: 1897). HuttonI J. E.1 '4 *History of Moravian Missions* (London: Moravian Publications Office, 1922)

Jacques-Garvey, Amy (ed.), ***Philosophy and* Opinions *of Marcus* Garvey Vols. I & Jl** (Dover, MA: The Majority Press, 1986).

Jacques-Garvey, Amy and Essien-Udom, E.U ., *More Philosophy* and *Opinions of Marcus Gawel* (London: Frank Cass, 1987).

Jakobsosonl S., Am I Not a Man and a Brother? British Missions and the Abolition of The Slave Trade and Slavery in West Africa and the West Innes 1786–1838 (Uppsala, 1972)

James, Cyril L. R,, *Beyond a Boundary* (London: Stanley Paul, 1969)., *The Black Jacobins* (London: Penguin Books, 1980 3rd edition).

Lampef Armando, *Christianity* in *the Caribbean* – Essays on *Church History* (Barbados: University of the West Indies Press, 2001).

Lewis, Rupert and Patrick Bryan (eds), Garvey.' *His* Wba *and* Impact (Trenton1 NJ: Africa World Press, Inc., 1994).

Manning, Frank (ed.) The Celebration of Society: Perspective on Contemporary Cultural Performance (Bowling Green, OH: Bowling Green State University Popular Press, 1983)

Martin, Tony (ed.), *The* PoetIc Works *of Marcus* Garvey (Dover, MA: The Majority Press, 1983).

Meeks, Brian Narratives of Resistance – Jamaica, Trinidad, the Caribbean (*Jamaica:* The University Press of the West Indies, 2000).

Osborne, Francis J. SJ, "Coastlands and Islands, First Thoughts on Caribbean Church History"; in Inez Nibb-Sibley, *The Baptists* im *Jamaica* (Kingston: Jamaica Baptist Union, 1965).

Naipaul, V. S. *The Middle* Passage (London: Deutsch, 1962).

***Negro World Newspaper* 14:6, 24 March 1923.**

Pares, Richard, *Planters and Merchants* (Cambridge, UK, published for the economic history review at the University Press, 1960).

Patterson, Orlando, Slavery and *Social Death* (Cambridge, MA: Harvard University Press, 1982).

***Rogozinski, yan, A Brief History of the Caribbean: From Arrawaks and Caribs to the Present* (New York: Lengrun, 1992).**

Robotham, Don, "The Development of a Black Ethnicity in Jamaica"; in Rupert Lewis and Patrick Bryan, Garvey; *His Work and Impact (Trenton,* NJ: Africa World Press, Inc., 1994).

Sherlock, Philip, *Shout for Freedom:* A *Tribute* to *Sam Sharpe* (London: Macmillan, 1976)

Sunshine, Catherine A,, *The Caribbean: Survival, Struggle and Sovereign* (Washington, DC: EPICA, 1985).

Thomas, Clive, *The Poor and Powerless* (New York: Monthly Review Press, 1984). *Taylor, Patrick (ed.), Nation Dance: Religion, Identity and Cultural DWerence in the Caribbean* (Bloomington, IN: Indiana University Press, 2001).

***Turner, M,, Slaves and Missionaries – The Disintegration of the Jamaican Slave Society 1787-1834* (Urbana, IL: University of Illinois Press, 1982).**

Walcott, Derek, *What the Twilight Says* – Essays (London: Faber & Faber, 1998). wniams, Eric, *Capitalism and Slavery* (London: Andre Deutsch, 1964).

Boothe, Hyacinth, 'A Theological Journey For An Emancipatory Theology'; *Caribbean Journal of ReLigious Studies* 17 (1), 15–21, April 1996.

Boodoo, Gerald M., "Gospel and Culture in a Forced Theological Context'; *Caribbean* Journal *of Religious Studies* 17 (2), September 1996.

Caribbean Conference of Churches (CCC) *Called* To Be document (n.d.).

Ching, Theresa L, "Latin American Theological Method and its Relevance to Caribbean Theology'; *Caribbean Journal of Religious Studies* 12 (1), April 1991.

Davis, Edmund, "'Contextualisation as a Dynamic Process of Theological Education';CarIbbean *Journal of Religious Studies* 2 (2), September 1979.

Davis, Kortright, *Emancipation Still Comin:* (New York: Orbis Books, 1990). *(ed)*, *Moving Into Freedom*, (Bridgetown, Barbados: The Caribbean Conference of Churches, 1977)., "Sunshine Christopher's' Bearers of Christ in the Caribbean'; *The Journat of* Religious *Thought* 49 (2), 7-24, Wnter Spring 1992–1993.

Erskine, Noel Leo, *DecoLonising Theology*, A Caribbean *Perspective* (Maryknoll, NY: Orbis Books, 1981).

Goodridge, *Sehon S.*, *Facing the Challenge of Emancipation: A Study of the William* Hart Coleridge First Bishop of Barbados, 1824–1842 (Barbados: Cedar Press, 1981).

Gordon, ErnIe, "Emancipatory Theology (A Theological Journey) Gospel & Culture'; *Caribbean Journal of Religious Studies* 17 (1), 22–37, April 1996.

Gregory, Howard *(ed.)*, *Caribbean Theology: Preparing for the Challenges Ahead* (Jamaica: Kingston Publishers, 1995).

Hamid, Idris (ed.), Out *of the Depths* (Trinidad: St Andrew's Press, 1977). **(ed.)**, *in Search of New Perspectives* (**Barbados**: **CADEC, 1971)**. (ed.), *Troubling ofthe* Waters (Trinidad: Rahaman Press, 1973). *fagessar, Michael N,, Full Life For All: The Work and Theology of Philip A. Potter – A* Historical Survey and Systematic Analysis *ofMajw* Themes (Zoetermeer: Uitgeverij Boekencentrum, 1997). "Unending the Bible: The Book of Revelation Through the Optics ofAnansi **and Rastafari"; unpublished paper presented at the Black Theology Annual** Conference on Reading and Re-reading the Bible, 27 July 2006 Queens College, **Birmingham**.

Jennings, Stephen, "Caribbean Theology or Theologies'i *Caribbean fournal of Religious* **Studies 8 (2), 1–9, September 1987**.

-, "The Word in Context: The Essential Criterion For Doing Theology and Reflecting Authentic Caribbean Theology'; *Caribbean Journal of Religious Studies* 9 (1), 3-20, April 1988.

Kirton, Allan, *Peace:* A *Challenge fo the Caribbean* (Barbados: CADEC, 1982). , *Peace, Human Rights and Development* (Barbados: CADEC, 1982).

Kirton, Allan and Watty, William, *Consuttationfor Ministry* in alVew Decade (Barbados: CADEC, 1985).

-, "Current Trends in Caribbean Theology and the Role of the Church'; *Caribbean* **Quarterly, 37 (1), 1991**.

Father Lett, Leslie, Speech Delivered to Caribbean Studies Association, St. Kitts/Nevis, 2 June 1984.

, *Third WorLd Theology, The Struggle for the Kingdom* (Cambridge: Jubilee Research Centre, 1986).

Mitchell, David I. (ed.), *With Eyes Wide Open* (Jamaica: Kingston Publishers, 1973). *(ed.), With Eyes Wide Open – A Collection of Papers by Caribbean Scholars on* Caribbean Christian Concern (Barbados: CADEC, 1973).

Murrell, Samuel, "Wrestling Wth The Bible in The Caribbean Basin: A Case Study On Grenada in Light of Romans 13:1-7'; *Caribbean Journal of Religious Stt£ciies* 8 (1), 12–23, April 1987.

Parsanal, Neil, "In Search of a Black Theology For The Caribbean: Rastafarianism and Revivalism'i in *Caribbean journal of Religious Studies* 17 (1), April 1996.

Potter, Philip, *Life in All Its Fullness* (Geneva: World Council of Churches, 1981). Russell, Horace O., "The Emergence of the 'Christian Black' the Making of a Stereo-type'i *Caribbean Journal of Religious Studies* 2 (1), April 1979.

Sankeralli, Burton (ed.), At *the Cross Roads – African Caribbean* Religion *and Christianity* (Trinidad and Tobago: Caribbean Conference of Churches, 1995).

Smith, Ashley, "The Christian Minister As Political Activist" *Caribbean Journal of Religious Studies* 2 (1), April 1979.

, "Theological Education in the Caribbean - A Critique and some Proposals': *Caribbean Journal of Religious Studies* 11 (1), April 1990.

, "Sin and Salvation a Contemporary View From a Corner of the 'South"; *Caribbean fournat of Religious Studies* 17 (2), September 1996.

Watty1 William1 *From Shore to Shore _ Soundings* in *Caribbean Theology* (Barbados: Cedar Press, 1981).

Weir+ Emmette J., "Towards a Caribbean Liberation Theology" *Caribbean Journal of Religious Studies* 12 (1), 46–48, April 1991.

Williams, Lewin, "What, Why and Wherefore of Caribbean Theology'; *Caribbean fournat of Religious Studies* 12 (D, 29–40, April 1991.

., "Caribbean Theology and Ministerial Formation'; *Caribbean Journal of Religious Studies* 18 (1), April 1997.

Aymer, Albert, "Mark's Understanding of Discipleship as a Paradigm for Christian Life and Witness in the Caribbean Today': *Caribbean Journal of Religious Studies* 12 (2), September 1991.

CADEC, *Called To Be, Report of Caribbean ConsuLtation$r Development, Trinidad, November 1971* (Barbados: CADEC, 1972).

Coleridge, William, *Charges Delivered to the Clergy ofthe Diocese ofBarbados and the* Leeward *IsLands* (London: J. G. & F. Rivington, 1835).

Gossai, Hemchand and Murrell, Nathaniel S., *Religion, CuLture and Tradition* in *the* CarIbbean (New York: St Martin's Press, 2000).

Gayle, Clement H., "The Crisis of the Pulpit': *Caribbean Journal of Religious Studies* 12 (2), September 1991.

Gayle, Clement H. and Watty William W., CarIbbean *Pulpit* (Barbados: Cedar Press, 1983)

General Baptist Repositorl, vol. 1, Supplement 1802.

fagessar, Michael N. Full Life for All – The work and theology of Philip Potter: A Historical Survey and Systematic Analysis of Major Themes (Zoetermeer: Uitgeverij Boekencentrum, 1997).

Jagessar, Michael and Anthony Iteddie, *Postcolonial Black British Theology – New Textures and* Themes (Peterborough: Epworth, 2007).

Kirton, Allan and Watty, William (eds), *Consultation for Ministry* in a New Decade (Barbados: CADEC, 1985).

Mulrain, George M., "Is There a Calypso Exegesis?': in R. S. Sugirtharajah (ed.), Voices *From the Margins – Interpreting the Bible in the Third World (Maryknoll, NY:* Orbis Books, 1995).

., "Hermeneutics within the Caribbean Context'; in R. S. Sugirtharajah (ed.), *Vernacular Hermeneutics* (Sheffield: Sheffield Academic Press, 1999).

Nathan, Ronald, "The Spirituality of Marcus'; *Black Theology* in *Britain* 3 (1999): 45. Nicholas, Joseph E., "West Indies Cricket and Biblical

Faith': *Caribbean Journal of Religious Studies* 13 (2), September 1992–April 1993.

"Feminine Presentation of God in the Bible" Caribbean *Journal of ReLigious Studies*, 16 (1), April 1995.

Persaud, Winston, "Hermeneutics of the Bible and Cricket as text: Reading as an Exile'; in Fernando F. Segovia (ed.) *Interpreting Beyond Borders* (Sheffield: Sheffield Academic Press, 2000).

Potter, Philip, *Life in All im its FulLness* (Geneva: World Council of Churches, 1981).

Rahim, Jennifer, "Patterns of Psalmology, in Lovelace's *The 14Z£ne of Astonishmentf Caribbean Journal of Religious Studies* 16 (2), 3–17, September 1995.

Wynnr, Doreen, "Vashti's Voice': *Caribbean Journal of Religious Studies* 17 (2), September 1996

Swanson, Theodore N,, "Clouds Like A Man's Hand – Emerging issues in Biblical Interpretation'; *Caribbean Journal of Religious Studies* 2 (1), April 1979.

Biblical Hermeneutics and Theology

Aminham, Samuel (ed.), A *Vision For Man*, Essays on *Faith, Theology and Society* im *Honour ojfoshwa Russell Chandran* (Madras: Christian Literature Society, 1978). Assmann, Hugo, *Theologl for A Normal Church* (New York: Orbis Books, 1976). Boff, Leonardo OFM, *Faith On the Edge – Religion and Marginalized* Existence (San Francisco, CA: Harper & Row Publishers, 1989).

Boone, Kathleen C,, *The Bible Tells Them So - The Discourse of Protestant F&rndamerrtalisrn* (London: SCM Press, 1990).

Camps, Arnulf, "The Bible and the Discovery of the World: Mission, Colonization and Foreign Development'; in S. Freyne, *The Bible As Cultural Heritage, (–Concilium")* (London: SCM Press, 1995/1).

Cone, James H. and Wilmore, Gayraud S., *Black Theology - A Documentary* History *Volume* Two: *1980-1992* (Maryknoll, NY: Orbis Books, 2003).

Coote, Robert B. and Mary P. Coote, Pow% Politics *and the Making of the Bible* **(Minneapolis, MN: Fortress Press, 1990).**

Coote, Robert B. David Robert Ord, is *the Bible True? Undnstanciing the Bible Today* (London: SCM Press, 1994).

Croatto, I. *Severino, Biblical Hermeneutics: Towards a Theory of Reading as the Production of Meaning* (New York: Orbis, 1987).

De La Torre, Miguel A., *Reading the Bible From the Margins* (Maryknoll, NY: Orbis Books, 2003).

Equiano, Olaudah, *The Interesting Narrative* and *Other Writings* (New York: Penguin Books, 1995).

Felder, Cain Hope (ed.), *Stony the Road* We *Trod: African* American *Biblical* **Interpretation (Minneapolis, MN: Fortress Press, 1991).**

Fretheim, Terrence, *Creation, Fall and Flood* (Minneapolis, MN: Augsburg, 1969). Genovese, Eugene D., *Roll yortlan Roll, The World the Slaves Made* (New York: Vintage Books, 1976).

Gilmore, Ga)Fraud S. *Black* Religion *and BLack RadicaLism* 3ʳᵈ. edn (Maryknoll, NY: Orbis Books, 1998).

Gottwald, Norman K. and Horsley, Richard A. (ed.), *The Bible and Liberation - Political and Social Hermeneutics* (Maryknoll, NY: Orbis Books, 1993 revised edn).

Hopkins, Bishop John Henry *The BibLe* View *of Slavery:* A Letter *From the Bishop of Vermont,* IVew England to *the Bishop of Pennsylvania* (London: Saunders, Ottley & Co., 1863).

–, *Scriptural, Ecclesiastical and Historical View of Slavery: From the Days of Patriarch Abraham to the Nineteenth Century* **(New York: Pooley & Co., 1864).**

Horsley, Richard A,, *yesus and the Spiral of Violence - Popular Jewish Resistance* in *Roman Palestine* (Minneapolis, MN: Fortress Press, 1933).

Jagessar, Michael and Reddie, Anthony, *Postcolonial Black British Theology* – New *Textures and Themes* (Peterborough: Epworth, 2007).

Kwok Pui Lan, "The Bible in the Non-Biblical World'; *Semeia* 59, 2000.

Liburd, Ron, " 'Like ... a House Upon the Sand?' ARican American Biblical Hermeneutics *in Perspective'; fourna! of the Interdenominationat Theological Centre xxii (V,* 71–91, Fall 1994.

Merton, Thomas *Faith and Violence* (Notre Dame, IN: University of Notre Dame Press, 1968).

Momla, ltumeleng S., Biblical Hermeneutics and Biblical Theology in Southern Africa (Grand Rapids, MI: Eerdmans, 1989).

, 'The Implication of the Text of Esther For African Women's Struggle For Liberation in South Africa,' *Semeia* 59, 2000.

Ord, David Robert and Robert B. Coote, is *the BibLe True? Understanding the Bible Today* (London: SCM Press, 1994).

Parrinder, G., *Religion* in *Africa* (New York: Praeger, 1969).

Placher, William C,, *Narratives ofA Vulnerable God* (Philadelphia, PA: Westminster John Knox Press, 1994).

Prior, Michael, *The Bible and Colonialism*, A *Moral* Critique (Sheffield: Sheffield Academic Press, 1977).

Ra%rick, George P,, From Sundown to Sunup, The Making of the Black Community (Westport, CN: Greenwood Publishing Company, 1972).

Roberts, J. Deotis, A *Black Political Theology* (Louville, KY: Westminster John Knox Press, 1974, reprinted 2005).

Rowland, Christopher and Corner, *Mark, Liberating Exegesis: The Challenge of Liberation to BibLical Studies* (London: SPCl<, 1991).

Scherer, James and Bevans, Stephen, New *Directions* im *Mission and Evangelism* (Maryknoll, NY: Orbis Books, 1999).

Schottroff, Willy and Wolfgang Stegemann, *God of the £owJy; Sociohlstorical Interpretations of the Bible* (Maryknoll, NY: Orbis Books, 1984).

Segovia, Fernando, *Decotonizing Biblical Studies, A View From the Margins* (Maryknoll, NY: Orbis Books, 2000).

, *Interpreting Beyond Borders* (Sheffield: Sheffield Academic Press, 2000).

Segovia, Fernando E and Tolbert, Mary Ann, *Reading From This Place vol* 1 – Social

Location and Biblical Interpretation in the United States (Minneapolis, MN: Fortress Press, 1995).

, *Teaching the BibLe - The Discourses and PoLitics of Biblical Pedagogy* (Maryknoll, NY: Orbis Books, 1998).

Segundo, Juan Luis, *Liberation of Theology* (New York: Orbis Books, 1976).

Shorter, Aylward, *Towards a Theology of Incutturation* (New York: Orbis, 1988). Shussler Fiorenza, Elizabeth, *in Memory of Her: A* FeministT*heological Reconstruction of Christian Origins* (New York: Crossroad, 1983).

Spencer Miller, Althea; O'Brien, Kathleen and Dube, Musa W. (eds), *Feminist* New

Testament Studies - Global and Future Perspectives (New York: Palgrave Macmillan, 2005)

Sugirtharajah, R. S. (ed.), *Voices From the Margins - Interpreting the Bible in the Third World* (Maryknoll, NY: Orbis Books, 1995).
(ed.), *Voices From the Margins - Interpreting the Bible in the Third World*, revised and expanded third edition (Maryknoll, NY: Orbis Books, 2006).

(ed.), *The Postcolonial Bible* (Sheffield: Sheffield Academic Press, 1998).

(ed.), *Asian BibLical Hermeneutics and Postcolonialism* (Maryknoll, NY: Orbis Books, 1998).

(ed.), *Vernacular Hermeneutics* (Sheffield: Sheffield Academic Press, 1999). -, *The Bible and the Third WorLd - Precotoniat, Colonial and Postcolonial Encounters* (Cambridge: Cambridge University Press, 2001).

. *Postcolonial Criticism and Biblical Interpretation (Oxford: Oxford University* Press, 2002).

-, *Postcolonial Recon$gwations: An ALternative Way of Reading the Bib te and Doing Theology* (London: SCM Press, 2003).

, *The* Postcolonial *Biblical* Reader (Boston, MA, Oxford, Victoria: Blackwell Publishing, 2006).

Thompson, Barry II (ed.), *Scripture: Method and Meaning, Essays Presented to Anthony Tyrell Hanson on his 70th-Birthday* (Hull: Hull University Press, 1987).

Ul<pong, Justin, "Developments in Biblical Interpretation: Historical and Hermeneutical Directions': *fomnal of Theology For Southern Africa* 108, November 2000.

Vaage, *Leif E. (ed.), Subversive Scriptures - Revolutionary Readings of the Christian Bible* in *Latin America* (Pennsylvania, PA: Trinity Press International, 1997).

Weems, Renita, "The Hebrew Women Are Not Like The Egyptian Women – The Ideology of Race, Gender and Sexual Reproduction in Exodus': *Semeia* 59, 25–34, 1992

Wallis, Jim, *God's PoLitics* (Oxford: Lion, 2005).

West, *Gerald O,, Biblical Hermeneutics of Liberation – Modes of Reading the Bible in* Southern *African* Context (Pietermaritzberg: Cluster Publications; Maryknoll, NY: Orbis Books, 1991).

, *Contextual Bible Study* (Pietermaritzburg: Cluster Publications, 1993).

. *The Academy of dIe Poor - Towards A DialogicalReadhrg ofthe Bible* (Sheffield: Sheffield Academic Press, 1999).

Wicker, Kathleen O'Brien, Spencer Miner, Althea and Dube, Musa W. (eds), *Feminist New Testament Studies, Global and Future Perspectives* (New York: Palgrave Macmillan, 2005).

Wimbush, Vincent L., "Biblical Historical Study as Liberation: Toward an Afro-Christian Hermeneutic': *fournat of Religious Thought* 42 (2), 9–21 (1985–1986).

, "Historical/Cultural Criticism as Liberation: A Proposal For An African American Biblical Hermeneutic'I *Serneia* 59, 2000.

Wolf, Hans Walter and Brueggemann, Walter, *The VItality of(Hd Testament Traditions* (Atlanta, GA: John Knox Press, 1982).

Interpretation of PhiLemon

Barton, S. C., "Paul and Philemon: A Correspondence Continued'; *Theology 90*, 98–99, 1987

Bieberstein, Sabine, "Disrupting the Normal Reality of Slavery: A Feminist Reading of the Letter of Philemon'i Journal *For the Study of the* New *Testament* 79, 105–16, 2000

Birneyy yames G.1 Sinfulness ofSlavehoLding in all Circumstances: Tested by Reason and Scripture (Detroit, MI: Charles Wilcox, 1846).

Blassingame, John W. (ed.), Frederick Douglas Papers, Series on: Speeches, Debates, *Interviews*, Vol. 3 *1855–63* (New Haven, CT: Yale University Press, 1985).

Equiano, Olaudah, *The Interesting Narrative and Other Writings* (London: Penguin Books, 1995).

Felder, Cain Hope, "The Letter to Philemon'i in *The New Interpreter's Bible* (Nashville, TN: Abingdon Press, 2000).

Fitzmyer, foseph A,, Sl, The Letter to Phi lemon: A New Translation with Introduction and Commentary (New York, London: The Anchor Bible, Doubleday, 2000).

Harris, Raymund, *Scriptural Researches* on *the Licitrress of the Slave Trade* (London: 1788)

Hopkins, Bishop John Henry, *Scriptural, Ecclesiastical and Historical View of Slavery: From the Days of Patriarch Abraham* to *the Nineteenth* Century (New York! Dooley & Co., 1864).

Lightfoot, J. B. *Saint Paul's Epistles* to *the* Colossians *anti* to *Philernon* (London: Macmillan & Co. Ltd., 1912).

Martin, Ralph II, *Interpretation* – A *Bible Commentary for Teaching and Preaching* - *Ephesians, Colossians and Pkrilernon* (Atlanta, GA: John Knox Press, 1991).

NordHng, John G., "Onesimus Fugitivus: A Defence of the Runaway Slave Hypothesis in Philemon': *Journal For the Stucil of the* New Testament 41, 79-119, 1991. Osiek, Carolyn, *Philippians and Philernon* (Nashville, TN: Abingdon Press, 2000). Petersen, *Norman R., Rediscovering Paul, Philemon and the Sociology of Paul's Narrative World* (Philadelphia, PA: Fortress Press, 1985).

Preiss, Theo, Life in Christ and Social Ethics in the Epistle to Phitemon; Studies in Biblical TheoLogy No. 13, *Life* in *Christ* (London: SCM Press, 1952).

Schussler Fiorenza, Elizabeth, *Searching the Scriptures* – A FemInist Commentary (London: SCM Press Ltd., 1995).

Weems, Renita J., "Reading Her Way Through the Struggle: African America Women and the Bible'; in Gottwald, Norman K. and Horsley, Richard A. (eds), *The Bible and Liberation – PoLitical and Social Herrnenet&tics* (Maryknoll, NY: Orbis Books, 1993 revised edn).

Wheaton, N. S., Discourse on St *Pants Epistle* to *Philemon* (Hartford, CT: Press of Case, Tiffany and Company, 1851).

Westerman, William, L., *The Slave Systems of Greek and Roman Antiquitl* (Philadelphia, PA: The American Philosophical Society, 1955).

Young, Rev. David, *Slavery Forbidden* by *the* Word *of God* (Aberdeen: G. & R. King, 1847)

First Century Social History and Theology

Beker, J. Christian, *Pants Apocalyptic* Gospel – The Coming *Triumph of God* (Philadelphia, PA: Fortress Press, 1982).

Carcopino, Jerome, *Daily Life in Ancient Rome – The PeopLe and the City at the Height of the Empire* (London: Penguin Books, 1991 3rd edition).

Cadoux, C. J., *The Early Church and the WorLd* (Edinburgh: T. & T. Clark, lst edn, 1925, Reprinted 1955).

Combe s L. A. H., "The Metaphor of Slavery in the Writings of the Early Church'; **Journal For the Study of the New Testament, Supplement Series 156** (Sheffield: Sheffield Academic Press,, 1998).

Crossan, John Dominic and Reed, Jonathan L. In Search *of Paul – How Jesus' Apostle Opposed Rome's Empire* with *Gods* Kingdom (London: SPCK, 2004).

Davis, David Brian, *The* Problem *of Slavery* in Western *CUlt&Ire* (New York, Oxford: Oxford University Press, 1966).

de Ste Croix, G. E. M., *The Class Struggle* in *The Ancient Greek World* (Ithaca, NY: Cornell University Press, 1980).

Esler, Philip F., The First Christian in their Social World – Scient@c Approaches to New **Testament Interpretation (London and New York: Routledge, 1994)**.

Crossan, John Dominic, *The Birth of Christianity* (Edinburgh: T. & T Clark, 1998). Freyne, Sean, Galilee.' *From Alexander to Hadrian* (Edinburgh: T. & T. Clarke, 1980). Finley, M. I,, *Ancient Slavery and Modern* Ideology (London: Chatto & Wndus, 1980).

, *Slavery* in *Classical Antiquity – Views* and Controversies (Cambridge: Heffer, 1968)

Hengel, Martin, *Judaism and HeLlerrism* (London: SCM Press, 1974).

Horsley, Richard A., *Sociology and the Jesus Movement* (New York: Continuum 1989).

-, **(ed.), Paul and Empire: Religion and Power in Roman Imperial society** (Harrisburg, PA: Trinity Press International, 1997).

, (ed.), *Paul and Politics – Ekktesia, Israel, Imperium, Interpretation* (Harrisburg, PA: Trinity Press International, 2000).

Kautsky, John H., *The Politics of Aristocratic Empires* (New Brunswick, NJ, London: Transaction Publishers, 1997, rev. edn).

Kyrtatas, Dimitris J., *The Social Strvrctrrre of EarLy Christian Communities* (London, New York: Verso, 1987).

Osiek, Carolyn, RSCJ, *What Are They Saying About the Social Setting of the New Testament* (New York/Mahwah, NJ: Paulist Press, 1992).

Patterson, Orlando, *Staverl and Social Death* (Cambridge, MA: Harvard University Press, 1982).

, *Freedom* Vol. I *Freedom in the Making of Western Culture* (London: I. B. Tauris & Co. Ltd., 1991).

Samply, J. Paul, *Walking Between the Times - Patrts Moral Reasoning* (Minneapolis, MN: Fortress Press, 1991).

Tidball, Derek, The Social Context of the New Testament (Exeter: The Paternoster Press, 1983).

Troeltsh, Ernst, *The Social Teaching of the Christian Churches*, trans. Olive Wyon (London and New York: 1931).

Westermann, William L., *The Slave Systems of Greek and Roman Antiquity* (Philadelphia, PA: The American Philosophical Society, 1955),

Sociology and Religion

Ashcrof{, Bill, Gareth Griffiths, Helen Tiffin, *The Postcolonial Studies Reader* (New York: Routledge, 1995).

Davis, Angela, *Women, Race and Class* (Reading: Cox & Wyman Ltd., 1981).

Douglass, Frederick, *Narrative of the Life of Frederick Douglass* (Boston, MA: Bedford/St Martin's, 1993).

Duncombe, Stephen, *CuLtural* Resistance *Reader* (London, New York: Verso, 2002). Equiano, Olaudah, *Equiano's Travels* (London: Heinemann, 1967).

Ferguson, Russell, Givens, Martha, Minh-Ha, Trin T. and West, Corne}, O af *There: Marginalisation* and *Contemporary C&attlre* (New York: The MIT Press, 1990). Freire, Paulo *Pedagogy ojthe Oppressed* (Middlesex: Penguin Books, 1972).

Gates Jr, Henry Louis. and William L. Andrews, PIoneers *of the Black Atlantic, Five Slave Narratives from the Entightenment 1772-1815 (Washington, DC:* Counterpoint: 1998).

Gramsci, Antonio, *Selection From* Prison *Notes* (London: Lawrence and Wishart, 1971)

hooks, bell, *Teaching* To *Transgress, Education* as *the* Practice *of Freedom* (New York, London: Routledge, 1994).

John Mc.Leod, BeginnIng - *Postcotonialiswl* (Manchester: Manchester University Press, 2000).

Mullard, Chris, *Race,* Power *and* Resistance (London, Boston, MA, Melbourne: Routledge & Kegan Paul, 1985).

Parrinder, G., *Religion* in *Africa* (New York: Praeger, 1969).

Weber, Max, *The Theory of Social and Economic Organisation* (London: Free Press, 1964).

Williams, M. and Bud% R. L., *Psychology For Language Teachers: A Social Constructivist Approach* (Cambridge: Cambridge University Press, 1997).

Journals

Asia Journal of TheoLogy
R. S. Sugirtharajah, "From Orientalist to Post-Colonial: Notes on Reading Practices'; 10 (1), 1996.
Black Theology in Britain
Alexander, Valentina, "Onesimus's Letter to Philemon" 4 (May), 2000.

Caribbean Journal of Religious Studies

Nicholas, Joseph, "West Indies Cricket and Biblical Faith" 13 (2), September 1992–April 1993.

Holder, John, "Some Deuteronomic Themes in a Caribbean Context" 14 (2), 12–16, 1993

Jennings, Stephen, "The Word in Context: The Essential Criterion For Doing and Reflecting Authentic Caribbean Theology" 8 (2), 1–12, April 1988.

Parsanlal, Neil, "In Search of a Black Theology for the Caribbean: Rastafarianism and Revivalism" 17 (1), April, 1996.

Caribbean Quarterly

Gonsalves, Ralph E., "Our Caribbean Civilisation: Retrospect and Prospect', 44, (3 & 4), 131–50, September-December, 1998.

Hill, Errol, "Traditional Figures in Carnival: Their Preservation, Development and Interpretation" 31 (2), 14-34, June,.'1985.

Kirton, Allan, "Current Trends in Caribbean Theology and the Role of the Church'; 37 (1), 98-107, 1991.

Lamming, George, Opening address Rex Nettleford cultural conference, U.WI. Jamaica March 1996, 43 (1&2), March–June 1997.

Roper, Garnet, "The Impact of Evangelical and Pentecostal Religion': 37 (1), 35-44, March 1991.

Concili tIm

DictIonary *of American Biography* (London: Oxford University Press, 1929, Vol. 2). *Ecbrmertica! Review*

Raiser, Konrad, "Celebrating an Ecumenical Pilgrimage: and Address to Honour Philip Potter on the Occasion of his 80th Birthday': October 2001.

Ethnic and Racial Studies

Cohen, Abner, "A Polytechnic London Carnival as a Contested Cultural Performance': 5 (1), 23-41, January 1982.

Interpretation

Brueggemann, Walter, "That The World May be Redescribed'; 56 (4), 359–67, October 2002

Dunham, Robert E., "Between Text and Sermon: Philemon 1-25" 52 (2), April 1998. *Jamaica Journal*

Reckford, Mary, "The Slave Rebellion of 1831'; June 1969: 26–28.
Journal of Biblical Literature

Porter, Frank C., "The Place of Apocalyptic Conceptions in the Thought of Paul" 41 (1/2), 183–204, 1992.

Feeley-Harnik, Gillian, "Is Historical Anthropology Possible? The Case of the Runaway **Slave" in Gene M. Tucker and Douglas A. Knight (eds)**, *Humanizing America's* Iconic Book, Society of Biblical Literature Centennial Addresses, 1980.

Frilingos, Chris, "For My Child Onesimus: Paul and Domestic Power in Philemon' 19 (1), 91–104, Spring 2000.

Gottwald, Norman K,, "Social Classes as an Analytical and Hermeneutical Category in Biblical Studies" 112 (1), 3–22, Spring 1993.

Glancy, Jennifer A,, "Slaves and Slavery in the Matthean Parables" 119 (1), 67–90, Spring 2000.

Journal of Caribbean History

Hall, Douglas, "Incalculabihty as a Feature of Sugar Production During the Eighteenth Century" 35 (1), 2001.

Journal of the Interdenominationat Theological Centre
Journal For the Study of the New Testament a, vo,f c,,ig s.p "once a Slave, Always a Slave? Slavery, Manumission and Relational

Patterns in Paul's Letter to Philemon: 23 (82), 89–105, 2001.

Biebersstein, Sabine, "Disrupting the Normal Reality of Slavery: A Feminist Reading of the Letter to Philemon" 23 (79), 105–16, September 2000.

Nordling, John D., "Onesimus Fugitivus: A Defence of the Runaway Slave Hypothesis in Philemon" 41 (1991), 97-119, February 1991.

Theissen, Gerdhard, "The Social Structure of Pauline Communities: Some Critical

Remarks on J.J. Meggit - Paul, Poverty, SurvivaF' 84 (2001), 65–84, 2001. *yov£rrlat For the Study of the New Testament, Supplement Series yournal of Theology For Southern Africa*

Bosch, David, "Paul on Human Hopes" 671 3–161 June 1989.

"Mission and the Alternative Community: How My Mind Changed" 41 (December), 6, 1982.

, "The Churches as the Alternative Community" 13 (December), 1975.

New Society

James, C. L. R., "Cricket in West Indian Culture" 36, 6 June 1963.

New Testament Stuciies

Barclay, John M. G., "Paul, Phi lemon and the Dilemma of Christian Slave-ownership" 37 (2), 161–86, April 1991.

Rapske, B. M., "The Prisoner Paul in the Eyes of Onesimus" 37 (2), 187–203, April 1991

Novum Testamenttrm

Deming Will 'A Diatribe Pattern in 1 Corinthians 7:21-22: A New Perspective on Paul's Direction to Slaves" 37 (Fasc. 2), 130-37, April 1995.

Re!!@on and American CuLture

Harrill, J. Albert, "The Use of the New Testament in the American Slave Controversy:
A Case History in the Hermeneutical Tension Between Biblical Criticism and Christian Moral Debate" 10 (2), 149–86, Summer 2000.

Religion in Life

Knox, John, "Paul and the 'Liberals'" 49, Winter 1980.

Religion and Theology

Taylor, N. H., "Onesimus – A Case Study of Slave Conversion in Early Christianity" 3 (3), 259–81, 1996.

Semeia

Callahan, Allan, "The Slavery of New Testament Studies" 83/84, 1998, Slavery in Text and Interpretation.

Callender, Jr., Dexter E., "Servants of God(s) and Servants as Kings in Israel and the Ancient Near East" 83/84, 1998, Slavery in Text and Interpretation.

Horsley, Richard A., "The Slave Systems of Classical Antiquity and their Reluctant

Recognition by Modern Scholars" 83/84, 1998, Slavery in Text and Interpretation. "Paul and Slavery: A Critical Alternative to Recent Readings" 83/84, 1998, Slavery in Text and Interpretation.

Milne, Pamela J., "What shall we do with Judith: A Feminist Reassessment of a Biblical Heroine" 62, 37-58, 1993.

Patterson, Orlando, "Paul, Slavery and Freedom: Personal and Social-historical Reflections': 83/84, 1998, Slavery in Text and Interpretation.

Wimbush, Vincent L,, "Reading Texts Through Worlds, Worlds Through Texts" 62, 129–40, 1993.

Social and Ecoyromic Studies

Gray, Obika "Discovering the Social Power of the Poor" 43 (3), 169-89, 1994.

Social Text

Certeau, M., "On The Oppositional Practices of Every Day Life" 3, 3–43, 1980. *Studies in BLack TheoLogy* Preiss, Theo, "Life in Christ and Social Ethics in the Epistle to Philemon" 13, Life in Christ (London: SCM Press, 1952).

Theology

*The Journal of Religious Thought*_
Davis, Kortright "'Sunshine Christopher's bearers of Christ in the Caribbean" 49 (2), 7–24, WIIter Spring 1992-1993.

Articles'

2006 Budget Statement entitled "Gearing Up For Growth" delivered Wednesday 30 November 2005 by Dr The Hon. L. Errol Cort, MP, Minister of Finance and The Economy.

Gottwald, Norman K,, "Socio-historical Precision in the Biblical Grounding of Liberation Theologies'i address to the Catholic Biblical Association of America at its annual meeting, San Francisco, August 1985.

Jagessar, Michael, Unpublished Master's Thesis entitled "A Theological Evaluation of Wilson Harris' Understanding of Community as reflected in the 'Guiana Quartet; An Interdisciplinary Study of Theology and Caribbean Literature" (Jamaica: University of the West Indies, 1992).

La Trobe, Benjamin, A Swaim a View *of the Missions Established Among the Heathens by the Church of the Brethren or Unitas Fratum, in a Letter to a Friend (London:* M. Lewis, 1771) Letter dated 26 November 1770.

O'Marde, Dorbrene E., "Calypso in the 1990s'; Antigua *Carnival Souvenir Magazine,* April 1990.

, "West Indies Cricket: is the Music Loud Enough?" speech delivered at the Carifesta Vll Symposium on "Continuing to Define Ourselves in a Changing World" 23 August 2000 held in St Kitts/ Nevis.

Lecture delivered by Dr Terrence Fretheim on "Is the Portrayal of God Reliable?" at the Vancouver School of Theology, Summer School Public Lecture Series, 6 July1995. Hall, Stuart, "Encoding and decoding in the Television Discourse'; Paper presented to the Council of European Colloquy on "Training in the Critical Reading of Television Language'; University of Leicester, September 1973.

Ruth Wust, "The Trinidad Carnival From Canboulay to Pretty Mass'; unpublished MA Thesis, Berlin (1987).

Newspapers

Negro World Newspaper

Outlet Newspaper Fan The Flame by Tim Hector: 17 April 1998

9 April 1999

25 June 1999

21 April 2000

1 December 2000

19 January 2001

9 March 2001

AFTERWORD

Steed Vernyl Davidson

Fifteen years after Oral Thomas published *Biblical Resistance Hermeneutics within a Caribbean Context,* much has changed, making this a relevant and critical book. This book falls within the theological tradition that sees Christianity and the Bible as influential factors in social formation, albeit one that recognizes the altered power of mainline traditional Christianity. With the Caribbean as its context, the assumption of majority Christian cultures and biblical literacy is not misplaced. Fifteen years later, those assumptions still hold true as the data shows small declines in the Christian population in Latin America and the Caribbean. In 1970, Christians comprised 94.3% of the population, and in 2020, that number slipped to 92.1%.[577] The nature of Christianity, however, changed over the years. Larger numbers of Christians are evangelical, with countries like Barbados (42%), Bahamas (36%), British Virgin Islands (32%), and Dominica (31%) recording the highest evangelical percentages.[578] The share of Anglicans in the population of Barbados declined from 37.5% in 1970 to 25.0% in 2020. While the percentage

---

[577] Gina A. Zurlo, "A Demographic Profile of Christianity in Latin American and the Caribbean," in *Christianity in Latin America and the Caribbean,* eds. Kenneth R. Ross, Ana Maria Bidegain, and Todd M. Johnson. (Edinburgh University Press, 2022), 3.
[578] Zurlo, 9.

of evangelicals increased from 27.8% in 1970 to 39.6% in 2020.[579] This redistribution of the Christian population suggests an audience with the literacy for this book but not necessarily disposed to its perspectives.

Several changes on the political front also occurred since this book was first published. While much of Latin America experienced a turn towards the left in the early years of the twenty-first century, the ensuing years have brought more right-leaning governments into power, "pushing back their predecessor's progressive reforms" and, in the process, repositioning Christianity within the society.[580] Rather than serving as an oppositional force to right-leaning governments, Christianity has tended to tilt in the same direction. With drifts towards the right, this means Christianity becomes more protectionist, more otherworldly, more conservative, and less militant. To the extent Christians became vocal, they do so to oppose advances in progressive causes, in particular reproductive and LGBTQ+ rights. The decisions to protect the traditional understanding of human formation reflect the general impulse to mirror external conservative theological positions. As to the project of indigenization and inculturation of Christianity in the Caribbean, "the Anglo-Caribbean Christ still appears to be 'a migrant from Europe' rather than being an Indigenous Saviour."[581] The current socio-political context of the Caribbean seems inhospitable to the type of resistance Thomas envisages in his book.

These changes and others do not diminish the value of this book. The spirit of this book precisely anticipates these bleak circumstances. This call to resistance in the form of Caribbean indigenization comes

---

[579] Roderick R. Hewitt, "Antigua and Barbuda, Bahamas, Barbados, Belize, Dominica, Grenada, Jamaica, Saint Kitts and Nevis, Saint Lucia, Saint Vincent and the Grenadines, Guyana, Anguilla, British Virgin Islands, Cayman Islands, Montserrat, Turks and Caicos Islands, Trinidad and Tobago" in *Christianity in Latin America and the Caribbean*, eds. Kenneth R. Ross, Ana Maria Bidegain, and Todd M. Johnson. (Edinburgh University Press, 2022), 205.

[580] Bibiana Ortega, "Social and Political Context," in *Christianity in Latin America and the Caribbean*, eds. Kenneth R. Ross, Ana Maria Bidegain, and Todd M. Johnson. (Edinburgh University Press, 2022), 372.

[581] Hewitt, 215.

not to the converted but to those who still need to embrace and continue the traditions of resistance to the Bible and with the Bible that are core to the Caribbean heritage. Perhaps Sam Sharp or Paul Bogle had an easier task to convince their peers of the need for resistance than current leaders who use the Bible as a form of social and political opposition to repressive policies and powers. And yet, we cannot take it for granted that oppressed people are sufficiently aware of their oppression and have not internalized their oppression to the point of indifference. Conscientization has always been a key feature of social and community organizations. While various forms of the prosperity gospel have created a clear link between economic well-being and forms of Christian virtue, a similar link between hardship and faith as the source for militant actions does not exist. The equation between their socio-political deprivation and resistance requires breaking the stranglehold of theologies that convince poor people to try harder because their own moral virtues will bring them the required reward. Interrupting the individualistic theologies that mine biblical texts that serve up quotable signifiers of virtuous living forms a critical next step in the work Thomas sets up in this book, given its look into the possibilities that emerge from congregational ministry.

Through the case studies that deal with real people and earnest readers of the Bible, Thomas reveals the potential to build "cultural literacy consciousness" that can form the foundation for resistance hermeneutics. Cultivating a different set of reading strategies for the Bible provides a way to envisage a different relationship with the Bible. Yet, the traditional processes of exegesis which Thomas employs can go only so far. In fact, he leaves his own thoughts around "exegetics and eisegetics" incomplete.[582] These seemingly mutually exclusive actions supposedly make the difference between good preachers and misusers of

---

[582] Oral Thomas, *Biblical Resistance Hermeneutics within a Caribbean Context,* (Equinox, 2010), 137.

the Bible. As any ardent churchgoer will attest, good preachers situate themselves amid life and illuminate real life with the help of the Bible. Since much of Thomas's concerns lie outside of the biblical text, he rightly raises a critical turn needed to produce the desired effect he anticipates.

Biblical scholars insist on centering the Bible. After all, can one continue to be a scholar of the Bible without the Bible as the central focus? The shifting place of the Bible within and without religious communities makes it possible for scholarly and other engagement that does not always center on biblical texts. Such engagement is not novel since artists and creatives have used the Bible as stepping stones to their work. Vincent Wimbush distinguishes exegesis and "excavation."[583] Exegesis controls meaning. Excavation provides material to create meaning. The adherence to the text that Wimbush describes as "ancient-cum-modern colonial-settler-imperial"[584] does not produce liberation. Nat Turner selectively read the Bible and supplemented his reading with direct divine revelation in the cause of his Christmas Day uprising. His critical relationship with the Bible suggests that Turner was aware of the forked nature of the book. Howard Thurman's grandmother and others like her saw the inconsistency in Paul as an advocate of the slaveocracy and believer in Jesus, making him an unreliable source of inspiration. Frederick Douglass certainly understood this when he declared his love for the "pure, peaceable, and impartial Christianity of Christ" and his rejection of "the corrupt, slaveholding, women-whipping, cradle-plundering, partial, and hypocritical Christianity of this land." The unknown authors of the Spirituals show the need to press the Bible into liberation, at times rewriting stories. Mary doesn't mourn for her

---

[583] Vincent Wimbush, "Tribunals of Jurists and Congresses of Gentlemen: Signifying (On) Biblical Studies as Colonial-Bureaucratic Masquerade," in *Black Scholars Matter: Visions, Struggles, and Hopes in Africana Biblical Studies*, edited by Gay L. Byron and Hugh R. Page, Jr. (SBL Press, 2022), 54.
[584] Wimbush, 56,

brother Lazarus as much as she bemoans Jesus's actions. Liberation means twisting temporal horizons to locate her at the crossing of the Sea: "Oh, Mary, don't you weep, don't you moan" adds the history of deliverance missing in the words of Jesus that would assure the oppressed that they will find deliverance: "Pharoah's army got drowned. Oh, Mary, don't you weep!"

Thomas evinces a passion for the quotidian: "the daily round the common tasks." These features define life and make it either bearable or unbearable. They also form the context within which the Bible is read. Contextual readings tend to elevate the Bible over these contexts and make them less defining than they can be either for producing meaning or meaningful action. Moving contexts beyond the Bible, particularly the surveillance of the Bible and its reading traditions, produces results that, in part, can be transformative. The theorist Sylvia Wynter wrote a novel long before her career in critical theory took off. The story represents much of her later theorizing. Wynter describes an emerging Black religion during Jamaican political independence in *The Hills of Hebron*. The fortunes of the separatist group to set up a promised land in remote hills mirror those of the emerging nation. They both confront the harsh economic realities. Prophet Moses, the central protagonist, after an initial attempt to fly to heaven fails, discovers that he has a stronger appeal to secure a following if he offers them the present world and a god incarnate that resembles them: "The idea of man being able to conceive of a God of his own provided Moses with the answer to his defeat."[585] This insight leads Moses to freely appropriate the Bible – no exegesis – and build a new community called Hebron in the hills. The first narration of his vocation mirrors the story of his namesake. On his second attempt to develop his community, he becomes Moses rather than the facsimile of the Bible: "he heard a voice calling him:

---

[585] Sylvia Wynter, *The Hills of Hebron*, (Ian Randle, 2010), 144.

'Come down, Moses! Come down to the sea!'"[586] In this novel, Wynter shows the colonizing power of Christianity and its missionary work. She constructs a character intent on freeing his people from the colonial state by using the Bible as a springboard.

Caribbean resistance has taken several forms. Rejection as a form of resistance leans into Caribbean traditions of maroonage, runaways, sabotage, or the choice to become unalive. What these traditions mean for a Caribbean hermeneutic of the Bible is a project that Thomas has opened with this book. Rejection as a form of critical distance enables the systemic analyses that Thomas calls for and the self-reflexive move that examines one's epistemologies and other forces of formation that predispose readers to colonize their imaginations of what freedom can be. Precisely because the Bible provides no clear and sustained vision that rejects empire, slavery, sexism, and all the oppressions that modern readers can quickly identify, resistant readers need to perform that function. That the Bible inspired revolts, conscientized political leaders that advocated for better working, social, and political arrangements, and stimulated teachers and other ordinary folk to work for freedom means that resistant readers can take what is valuable from the Bible to build spaces of freedom with other material. The folk traditions of the Caribbean, the genius of songwriters, artists' creativity, and the Bible's strength are some of the other sources that can enhance biblical resistance readings.

---

[586] Wynter, 145.

Printed in the United States
by Baker & Taylor Publisher Services